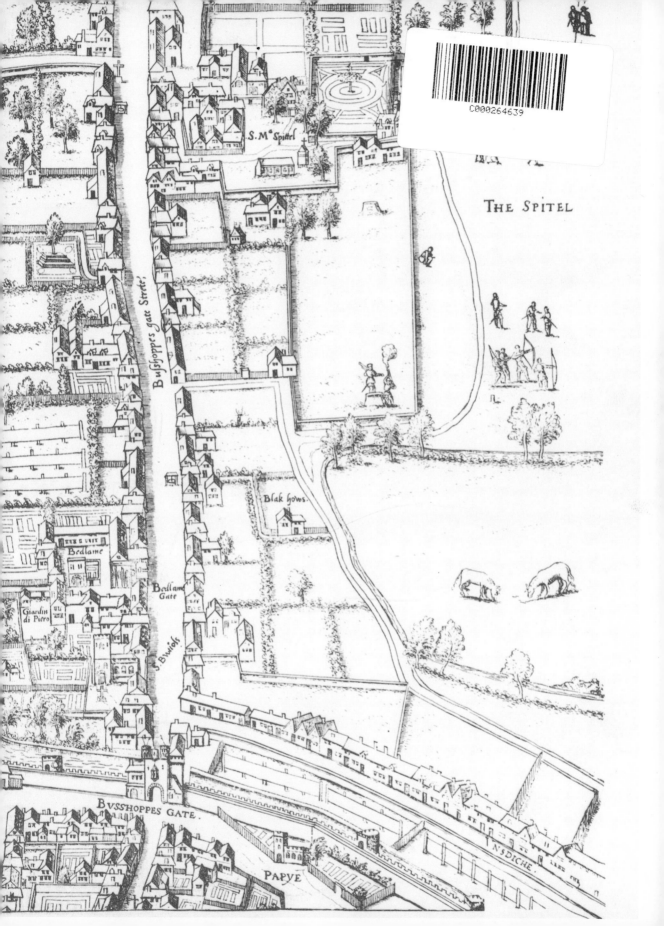

C000264639

THE SPITEL

S.M̃ᵃ Spitel

Busshoppes gate Strete.

Blak hows.

Bedlame

Bedlame Gate

Giardin di Pietro

S. Butiols

BVSSHOPPES GATE.

PAPYE

NSDICHE.

A History of the Carpenters' Company

BY THE SAME AUTHOR:
Nicholas Ridley
Thomas Cranmer
John Knox
Lord Palmerston
Mary Tudor
Garibaldi
The Roundheads
Napoleon III and Eugénie
The History of England
The Statesman and the Fanatic
Henry VIII
Elizabeth I
The Tudor Age
The Love Letters of Henry VIII
Maximilian and Juárez
Tito

Opposite:
The Coat of Arms of the Worshipful Company of Carpenters.
Reproduced from a property survey made in 1750.

A History of the Carpenters' Company

by

Jasper Ridley

CARPENTERS' HALL

© Jasper Ridley 1995

Published in 1995 by the Carpenters' Company, Carpenters' Hall, Throgmorton Avenue, London EC2N 2JJ

ISBN 0–906290–12–0

In association with Unicorn Press Ltd, London SW11

Filmset in Plantin and printed in England by Butler & Tanner Ltd, Frome, Somerset

All rights reserved. No part of this publication may be reproduced or transmitted in any form or by any means without prior permission of the publisher in writing

The right of Jasper Ridley to be identified as the author of this work has been asserted by him in accordance with the Copyright, Designs and Patents Act, 1988

ACKNOWLEDGEMENTS FOR ILLUSTRATIONS

We are indebted to the following institutions and individuals for permission to reproduce photographs: the British Library (no. 9: Cotton Augustus III, f.19); the Trustees of the British Museum (no. 7); the Drapers' Company (no. 12); Mr. Alfred Fisher, Chapel Studio, Hertfordshire (no. 83); Guildhall Library, Corporation of London (nos. 10, 31, 45, 48 and 49); Guildhall Library, Corporation of London/The Bridgeman Art Library, London (nos. 1, 34 and 36); the Mansell Collection (nos. 29 and 47); the Museum of London (endplates and nos. 5, 26 and 27); Mrs Patricia Neild, Matron at Rustington (nos. 52 and 53); and the Royal Collection ©: Her Majesty the Queen (no. 11). All other illustrations are the property of the Worshipful Company of Carpenters, London.

Photography of Company material was been carried out by Mr. Tony Shipton and Butler and Tanner Ltd with a few exceptions. Mr. Richard Bateman of Industrial and Architectural Photography took the photograph of the Dining Hall (no. 73); Mr. Geremy Butler was responsible for the photography of Company items on loan to the Manuscript Section of Guildhall Library (nos. 6, 15 and 25); Mr. Dennis Jordan of Gerald J. Sharp Photographers photographed the Court (no. 4); and Mr. Toby Crisp photographed the newly-refurbished reception area (no. 85).

CONTENTS

1 ELECTION DAY   13
Election Day in the Carpenters' Company – service at Church of All Hallows-on-the-Wall which has been held continuously since 1499 – ceremonies at the election dating back at least to 1738 – the links between the senior members of the Livery and past generations.

2 THE CARPENTERS OF LONDON   21
The City of London in 1300 – influx of "foreigns" into London resented by the citizens – the origin of Livery Companies – the Carpenters' Company formed before the end of the thirteenth century – The Book of Ordinances of 1333 – the great merchant Livery Companies taken over in the fourteenth century by country gentlemen and career City politicians – the Carpenters' Company remains closely linked to the craft – the first Carpenters' Hall built in 1429 – the Company's ordinances of 1455 – the Carpenters' Company receives its charter of incorporation in 1477.

3 THE KING'S MASTER CARPENTERS   35
Prominent members of the Carpenters' Company hold important positions at Henry VIII's court – Humphrey Cooke builds the pavilions for the Field of Cloth-of-Gold – Cooke averts a diplomatic crisis by completing the buildings on time – James Nedeham, the King's Master Carpenter and afterwards Clerk and Surveyor of the King's Works in England – Nedeham's influence with Henry VIII – secret meeting of Thomas Cromwell and the Emperor Charles V's ambassador in Nedeham's half-built house – Nedeham is granted monastic lands and the lands of executed traitors.

4 DANGEROUS TIMES   47
The Carpenters' Company's attitude to the religious changes and persecutions in the sixteenth century – the Carpenters' Company supports the Lords of the Council's coup d'état against Protector Somerset in 1549 – The Carpenters' Company forced to pay for new charters – The Dutch Church in London, and the Dutchmen's relations with the Carpenters' Company – The Carpenters' Charter and Ordinances of 1607 – The Carpenters refuse to help colonize Virginia, but acquire land in Ulster – Richard Wyatt founds the almshouses in Godalming in 1619.

5 CIVIL WAR   59
The plague of 1625 – The City, and the Carpenters' Company, fined for the murder of Dr. Lamb – demarcation disputes between the Carpenters' Company and the Joiners' Company – Charles I welcomed by the City on his return from Scotland in 1641 – The Civil War – the Carpenters contribute money repeatedly to the Roundhead cause – the Carpenters support the Presbyterians against the Independents in the Second Civil War – The Carpenters prevent Carpenters' Hall from being requisitioned by Cromwell's troops when the Army occupies London in December 1648 – the Carpenters accept the Commonwealth and Cromwell as Lord Protector – the Carpenters welcome Charles II at his Restoration in 1660.

6   PLAGUE, FIRE AND QUO WARRANTO   71

The numbers on the Court of Assistants are greatly reduced because of deaths from the Great Plague of 1665 – new members co-opted to the Court – Carpenters' Hall escapes the Great Fire of London in 1666 – the Carpenters offer the use of their Hall to the Lord Mayor – Charles II crushes the Whig Opposition in London by confiscating the charters of the City and of the Livery Companies – the Quo Warranto proceedings and Judge Jeffreys – The Revolution of 1688 restores the old charters to the City and to the Carpenters' Company.

7   THE EIGHTEENTH CENTURY   83

The Carpenters erect Carpenters' Buildings in 1737 – Carpenters' Hall leased permanently to tenants – The Carpenters do well in the South Sea Bubble, selling out before the shares become valueless – The Carpenters' Company purchases lands at Stratford in East London – Changing attitudes towards charitable giving – the Carpenters' hold their dinners at the London Tavern and elsewhere – Sir William Staines becomes the first Carpenter Lord Mayor in 1801.

8   MR. SIMMONS AND CAPTAIN YALLOWLEY   93

Radical influence in the City of London – Matthew Wood as Lord Mayor leads the Radicals – The country is split by the matrimonial disputes between King George IV and Queen Caroline – the issue splits the Carpenters' Company – on the Court of the Carpenters' Company, John Simmons denounces Joseph Yallowley as a Nonconformist and a supporter of Queen Caroline – Simmons expelled from the Carpenters' Company.

9   THE NINETEENTH CENTURY   99

Increased wealth of the Carpenters' Company – the Carpenters sell land to the Great Eastern Railway – the Company opens almshouses for its freemen at Twickenham in 1841 – increased wealth and higher social standing of the liverymen of the Carpenters' Company – Richard Webb Jupp and Edward Basil Jupp as Clerks of the Carpenters' Company for seventy-nine years – Sir William and Sir James Clarke Lawrence as Lord Mayors and Masters of the Carpenters' Company – the origin of the Lord Mayor's attendance at the Carpenters' Company's annual dinner in November.

10   THE ATTACK ON THE LIVERY COMPANIES   107

The Radicals' demand for a reform of the government of the City of London after 1832 – the leading role played by Sir James Clarke Lawrence of the Carpenters' Company in defending the City institutions from the Radical attack – the arrival of Princess Alexandra of Denmark in London in 1863 – J. F. B. Firth's attack on the Livery Companies – the appointment of a Royal Commission to inquire into the Livery Companies in 1882 – the failure to take any action to reform the City from 1882 to 1995 shows the lack of public support for the attacks on the City – Under Disraeli, the Conservatives gain the political support of the City of London.

CONTENTS

11 VICTORIAN PHILANTHROPY   117

The Carpenters' Company build a new Hall in 1876 – dinner in the new Hall in 1880 – Past Master Stanton Preston becomes Clerk – Alderman Nottage becomes Lord Mayor – Queen Victoria's Jubilees in 1887 and 1897 – The coronation of Edward VII in 1902 – The Carpenters' Trades Training School opened in 1893 – Henry Harben joins the Carpenters' Company – He buys land at Rustington to found the Carpenters' Convalescent Home there – the Honorary Freemen of the Carpenters' Company 1888–1910.

12 THE FIRST WORLD WAR AND THE INTER-WAR YEARS   131

The Carpenters' Company in the First World War – the Carpenters' Trades Training School damaged in air raid by German Zeppelins in 1918 – Field Marshal Haig made an Honorary Freeman of the Carpenters' Company – The Carpenters' Company and the General Strike of 1926 – the Marquess of Reading made an Honorary Freeman – the Prince of Wales at the six hundredth anniversary dinner in 1933 – the Assistant Clerk's frauds involve the Carpenters' Company in a leading legal case in the Court of Appeal – Henry Carl Osborne becomes Clerk to the Company in 1935.

13 THE SECOND WORLD WAR   143

Preparations for war in the summer of 1939 – the Carpenters' Company in the Second World War – the Carpenters' Company offers the use of their Hall to the Lord Mayor and other Companies after the destruction of the Guildhall and the Livery Company Halls in air raids in October to December 1940 – Carpenters' Hall destroyed in air raid on the night of 10 May 1941 – the Drapers' Company grant the Carpenters the use of their Hall after the destruction of Carpenters' Hall.

14 CONTESTED ELECTIONS   147

The system of choosing the Masters of the Carpenters' Company before 1721 – the present system of appointment by seniority begins in 1721 – contested elections of Masters and Wardens between 1741 and 1947 – a troublesome liveryman – Sir Leslie Boyce, Sir Cuthbert Ackroyd and Sir Edmund Stockdale of the Carpenters' Company become Lord Mayor – The Carpenters' Company's Clerks since 1960.

15 THE POST-WAR YEARS   159

General Smuts becomes an Honorary Freeman in 1941 – the Honorary Freedom is not offered to Ernest Bevin – the attempt to ban Communists from benefitting from education under the Read's Trust – Field Marshal Montgomery granted the Honorary Freedom in 1951 – Queen Juliana of the Netherlands an Honorary Freeman and Liveryman – the new Hall opened in 1960 – Queen Juliana uses Carpenters' Hall for a dinner given to Queen Elizabeth II in 1972 – The Prime Minister of Malaysia made an Honorary Freeman in 1989 – relations with the Carpenters' Company of Philadelphia – The Rustington Convalescent Home – sale of the Twickenham Almshouses – the Godalming Almshouses – less lengthy Company dinners.

16   THE CARPENTERS' COMPANY TODAY   177
Participation of junior liverymen in the running of the Carpenters' Company – arguments as to the power to co-opt liverymen who have not been Master or Warden to serve on the Court, 1665 to 1993 – opposition to the proposal to co-opt liverymen to Court Committees in 1962 – the principle accepted in 1992 – the attendance of ladies at dinners and social events, 1477 to 1985 – the admission of women to the Livery rejected in 1977 – there is no justification for the criticism of Livery Companies today – the Carpenters' Company's future.

APPENDIX I   187
List of Dates

APPENDIX II   189
List of Honorary members

APPENDIX III   191
List of Masters and Wardens

APPENDIX IV   209
List of Clerks and Beadles

BIBLIOGRAPHY   211

INDEX   215

LIST OF ILLUSTRATIONS

1.	Interior of All Hallows-on-the-Wall, c.1800	14
2.	Election Day, c.1935	16
3.	The Tudor Crowns	18
4.	The Court, 1995	19
5.	Detail from the Copperplate Map, London, 1558/9	20
6.	Extract from the Bible, c.1250	22
7.	Tudor wall paintings	26
8.	Grant of Arms, 1466	30
9.	Designs for English royal tents, c.1520	34
10.	Panorama of London, 1520	36
11.	The Field of Cloth-of-Gold, 1520	38
12.	Cromwell's house, c.1540	42
13.	The Lord Mayor's Show, c.1650	43
14.	Interior of Austin Friars, 1919	50
15.	Building licence for carpentry work, 1588	51
16.	Royal Charter, 1607	52
17.	Richard Wyatt, Master and Company benefactor	54
18.	Plan of estate at Bramshott, Hampshire, 1727	55
19.	Godalming almshouses; view of the front	56
20.	Godalming almshouses: view of the back	57
21.	Plan of estate at Shackleford, Surrey, 1727	58
22.	Master and Wardens' cups	60
23.	Detail from Royal Charter, 1640	62
24.	Wyatt's tankards	63
25.	Extract from list of Company plate sold, 1643	66
26.	The Great Fire of London, 1666	70
27.	Plague scenes from a broadsheet, 1665	72
28.	Reversal of Quo Warranto, 1690	75
29.	"Judge Jeffreys", Lord Chief Justice	78
30.	Carpenters' Hall, 1830	82
31.	Sir John Cass, 1710	85
32.	Plan of Stratford estate, 1769	86
33.	Plan of Carpenters' Hall and buildings, 1727	87
34.	Sir William Staines, Lord Mayor, 1804	90
35.	Interior of Carpenters' Hall, 1877	92
36.	London Wall, 1811	95
37.	Design for Twickenham almshouses, 1842	98
38.	Twickenham almshouses, c.1890	101
39.	Richard Webb Jupp, Clerk 1798–1852	102
40.	Sir William Lawrence, Lord Mayor	103
41.	Sir James Clarke Lawrence, Lord Mayor	103
42.	The Lord Mayor at Carpenters' Hall, 1992	104
43.	The Master's chair	105
44.	Some of Mr George Faith's Fleet	106

45. J.H. Bank's balloon view of London, 1851 — 108
46. Dining Hall, 1927 — 111
47. J.F. Bottomley Firth, MP — 112
48. The Fatal Effects of Gluttony, 1830 — 113
49. Detail from Ordinance Survey map, 1874 — 118
50. Dining Hall, 1939 — 120
51. Stanton William Preston, Master — 122
52. Rustington Convalescent Home, c.1920 — 124
53. The Dining Hall at Rustington, c.1920 — 124
54. Invitation to the Foundation Ceremony for the new Hall, 1876 — 126
55. Building Crafts Training School, c.1950 — 129
56. Court meeting in Court Room, 1903 — 130
57. Mary Woodgate Wharrie, Company benefactress — 132
58. Menu for the Company's Sixth Centenary Dinner — 134
59. Memorial roll: members killed in the First and Second World Wars — 135
60. Honorary Freedom to the Marquess of Reading, 1926 — 137
61. Henry Carl Osborne, Clerk 1935–1960 — 138
62. Master's Badge, 1933 — 141
63. Bomb damage to the Hall, London Wall — 142
64. View of Hall from the eastern end of London Wall — 145
65. Ballot Box — 146
66. Record of voting for the Estates Committee, 1914 — 148
67. Livery List, 1788 — 149
68. Sir Cuthbert Ackroyd, Lord Mayor — 150
69. Carpentry tools — 154
70. Sir Edmund Stockdale, Lord Mayor — 155
71. Honorary Freedom to Field Marshal Viscount Montgomery of Alamein, 1951 — 161
72. The Dining Hall, 1992 — 162
73. Carpenters' Hall, Philadelphia, 1992 — 163
74. Presentation of the Honorary Livery to Queen Juliana of the Netherlands, 1966 — 164
75. Presentation of the Honorary Livery to HRH The Prince of Wales, 1995 — 166
76. Carpenters' and Dockland Centre, Stratford, 1993 — 167
77. Building Crafts Training School, 1970 — 168
78. Sitting Room, Rustington, 1992 — 170
79. Court visit to Godalming, 1994 — 171
80. Livery Dinner Menu, 1914 — 174
81. City and Guilds College Association Dinner, 1995 — 178
82. Designs for stained glass windows — 179
83. Students at Building Crafts College, 1994 — 182
84. HMS Norfolk — 185
85. Hall reception area, 1995 — 186
86. HRH The Prince of Wales meets students from Building Crafts College, 1995 — 188

ACKNOWLEDGEMENTS

I wish to thank the Master of the Carpenters' Company (Captain K. G. Hamon, RN) and the Clerk (Major General Paul Stevenson, OBE) for their encouragement and advice on the typescript; the Assistant Clerk (Mr. Ian Lester) for all the help he has given me in the research among the documents of the Carpenters' Company at Carpenters' Hall and from his extensive knowledge of the history of the Company; Mr. Tony Shipton for his advice on editorial problems; the Company Archivist (Mrs. Lieselotte Clark) for researching the illustrations and writing the captions; Mr. Roger Miller for help with the proof-reading; and Mrs. Patricia Hymans for compiling the index.

My colleagues on the Court of Assistants of the Carpenters' Company, Dr. R. L. Woolley and Mr. Hugh Barnes-Yallowley, and the Matron of the Carpenters' Convalescent Home at Rustington (Mrs. Patricia Neild) for lending me rare documents in their possession dealing with the history of the Company in the first half of the twentieth century.

My stepmother Mrs. Jane Ridley for lending me documents and recounting to me her personal recollections of the time when her husband Geoffrey Ridley (my father) was Master of the Company in 1955, and from earlier and later periods.

My colleagues on the Court, Mr. V. J. G. Stavridi, Mr. D. R. Stuckey, Dr. W. F. Felton and Sir Desmond Heap, for their personal reminiscences.

The Senior Warden of the Carpenters' Company (Mr. Malcolm Francis), the Director of the Carpenters' Building Crafts College (Mr. P. C. Quick), and Mrs Lorraine Cavanagh of the Carpenters and Dockland Centre for their help with the research.

The librarian and staff of the British Library, the City of London Library at the Guildhall, the Kent County Library at Tunbridge Wells, the Littlehampton Museum, the London Library, and the Registry of Births, Deaths and Marriages at St. Katherine's House; the staff at Carpenters' Hall for their kindness at all times; my wife Vera for her advice on the typescript; and my son John for his help with the proofs.

My sources of information are listed in the Bibliography. I have relied chiefly on the Carpenters' Company Court Minutes. The most important printed book is the scholarly History of the Carpenters' Company written in 1848 by the Company's Clerk, Edward Basil Jupp. For Chapter 10, a particularly useful source is the account of the Radicals' campaign against the City of London and the Livery Companies in I. G. Doolittle's The City of London and its Livery Companies.

Until 1752, the Old Style Julian Calendar was in force in England. The year began on 25 March, not 1 January, and the days of the year were ten days behind our present calendar in the sixteenth and seventeenth centuries and eleven days behind between 1700 and 1752. Thus in 1500 the Carpenters' Company's Election Day, 10 August, was 20 August by our modern calendar. I have adopted the usual practice of giving the days of the month before 1752 in the old calendar and the year in our modern calendar. Thus I say that the first Carpenters' Hall was built in January 1429, not (as the contemporaries wrote) in January 1428, two months before the end of the year 1428 on 24 March.

I have also followed the usual practice in referring to the date when a liveryman was

Master of the Carpenters' Company (or Lord Mayor), giving the date when his year of office began. Until 1873 the Master took office in September and since 1873 in August. So the statement that Sir John Cass was Master in 1711 and Alan Preston in 1957 means that Cass was Master from September 1711 to September 1712 and Preston from August 1957 to August 1958. In the list of Masters and Wardens in Appendix III, there are some cases where a Master died during his year of office and was succeeded by another as Master. Both Masters are listed as having served in the year when the first Master's term began, even if the second Master succeeded him in the following calendar year. Thus it is stated that in 1860 (i.e. the year beginning in September 1860) the Masters were Thomas G. Smith, Thomas Finden and Sir James Clarke Lawrence, although Lawrence became Master in February 1861.

The spelling of surnames had not been standardized in the sixteenth century, and people wrote other persons' names, and even their own names, differently on different occasions. Thus James Nedeham's name is spelt "Nedam" in the Carpenters' Company's records, but in contemporary letters and other documents it is also spelt "Nedeham", "Needeham" and "Nedham". I have adopted the spelling "Nedeham" as this is certainly how it was pronounced. Sir Edward Coke, like Humphrey Cooke, pronounced his name "Cook", but in his case I have spelt his name "Coke", as this is the universally accepted spelling of the name of this famous Chief Justice.

Tunbridge Wells,
31 July 1995   Jasper Ridley

1
Election Day

Election Day in the Carpenters' Company – service at Church of All Hallows-on-the-Wall which has been held continuously since 1499 – ceremonies at the election dating back at least to 1738 – the links between the senior members of the Livery and past generations.

On the last Tuesday but one in July every year, a General Court of the Livery of the Worshipful Company of Carpenters is held to elect the Master and Wardens for the forthcoming year. The members of the Livery assemble at Carpenters' Hall in London Wall in the City of London at 11.40 a.m. The members of the Court of Assistants, the governing body of the Company, are present; there are some fifteen or twenty of them, and apart from the Master and the three Wardens nearly all are Past Masters of the Company. About 30 of the 150 liverymen of the Company will have come for the occasion; the rest are working in their offices or elsewhere, carrying on their profession and earning their living.

The Assistant Clerk hands each of them one shilling. Several centuries ago, this was the daily wage of a skilled carpenter. The liverymen attending the General Court continued to receive a shilling till 1971, when it became a 5p coin. Since 1991 they are given the new, tiny 5p coin.

The members line up for the procession to the church. At the head goes the Beadle, the officer of the Company whose duty is to clear the way for the Master. Behind him come the Master, the three Wardens and the Clerk, who, like the Beadle are dressed in their robes of office; then the members of the Court and then the liverymen. They walk two abreast in order of precedence; between each pair, the first in precedence takes the place of honour on the right. They set off for the church of All Hallows-on-the-Wall, about a hundred yards away on the other side of London Wall. A policeman, who has been warned that they are coming, holds up the traffic to let them cross the road.

The Carpenters' Company has probably been going to the church of All Hallows-on-the-Wall on election day at least since 1499. They have missed a few years. On several occasions in the sixteenth and seventeenth centuries the attendance at church was cancelled because of the plague; the Lord Mayor and the City authorities had ordered that people should assemble in crowds only when it was absolutely necessary. In 1941 the service was held in a small nearby building because the church had been damaged in the air raid on the night of 10 May. In 1989 the Court and the Livery did not go to the church because a transport strike made it necessary to change the date of the General Court, and the church was not available on the new date. In 1993 they went to the Dutch Church in Austin Friars, with which the Carpenters' Company has had links since the sixteenth century, because the church of All Hallows had been damaged by an IRA bomb.

The Carpenters enter the church, and the Master, Wardens and members of the Court sit in their appointed places; the Livery sit in the seats behind them. The Master will have chosen the hymns, and he reads the lesson. Today is the last important function which he

1. Interior of All Hallows-on-the-Wall, c.1800: in 1764, a few days after their annual election service, members of the Carpenters' Company complained that All Hallows was in poor condition. It proved cheaper to rebuild rather than repair the church and Mr George Dance, the Younger (1741–1825), was selected as architect for the new church; his plan costing £2,941 to implement. The most striking difference between the watercolour of Dance's interior and the Church today is the removal of the pews and bookcases.

14

will attend as Master, for his year of office will end in a fortnight's time. He will remember this same occasion last year, when he was about to be elected Master and his year lay ahead of him. The Company listen to a sermon in the church. Seventy years ago it was often preached by a bishop; now the preacher is always the Rector of All Hallows, unless he has asked the pastor of the Dutch Church to preach the sermon.

The Carpenters return in procession to Carpenters' Hall and have an excellent four-course lunch with sherry, white wines, claret and port. At the end of the lunch, after the Master has proposed the Queen's health, the Deputy Master, who was Master on this same occasion a year ago, proposes the health of the Master in a short speech in which he pays tribute to the Master's work during his year of office; and the Master replies in another short speech.

The Company then go to the Court Room for the General Court of the Livery. The Master sits almost for the last time in the great Master's chair and presides over the meeting. He opens the proceedings with the bidding prayer with which he also opens all the monthly meetings of the Court: "May we, in all our deliberations and in our decisions this day, be ever mindful of our Company's ancient motto, 'Honour God' ". The motto "Honour God" is indeed ancient; it dates back at least to the fifteenth century. But the bidding prayer is of much more recent origin. At the meeting of the Court on 7 December 1954 the Master, W. W. Dove, suggested that the meetings of the Court should open with a prayer which incorporated the Company's motto "Honour God". His motion was carried by 12 votes against 1, and it was agreed that the Master should be asked to draft the words of the prayer. It was first used at the meeting of the Court on 1 March 1955.

After a very short discussion on the annual report that the Court has presented to the Livery, they proceed to the election first of the Master and then of the three Wardens. During the Company's first four hundred years, the Wardens were called the Upper Warden, the Middle Warden and the Youngest Warden. At the beginning of the eighteenth century, the name of the Youngest Warden was changed to the "Renter Warden" – a name which is given to the most junior warden in many Livery Companies today. Since 1845 they have been known as the Senior Warden, the Middle Warden and the Junior Warden.

By the Ordinances issued for the Company in 1607 by the Lord Chancellor, the Lord Treasurer and the two Chief Justices, the right of the members of the Livery is limited to voting for one of the candidates nominated for office by the Court. The Court will have put forward three names for each of the offices. The first name on the list is the candidate whom the Court wishes to see elected; he has in fact been chosen by the Court because of his seniority in the list of liverymen according to the date on which he became a liveryman. The other two candidates have only been nominated so that an election can be held, they do not expect to be elected.

The liverymen vote by putting little wooden balls in the ballot box. There is a large hole in the centre of the ballot box, and any ball placed in this hole will be a vote for the Court's chosen candidate whose name appears first on the list. In order to vote for either of the other two candidates, a voter must perform the slightly difficult, though not impossible, task of putting his hand through the hole and slipping the ball to one side or the other of the hole. By modern standards it is hardly a democratic election; but one could not expect a voting

15

2. Election Day, c.1935: the election procession crosses London Wall on the way to All Hallows-on-the-Wall, led by the Beadle, Frederick William Powell (1928–1964).

system devised by royal officials in the reign of James I, that champion of royal absolutism and the divine right of Kings, to be in accordance with twentieth-century ideas of democracy. The Court's chosen candidate is usually elected unanimously.

After the Master has been elected, the same procedure is followed in turn with the election of the Senior Warden, the Middle Warden and the Junior Warden. The outgoing Master and Wardens and the newly-elected Master and Wardens line up side by side, with their cup-bearers standing beside them; the cupbearers are the four most junior members of the Livery who are present. The outgoing Master and Wardens drink to their successors in a loving cup and "crown" them with the sixteenth-century hats which they wear only on this occasion. They then walk in procession out of the room through one door and back into the room by the other door, which may perhaps represent beating the bounds of the Company's properties. The Master then closes the meeting and the liverymen disperse, while the members of the Court hold another meeting to elect the members of the various committees for the next year.

16

A fortnight later, on the first Tuesday in August, the monthly meeting of the Court takes place. The retiring Master vacates office at the beginning of the meeting. He invests the new Master with the chain of office; until a few years ago he also handed him the key of the Company's seal. The new Master then presents the retiring Master with his Past Master's badge, and takes his place in the Master's chair to begin his year as Master. The most senior of the Past Masters makes a speech in which he pays tribute to the retiring Master, who replies. The Court then proceeds to other business, with the new Master presiding for the first time.

This procedure at the General Court of the Livery and at the August Court has been going on for many centuries, though some changes have been introduced over the years. The date of the election day has been changed. In 1455 it was fixed for St. Lawrence's Day, 10 August, one of the high holy days of the medieval Church. After the Reformation in the sixteenth century it was changed to the second Monday in August; and in 1621 to the second Tuesday in August. The new Master and Wardens took office at the end, not the beginning, of the meeting of the Court on the first Tuesday in September; but in 1873 the September Court was abolished, and the Master and Wardens henceforth took office immediately after the General Court of the Livery on the second Tuesday in August; the tribute to the retiring Master took place at the October meeting of the Court. In 1886 the date of the General Court of the Livery was changed to the penultimate Tuesday in July, and the installation of the new Master and Wardens and the tribute to the retiring Master became the first business at the meeting of the Court on the first Tuesday in August. This has been the rule ever since.

The practice of holding the regular meetings of the Court on the first Tuesday in the month is the oldest unbroken custom of the Carpenters' Company; it has been going on for more that 360 years since the reign of Charles I, though the Ordinances of the Company of 1455 laid down that the Court should meet on Fridays. The rule about the meeting on the first Tuesday in the month was originally strictly adhered to: when 1 January was a Tuesday, the Court met on New Year's Day. It was not until 1883 that it was decided that if New Year's Day was a Tuesday, the Court should meet on 8 January.

The ceremony of crowning the new Master and Wardens with the caps, drinking their health in the loving cup, and walking in procession out of the room and in again, dates at least from 1738 and is probably much older. In the fourteenth and fifteenth centuries the day's proceedings began with Mass in the church, but the election was held before dinner. The result was not announced at the time, and the liverymen went to dinner not knowing who had been chosen to be their Master and Wardens next year. It was only at the end of the dinner that the Master announced the election results. After dinner the liverymen watched a play performed by actors, which in the fifteenth and early sixteenth centuries was certainly a religious morality play. The proceedings ended with all the members of the Livery escorting the Master Elect to his home, because the Master Elect, like all the other members of the Livery, always lived in the City.

The liverymen who attend on election day will have varying thoughts about the occasion. A young liveryman, coming for the first or second time, will be interested and impressed and a little awe-struck by the occasion, by the tradition and by the ceremony. It will probably not occur to him that one day he himself will be elected Master. The Master and Wardens

3. The Tudor Crowns: the embroidered velvet Master's crown, the oldest documented livery crown of its kind, was given to the Company by John Tryll in 1561, the year in which he was Master. The Crown bears Tryll's carpentry mark and initials (I.T.). The three Wardens' crowns date from the early seventeenth century and bear the initials of John Ansell, Peter Thornton and William Wheatley.

Elect will be deeply conscious of the honour that has been conferred on them, and eager to perform their new duties. The Master presiding over the meeting will certainly feel a pang of regret that his year of office is about to end. The members of the Court will have many memories of the other election days that they have attended during the past forty or fifty years. They will be thinking of their fathers and grandfathers, and of their former colleagues on the Court who are no longer there.

The oldest members of the Company are the link between the younger liverymen and the past. In 1995 the Senior Past Master – in earlier times he would have been called "the Father of the Company" – was V. J. G. Stavridi. He became a liveryman in 1929, when the eldest liveryman was Minden Smith, who joined the Livery in 1868. The Father of the Company in 1868 was Thomas Flight, who joined in 1812, three weeks before Napoleon invaded Russia, when there were no railways, and thieves were hanged in public for stealing a shilling. So the Carpenters' Company has continued from one election day to another, from one generation to another, and from one century to another. It will probably continue for many more election days, for many more generations, and for many more centuries.

4. The Court, 1995: the Installation Court chaired by the retiring Master of the Company. (Left to right) H.M.F. Barnes-Yallowley, J.G. Ridley, H.J. Osborne, R.B.A. Smith, D.R. Stuckey, F.D. Hornsby, M.R. Francis, the Beadle (Lieutenant-Commander B.F. Dutton RN), the Master – Captain K.G. Hamon RN, the Clerk (Major General P.T. Stevenson), H.M. Neal, the Assistant Clerk (I. Lester), Dr R.L. Woolley, A.T.C. Binny, Dr W.F. Felton, P.C. Osborne, V.F. Browne, Sir Desmond Heap, and C.W. Preston.

5. *The Copperplate Map, 1558/9: the map is one of the earliest impressions of the City and only two of the original plates have survived. The "Dogge Hows" on Moor Field refers to the kennels of the Lord Mayor's hunt. Carpenters' Hall is believed to be the building and gardens on London Wall, midway between Moor Gate and All Hallows-on-the-Wall.*

20

2
The Carpenters of London

The City of London in 1300 – influx of "foreigns" into London resented by the citizens – the origin of Livery Companies – the Carpenters' Company formed before the end of the thirteenth century – The Book of Ordinances of 1333 – the great merchant Livery Companies taken over in the fourteenth century by country gentlemen and career City politicians – the Carpenters' Company remains closely linked to the craft – the first Carpenters' Hall built in 1429 – the Company's ordinances of 1455 – the Carpenters' Company receives its charter of incorporation in 1477.

London has always been the largest and most important city in England. By the year 1300 its population had increased to 40,000; no other town in England had more than 15,000 inhabitants. It covered an area stretching for one mile from Ludgate in the west to the Tower and Aldgate in the east, and for half a mile from Aldersgate, Moorgate and Bishopsgate in the north to the River Thames in the south. It was surrounded on three sides by London Wall, two and a half miles in length; there were ten gates in the Wall through which people could enter and leave London, except at night, when the gates were closed. On the south side the City was protected by the river, with London Bridge, the only bridge across the Thames between Kingston and the sea, reaching to the little borough of Southwark. There were houses on both sides of the bridge, and a gate at the southern end.

Nearly all the houses in London, and in England, were built of wood; castles, cathedrals and churches were built of stone. The houses rarely lasted for more than a hundred years; before then someone usually left a candle burning at night and the flame, blown by the wind, set fire to the wooden house.

These houses were built by carpenters. A master carpenter, the entrepreneur, was responsible for the planning and erection of the building, combining the functions of the architect and the builder today. He employed journeymen carpenters and apprentices, who were being taught the trade so that they could one day become master carpenters. The journeymen were paid threepence a day; the apprentices were unpaid, and paid money to their master carpenter to train them. A skilled carpenter, if he worked as an employee for another master carpenter, could earn up to eight pence a day. The master carpenter who employed other carpenters and ran his own business could make quite a lot of money.

The population of London rose continually, and had doubled between 1100 and 1300. Outside the cities the great majority of the people of England worked on the land as serfs of their feudal overlords, from whom they held their land by labour service; they worked for a certain number of days in the year on their lord's land and the other days on their own land. The lords held their lands from the King, being bound to bring a certain number of men to fight for him in wartime. But from the earliest times many lords found it convenient to receive rents in money instead of labour service. The King and the lords who owned the land on which the towns were built were pleased that the citizens in the towns paid them

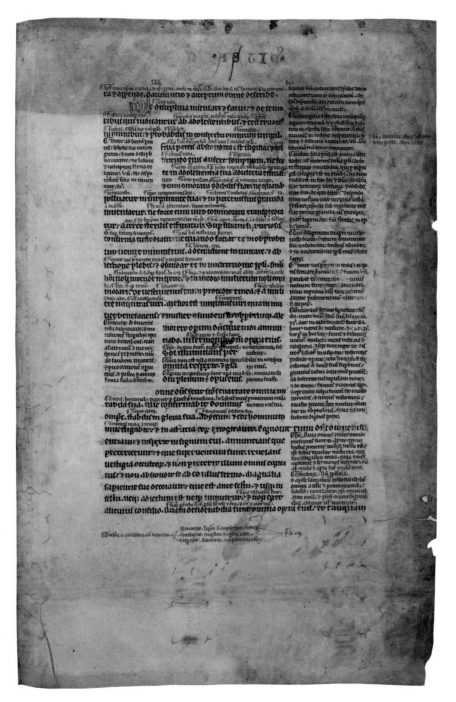

6. *Bible extracts, c.1250: a mid-thirteenth century copy of the Apocryphal Book of Ecclesiasticus XLII, v.8–22, annotated in the inner margins. These extracts were found in the binding of the Wardens' Accounts, 1614–1647.*

rent in the money which they had obtained from trading with other English and foreign merchants. So the towns came out of the feudal system.

Many serfs preferred the idea of working as citizens in the towns rather than labouring in the country for their lords. They were helped by the law that a serf gained his freedom if he escaped from the land and remained free and undetected for a year and a day. Some of the serfs who came to London became carpenters. But the immigrants did not wish other immigrants to follow them; and as so often happens, the most recent immigrants were more eager than anyone to prevent further immigration, to keep the "foreigns" from other parts of England out of London. The London carpenters were determined to prevent these "foreigns" from working as carpenters in London.

In London as in every other city in Europe, some of the inhabitants were merchants and others were craftsmen. The merchants who bought and sold things were wealthier than the craftsmen who made things, and because they were wealthier they were more powerful. They nearly always managed to gain control of the government of the cities. The craftsmen resented this, and often rebelled against the rule of the merchants and their city officials.

The struggle between the merchants and the craftsmen was less acute in London than in many European cities, and though there was constant friction, the craftsmen did not often openly rebel. On the few occasions when they did, it was at a time when their superiors, the feudal lords, were in rebellion against the King, for revolution is usually infectious. In 1308, after the death of the formidable Edward I, the nobles rebelled against his weak and homosexual son, Edward II, and during the next nineteen years they put to death his favourite ministers before eventually deposing and murdering the King himself. Almost immediately the craftsmen in London followed their example, and in 1309 there were serious disorders in London. The carpenters played a leading part in these disturbances.

Perhaps the chief reason why there were so few revolts of the craftsmen against the merchants in London was because the representatives of the merchants in the City Corporation skilfully enlisted the support of the leading craftsmen in preserving order. In 1271, when Walter Hervey (a mercer) was Mayor, the city authorities asked a number of leading carpenters and masons to prevent the members of their crafts from breaking the regulations and paying more than the prescribed level of wages. The help of the wealthy carpenters and masons was again enlisted for this purpose in 1284; and in 1299, when a number of carpenters assembled at Mile End and swore an oath to defy the City regulations, the Mayor and Corporation chose two wealthy carpenters to keep the other carpenters in order.

It was probably about this time that the Carpenters' Company was first formed, though the earliest record of the Company that we have is its Book of Ordinances of 1333. Several other Livery Companies were formed in the thirteenth century. The earliest of them all was the Weavers' Company which was formed in 1130 and received a charter of incorporation from the young King Henry II in 1155; but the Weavers were soon eclipsed by the merchants and their Livery Companies, who dominated the government of London.

Originally, London was governed by an official who was known as the Bailiff of London; but in 1189 the Bailiff took the title of Mayor of London. In the course of the next few centuries the Mayor became one of the most important officials in England, though he was never officially granted the title of Lord Mayor, and was usually called "the Mayor" as late as the sixteenth century. The first Mayor, Henry Fitzailwin, who was re-elected annually for twenty-one years, was a mercer; and during the next hundred years the Mercers, the Drapers and to a lesser extent the Fishmongers supplied nearly all the Mayors. The Mercers and Drapers sold cloth; the Grocers sold foodstuffs; the Taylors and Linen Armourers, who later became the Merchant Taylors, sold garments; the Fishmongers sold fish. The only association of craftsmen which could compete in influence with these merchants were the Goldsmiths, who made the gold coins which have been universally accepted as the medium of exchange in trading transactions, and the gold rings and trinkets which wealthy men and their wives wished to wear as a sign of their affluence.

The members of all these trades exercised their influence through their Livery Companies. Six hundred years later, there was a bitter political controversy about why the Livery Companies were formed. Were they trades unions? Were they official bodies, "State departments" formed to administer the government of London under the authority of the Mayor and corporation and the King? Were they friendly societies, whose object was to help their members in distress? Were they organisations of laymen who helped the clergy to carry out religious duties, like a modern parochial church council? Were they charitable trustees? Were they social clubs, where members of the same occupations met to discuss their common interests and to eat and drink together? They were in fact a combination of all these things, because a thirteenth-century Livery Company, not surprisingly, did not exactly correspond to any nineteenth or twentieth century organisation.

Although it has sometimes been said that the Livery Companies were trade unions, they were never trade unions in the modern sense of an organisation formed to protect the interests of employees against their employers. They were more like an employers' organisation, for usually only the wealthier and more successful members of a trade were members of the Livery Company. At the beginning of the fifteenth century only forty carpenters were freemen of the Carpenters' Company at a time when there were probably about four hundred carpenters working in London.

In 1333 the Carpenters drew up a Book of Ordinances which stated the objects for which the Company had been formed. It was probably not their first set of rules, but unlike the earlier ones it survived, because the Carpenters' Company produced it in 1389 when King Richard II ordered all the City Livery Companies to produce their ordinances; he was hoping to exercise more control over the City by granting licences to the Livery Companies. These ordinances of 1333 show that the "Brotherhood of Carpenters of London", which included both "brethren and sisters", was primarily a friendly society. It used the funds which had been contributed by members' admission and other fees to grant relief to the members who were in need because of poverty or sickness; after a member had been sick for a fortnight, he was to be paid 14d. a week, which was about half his weekly wage when he was fit enough to work. The Book of Ordinances directed that if this was not enough to relieve his distress, a collection was to be made among the other members of the Company to raise the money which he needed.

Religion played a very important part in the lives of the people in the fourteenth century. They believed that if they died unrepentant sinners their souls would burn in Hell for all eternity, and they interpreted the pains of Hell fire in the most literal sense. The influence of the Roman Catholic Church was very strong. People thought they would only be saved if they performed "good works", that is to say, gave gifts to charity, especially to monks to pray for souls. Nearly every organisation and activity was associated in some way with the Church. The Ordinances of 1333 described the Brotherhood of Carpenters of London as being "a Fraternity to be holden in the church of St. Thomas of Acon beside the Conduit of London and the church of St. John the Baptist at Holywell beside London". The church of St. Thomas of Acon was near the Fleet river in what today is Fleet Street; the church of St. John the Baptist at Holywell beside London was in Shoreditch, just off the modern Great Eastern Road, a little to the north of Liverpool Street Station. The Ordinances stipulated that all the liverymen and freemen should attend Mass every year on the twelfth day of Christmas (6 January) and on the Feast of St. John the Baptist (Midsummer Day, 24 June). They were to be paid one penny if they came, and fined one pound of wax if they were absent.

There were no regulations in the Book of Ordinances which indicated that the Brotherhood of Carpenters exercised any control over the craft and the carpenters of London; but there was a provision that every master carpenter who wished to employ a carpenter should offer the job first to a member of the Fraternity, and should employ an outsider only if no liveryman or freeman was competent to fill the position.

Nor was there anything in the Ordinances which suggested that social life or dinners played a part in their activities, though some Livery Companies, such as the Merchant Taylors, expressly stated in their charter that holding dinners was one of the objects of the Company. But the Brotherhood of Carpenters probably met from time to time at dinners. In the nineteenth century the Livery Companies were denounced by Radical reformers as "dens of gluttony" whose only object was to indulge in feasting and drinking; and in the twentieth century most Livery Companies are eager to play down this aspect of their Company's activities. But the Carpenters in the fourteenth century were following a well-established tradition by having dinners, for it seems to be a fundamental instinct of human beings in every part of the world to wish to eat and drink together. The dinner was a midday meal, held on one of the many holy days in the year when neither carpenters nor anyone else performed any work. After rising at 5.00 a.m. in summer and 6.00 a.m. in winter, the liverymen sat down to dinner at about 10.30 or 11.00 a.m. and did not finish till 2.30 or 3.00 p.m.

There were two classes of members of the Carpenters' Company – freemen and liverymen. No one could become a liveryman unless he had first been admitted as a freeman; but not every freeman was allowed to proceed to become a liveryman. The Company's regulations of 1455 imposed a property qualification for liverymen; no one was to be admitted to the Livery unless he owned property or assets worth 20 marks (£13.33) a year, which was more than the most highly-paid carpenter earned in ten months. The members of the Company were called liverymen, and the Companies were called Livery Companies, because when the members became liverymen they were given a gown to put on which was the Livery of their particular trade. It was a uniform. In the Middle Ages all classes in effect wore a uniform, for a series of Acts of Parliament, known as the Sumptuary Laws, regulated in the most minute detail what clothes, furs, ornaments and colours the members of each class in society was allowed to wear. So it was natural that the carpenters should wear the carpenters' livery.

There were three ways in which a man could become a freeman and a liveryman. If he

a. Noah and the Building of the Ark [now disintegrated]

7. Tudor wall paintings: in 1845, workmen in the Hall uncovered a wall painting. Artist Frederick William Fairholt (1818–1866) was summoned to make watercolour sketches and a full scale facsimile of these murals. The murals date from the second part of the sixteenth century and depict scenes from the Bible. During the Second World War the frescoes were on loan to the Museum of London and one, Noah and the Building of the Ark, was damaged during the air raids.

b. King Josiah gives instructions for the rebuilding of the Temple in Jerusalem

c. Christ in the Carpenter's Shop

d. Christ teaching in the Synagogue

27

had been apprenticed to a master carpenter in the City of London, he could join by servitude. The son of a freeman could become a freeman by patrimony automatically by right, but only if he was born after his father became a freeman – a rule which still applies today and sometimes has the effect of admitting a younger and excluding an elder son. The son of a liveryman could become a liveryman by patrimony, but only if the Company decided to accept him. It was possible for someone who had neither been apprenticed to a master carpenter nor was the son of a freeman or liveryman to become a freeman or a liveryman by redemption if he paid the necessary admission fees and the Company decided to accept him. This was a method by which new members with no previous connection with the Company could be brought into it.

Over the course of the years and the centuries a number of people who were not carpenters by trade became members of the Carpenters' Company. In the Middle Ages sons usually followed their father's occupation, and most carpenters' sons became carpenters; but a few did not, and they were nevertheless entitled to become freemen of the Carpenters' Company by right. It also became the practice for the Company to allow the sons of liverymen to become not merely freemen but also liverymen by patrimony even when they had chosen some other occupation and were not carpenters. But it was chiefly through admission by redemption that non-carpenters became liverymen of the Carpenters' Company, though this development took place later in the Carpenters' Company than in some other Livery Companies.

Important developments took place in London during the fourteenth century. In 1348 the plague known as the Black Death reached England from Eastern Europe, Italy and France, and it was followed by other outbursts of plague during the next ten years. Between one-third and half of the English people died from these plagues, reducing the total population from 4,000,000 to a little over 2,000,000. The population of London also fell, but had risen again to 35,000 before the end of the century.

The fall in population had important economic and social consequences. The shortage in the supply of labour made it possible for all artisans, including carpenters, to demand higher wages. The government tried to prevent the rise in wages. Both the regulations of the corporation of the City of London and a series of Acts of Parliament fixed the maximum wages payable to the artisans in the different trades, and made it a criminal offence to pay or receive higher wages; but the statutes and regulations were only partly successful in preventing the rise in wages, for many employers were prepared to break the law and secretly pay more than the law allowed them to pay, in order to obtain the labour.

In the countryside, serfdom was quietly disappearing. The peasants who followed Wat Tyler in 1381 and captured London demanded the abolition of serfdom; and though the revolt failed, and their status as serfs was re-emphasized, serfdom had almost disappeared by the beginning of the fifteenth century, nearly four hundred years before it ceased to exist in many other European countries.

Despite the Black Death and the Peasants' Revolt, London became wealthier during the fourteenth century. The export of wool ensured English prosperity. Country gentlemen, who were increasingly employing paid labourers instead of serfs, sold their wool to merchants who exported it to the Netherlands, and both the gentlemen and the merchants made a great deal of money. Many London merchants, who were engaged in other trades and belonged to their particular Livery Companies, also bought and sold wool for export, either as a profitable sideline or as their principal source of wealth. Before the end of the fourteenth century many liverymen of the Taylors and Linen Armourers, the Mercers, the Grocers, the Fishmongers and the Goldsmiths were concentrating chiefly on exporting wool to the Netherlands.

The wool trade linked the country gentlemen to the London merchants. Many country gentlemen were invited as guests to Livery Company dinners. After a time the gentlemen suggested that they might join the Livery Companies by redemption. This would give them influence in the City, and a voice in electing the Sheriffs and the Mayor, and strengthen their ties with the merchants on whom they depended to sell their wool on the continent. The Livery Companies were very pleased to have them. A gentleman was socially superior to a merchant, even if he were not as rich. His status as a gentleman was safeguarded by law, which allowed him to wear clothes and eat dishes for dinner which were forbidden to those below him in rank. It was a boost to the prestige of the Livery Companies if they had gentlemen among the Livery.

By the end of the fourteenth century many liverymen had no connection at all with their Company's trade. They joined the Company merely to gain influence in the City, like a modern politician gets himself elected to Parliament as MP for a constituency where he does not live and with which he had no connection at all until he was adopted there as a Parliamentary candidate. In 1370 less than half the liverymen of the Taylors and Linen Armourers were tailors or engaged in selling clothes. One of their liverymen was King Edward III himself. He needed money to pay for the Hundred Years War which he was waging in France, and was prepared to do anything to please and flatter the City merchants who lent him money although they knew that it was unlikely that he would repay it. He was very happy to become a liveryman of the Taylors and Linen Armourers.

The Carpenters' Company remained more closely connected with their craft than many other Companies. Because the Carpenters were poor in comparison with the great merchant Companies, the gentlemen and the ambitious City politicians did not wish to join the Carpenters, and it was not until the nineteenth century that the Company attracted the wealthy outsiders and members of a higher social class.

But if the Carpenters' Company could not compete with the merchant Livery Companies, it was prospering. Only forty carpenters were freemen of the Company, but these forty freemen were the wealthiest and most eminent carpenters in the City. By the beginning of the reign of Henry VI, when Joan of Arc was trying to persuade the French authorities that God had sent her to save the town of Orleans from the English, the members of the Carpenters' Company were sufficiently prosperous and confident to buy property and build themselves a Hall.

On 22 January 1429 the leading members of the Company took a lease from the Priory and Convent of St. Mary's Hospital in Bishopsgate for 98 years of a plot of land near the Church of All Hallows-on-the-Wall, just inside the northern wall of the City between the great gate of Bishopsgate and the postern gate of Moorgate. It was on the same site, in the modern street "London Wall", on which Carpenters' Hall stands today. The rent of the land

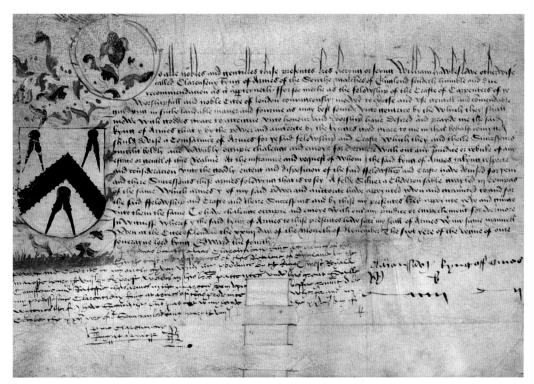

8. Grant of Arms 1466: the right for the Company to bear a coat-of-arms was granted by William Hawkeslowe, Clarenceux King of Arms, on 24 November 1466 with additional confirmation on 28 October 1530.

was twenty shillings a year. There were five cottages on the land, but the Company pulled them down and built a Hall on the site. They also built four new cottages around the Hall, three on the east and one on the west side. A few years before the expiry of the lease, Thomas Smart, a Past Master of the Company, bought the freehold of the land and left it in his will to the Company in 1520. It is still owned by the Carpenters' Company 475 years later in 1995.

One of the trustees who took the lease for the Company in 1429 was the prominent carpenter, William Serles. A few months after the lease was signed, the Grocers' Company asked Serles to build a roof for their Hall. He was required to complete the work in four months, and did so. The Grocers paid him £100 for the work. It would have taken a skilled carpenter, earning the maximum permitted wage of eightpence a day, nearly ten years to earn £100.

Not every Livery Company had a Hall, and the Carpenters in the fifteenth century made money by letting other Companies use their Hall, as they still do in the twentieth century. In 1458 they let the Hall for two shillings to the "Dutchmen". This was the beginning of a long association between the Carpenters' Company and Dutchmen living in London which is still highly valued by the Carpenters, although the term "Dutchmen" in the fifteenth century was not limited to the inhabitants of the country which the English today call "Holland". "Dutch" was the anglicised form of the German word "Deutsch", and included people from Holland, Belgium and the Hansa towns of North Germany.

The members of a trade, having formed their Livery Company, were always eager to obtain a charter of incorporation from the King who alone could grant one. Until a charter was obtained, their Company could not exist as a separate legal entity from its individual members, and all property had to be held by the leading liverymen as trustees for the other members. There were various legal restrictions on the operations of an unincorporated association, and it was easy for the trustees inadvertently to break the law and perhaps be prosecuted at the instigation of jealous rivals. There was also the prestige factor: as other Companies had obtained a charter, it was important that their Company should also have one.

But charters were not readily granted, and nearly all the Livery Companies had to wait many years for their charters. The King had to be persuaded to grant the charter when he was in a good mood and not too busy hunting or making war. This meant that his secretaries had to approach him about it at a suitable time, and the secretaries would do this only if they received a suitable gift from the liverymen in return for their services. We today would say that they had to be given bribes; but the practice was as universal in medieval England as it is today in certain foreign countries, and no one expected anything else or thought the worse of those who gave or accepted the gift. It was the principal source of income for royal officials who were paid a very small salary, if they received any salary at all. When a Company applied for a charter, there was often opposition from the Corporation of London and from the other Livery Companies. Those Companies which had already been granted a charter, after waiting a long time for it, thought that this distinction would be cheapened if charters were granted too readily to other Companies.

Even the most powerful Livery Companies of the great merchants had to wait more than a century for their charters. The Mercers and the Fishmongers were already a fraternity in the reign of Henry II; but the Fishmongers had to wait a hundred years before they obtained their charter from Edward I, and the Mercers for more than two hundred years till 1393. The Drapers were a fraternity for many years before they received their charter in 1364. The Goldsmiths waited from 1180 to 1327, though the Taylors and Linen Armourers waited only about sixty years, from before 1267 to 1327.

So it cannot have surprised the Brotherhood of Carpenters that they had still not obtained a charter in 1455 when they drew up new regulations to replace their book of Ordinances of 1333. The Ordinances of 1455 were more precise than the earlier regulations. The Ordinances of 1333 stated that the Brotherhood was to be governed by "masters", but did not mention a procedure for electing them; the regulations of 1455 laid down that the Company was to be governed by a Master and three Wardens who were to be elected annually on the Feast of St. Lawrence (10 August) and hold office for one year. The Master and Wardens could appoint eight Assistants to form a Court of Assistants to help them manage the Company's affairs. These Assistants must either have held office in the Company as Master or Wardens, or else be "most honest persons". The Court was to meet once a week on Fridays.

31

The Carpenters Company's Ordinances of 1455, unlike their Book of Ordinances of 1333, showed that the Company was attempting to exercise control over the way in which carpenters carried on their work. The new regulations contained provisions for settling demarcation disputes with other crafts. No freeman or liveryman was to undertake the work of a mason, a plumber, a plasterer or a tiler, in return for reciprocal agreements with the Masons, the Plumbers, the Plaisterers and the Tylers. The Master and Wardens were given power to search the carpenters' workshops to make sure that all timbers and boards corresponded to the standard, sizes and qualities laid down by the City Corporation. Only freemen of the Carpenters' Company were to be eligible to hold the office of Master Carpenter at the Guildhall, who supervised all the carpenters' work at the Guildhall, or Master Carpenter of the Bridge House, who supervised the work on London Bridge.

While the Carpenters' Company was drawing up its new ordinances, the wars broke out between the houses of Lancaster and York which were afterwards called the "Wars of the Roses", when Richard, Duke of York, claimed to be the rightful heir to the throne in place of the weak and saintly King Henry VI. The citizens of London sympathised with the Yorkists because Henry VI had failed to maintain law and order and had lost the English territories in France. The Londoners were also aware that the Yorkist armies were more disciplined than the wild levies that the Lancastrians recruited in Lancashire and Wales. By 1461 Richard, Duke of York, had been killed, but his son Edward had won the war and had become King Edward IV; and though the Lancastrians drove him out in 1470 he returned triumphant within a year and ruled in peace for another twelve years.

There was a mood of optimism in London and a good deal of housebuilding. In Edward IV's reign people first began to build houses in brick; but as this was expensive, the houses of the common people were still mostly built in wood, and there was a considerable amount of woodwork in the brick houses. Enterprising master carpenters moved with the times and began to supervise the building of brick houses. Some of these carpenters became very wealthy.

It was a suitable time for the Carpenters to press more energetically to obtain their charter. Edward IV was eager to remain on good terms with the citizens of London, and became personally friendly with many of them. He became even more friendly with some of their wives, though it was undoubtedly an exaggeration to say, as many of his subjects said, that every merchant's wife in the City of London had been the King's mistress.

In 1466 the Carpenters' Company took a step towards their goal when they obtained a grant of a coat-of-arms from the College of Heralds. It was "a field silver, a chevron sable grailed three compasses of the same". These are still the Company's arms today. The Company was not granted supporters or a crest, and has never had them. Later, it chose as its motto "Honour God".

By 1472 the Company had actually drafted the charter and was only waiting for the King to sign and seal it. This took another five years. It was of course necessary to make gifts to the royal officials; altogether obtaining the charter cost the Company £26.5s.8d. (more than £12,000 in terms of 1995 prices). But at last the King granted the charter on 7 July 1477; it was the day of the greater feast of St. Thomas of Canterbury (Thomas Becket), one of the most important saints' days in fifteenth-century England.

The charter stated that the Company was to be incorporated under the name of "the Freemen of the Mystery of Carpentry of our City of London". The charter was granted to the freemen so "that they, or any of them, to the praise glory and honour of the omnipotent God and the glorious and undefiled Virgin Mary, may make, found, and establish one perpetual brotherhood, or guild, within the said city, to remain for ever, to consist of one Master, three Wardens, and commonalty of freemen, of the mystery of carpentry, abiding and to be dwelling within the said City of London and the suburbs and precincts of the same, and of the brethren and sisters of freemen of the said mystery, and of others which of their own devotion will be of the same brotherhood or guild". The Master and Wardens were given powers to control the working practices of carpenters.

It was usual for Livery Companies to choose a patron saint. The Carpenters chose the Virgin Mary, probably because of her association with her husband Joseph the carpenter, and because Jesus Himself worked for a time as a carpenter; the Carpenters' Company has never forgotten that Our Saviour chose carpentry as His trade. Now that they had a Hall near London Wall between Bishopsgate and Moorgate they transferred their association from the churches of St. Thomas of Acon beside the Conduit and of St. John the Baptist in Shoreditch to the church of All Hallows-on-the-Wall, about a hundred yards from Carpenters' Hall.

The obtaining of the charter was a boost to the Company's prestige, and immediately attracted new members; the membership doubled from about 50 to 106. But then disaster struck the Company; within a few years the membership had fallen again to about forty. This was probably due to the very serious outbreak of plague in 1479, for there is no other apparent explanation of this sudden and drastic fall in membership. It is certainly not impossible that half of the liverymen and freemen of the Carpenters' Company died of plague in 1479. But the Company survived the recurrent outbreaks of plague, just as it survived all the revolutions and religious and political upheavals in the fifteenth, sixteenth and seventeenth centuries.

9. Designs for English royal tents, c.1520: these tents have been designed in the Tudor livery colours of green and white. This design is one in a series of three "magnificent tents" believed to be those commissioned by Henry VIII for the Field of Cloth-of-Gold. These designs were acquired by Sir Robert Bruce Cotton (1571–1631), an antiquarian who gathered and preserved many of the records dispersed by the dissolution of the monasteries. Cotton's collection is now held by the British Library.

3
The King's Master Carpenters

Prominent members of the Carpenters' Company hold important positions at
Henry VIII's court – Humphrey Cooke builds the pavilions for the Field of
Cloth-of-Gold – Cooke averts a diplomatic crisis by completing the buildings
on time – James Nedeham, the King's Master Carpenter and afterwards Clerk
and Surveyor of the King's Works in England – Nedeham's influence with
Henry VIII – secret meeting of Thomas Cromwell and the Emperor Charles
V's ambassador in Nedeham's half-built house – Nedeham is granted monastic
lands and the lands of executed traitors.

On 22 August 1485 Henry Tudor, Earl of Richmond, defeated and killed King Richard III
at the Battle of Bosworth, and on 3 September he entered London in triumph as King
Henry VII. The Carpenters' Company came out to welcome him with all the other Livery
Companies; the day's entertainments cost the Company 7s.7d. They also took part in the
other important state events in London during his reign – in the coronation of his Queen,
Elizabeth of York; the marriage of his son Arthur, Prince of Wales, to Catherine of Aragon,
the daughter of the King and Queen of Spain; and the funerals of Queen Elizabeth and
Henry VII himself.

They duly paid their contribution to the loan which the City granted to the King for his
war against France in 1488. All the Livery Companies, being eager to win the King's favour,
gave as much as they could afford, and their contributions show their respective wealth. The
Carpenters gave £8, more than the £4 given by the Masons and the twenty shillings by the
Wheelwrights; but the Goldsmiths gave £280, the Drapers £420, the Grocers £455, and
the Mercers headed the list with £740.

In 1518 there was an outbreak of violence against the French and other foreigners living
in London. A second-hand dealer and a London vicar incited the people against the foreigners
in inflammatory speeches and sermons. One of their grievances was that a Frenchman had
forced a shopkeeper to sell to him two pigeons which had already been sold to a poor
carpenter. It is very unlikely that this poor carpenter was a member of the Carpenters'
Company, for their freemen and liverymen were the more prosperous carpenters.

The apprentices played the leading part in the attacks on the foreigners on "Evil May
Day", the May Day holiday on 1 May 1517. Henry VIII clamped down vigorously on the
rioters. He sent the Duke of Norfolk with 2,000 soldiers to occupy London, and the rioters –
some of whom were as young as thirteen – were tried for high treason at the Guildhall. Two
hundred and seventy-nine were sentenced to death, but after fourteen had been executed
the King pardoned the others. There was great sympathy in London for the victims,
particularly for the young apprentices who had been condemned to be hanged, drawn and
quartered; but the Carpenters' Company was on the side of the King and the Lord Mayor,
of authority and law and order.

Some of the leading carpenters, who were prominent members of the Carpenters'

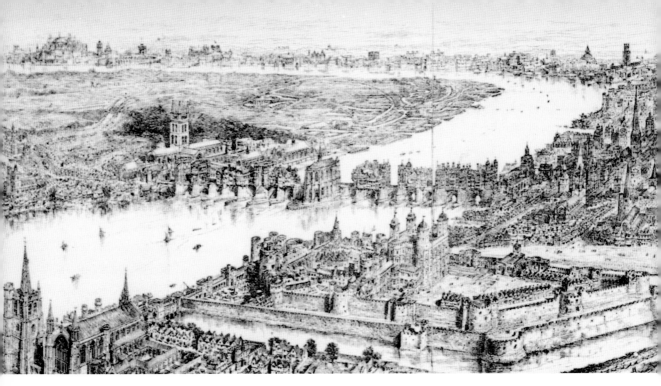

10. Panorama of London, 1520: this reconstruction of London as it was in the time of Henry VIII was made by H.H. Brewer in December 1887. London has been viewed from the east.

The prominent buildings in the foreground, outside the City wall, are: (left to right) St Katharine's church (now St Katharine's dock), the Tower of London, East Minster, the Abbey of St Clare (also known as the Minories). The first bridge into the City from the east is Aldgate (bottom right) leading from St Botolph, Aldgate over to the Priory of the Holy Trinity inside the wall. The next gate is Bishops Gate (centre, far right). St Botolph is outside the wall and behind the church lies

Company, were making a great deal of money and rising to important positions. In 1509 Humphrey Cooke was appointed Master of the Bridge House and also Master Carpenter of the Savoy Hospital. In 1511 he drew up plans to enlarge the cloister at Eton College. In 1514 he became Master of Carpentry at Corpus Christi College, Oxford, to the great satisfaction of Bishop Foxe, the former Lord Privy Seal, who had founded the College. In 1519 Cooke became King's Carpenter. He was a Warden of the Carpenters' Company in 1506, 1507, 1510 and 1519, and probably later became Master, though we cannot be sure of this because the Company's records from 1520 to 1532 are missing.

Soon after he became King's Carpenter, and in the year when he was Upper Warden of the Carpenters' Company, Cooke was entrusted with the duty of erecting the pavilions for Henry VIII's meeting with Francis I of France at the Field of Cloth-of-Gold. Henry, having begun his reign by going to war with France, was now pursuing a policy of friendship with Francis, though he was already considering making war on France again in alliance with the Emperor Charles V, who ruled Spain and the Netherlands. Henry and Francis agreed that they should meet on the frontier between France and the English territory around Calais, which was the only part of France still held by the King of England.

Moorfields, a swampy ground that was drained in 1527. The large building opposite Moorfields, on modern Broad Street is the Church of the Augustine Friars (Austin Friars). Beyond Moorfields, on the outside of the City walls, is an abandoned fortress known as the Barbican. Other landmarks are London Bridge, leading over the Thames to Southwark, the Palace of Westminster (top left) *and the medieval St Pauls Cathedral* (top centre). *London, like Oxford, was a city of spires and, in 1520, there were 107 parish churches within the City walls.*

The meeting took a long time to arrange, for there were lengthy discussions between the English and French ministers about exactly where the meeting should take place, which King's shield should hang higher over the meeting ground, and whether Henry or Francis, when they walked together side by side, should take the place of honour on the right; but eventually everything was settled by compromises on both sides. There was a good deal of argument about the date of the meeting, but in the autumn of 1519 it was agreed that Henry would cross to Calais no later than 31 May 1520, and that the two Kings should meet on 6 June on the border between English and French territory. They would gallop towards each other and would meet exactly on the border line, where they would dismount and embrace.

Henry ordered Cooke to build a splendid pavilion where he would stay during the two and a half weeks that the meeting was to last and smaller pavilions for his nobles and escort, though most of the King's attendants would sleep in tents. Cooke set to work, but there were delays, and in March 1520 the English Ambassador had to tell Francis that the work would not be finished by the beginning of June. He asked Francis to postpone the meeting. Francis had made many concessions to please Henry, but he absolutely refused to agree to a postponement. It had been agreed that his Queen, like Henry's Queen, Catherine of Aragon,

11. *The Field of Cloth-of-Gold, 1520: Henry VIII rides into Guisnes with his forces. The large building (centre right), fronted by two fountains, has been erected as a reception for the English King and his retinue. The golden tent immediately behind this temporary palace is the royal dining tent. Behind the golden dining tent is a circle of green and white tents with a golden tent in the centre*

38

(top centre). *Henry and Francis I are shown greeting each other in front of this encircled golden tent. Additionally, the two kings and their queens watch a jousting tournament, the tree nearby having been decorated with the contestants' shields* (top right). *Artist(s) not known.*

would be present at the meeting; but the French Queen was pregnant, and after June her pregnancy would be too far advanced for her to be able to come. Francis probably thought that Henry was making an excuse when he said that the buildings would not be ready in time, and that Henry was plotting with Charles V and wished to call off the meeting. Henry was indeed plotting with Charles V, but he wished the meeting with Francis to take place. So he agreed to meet Francis on 6 June, and told Cooke that at whatever cost the pavilions must be finished by the end of May.

Cooke was up to the task, and the pavilions were ready on time. Henry's pavilion was a magnificent building. The base was of stone, the walls were of brick up to a height of 12 feet from the ground, and the rest was of wood. Three of the rooms were longer than any room in Henry's palaces in England. The great chamber was 124 feet long, 42 feet wide and 30 feet high. The dining room was 80 feet long, 34 feet wide and 27 feet high, and the drawing room 60 feet long, 34 feet wide and 27 feet high. There was also a chapel and a cellar with 3,000 bottles of the most expensive wines. The building was surrounded by 2,800 tents for Henry's retinue.

Cooke went with Henry to the Field of Cloth-of-Gold, and was there for the seventeen days that the meeting lasted. He knew that it was his efforts which had made the meeting possible, and that he had prevented a major diplomatic rupture between England and France.

In 1525 Cardinal Wolsey employed Cooke to build the roof of the great hall of the new college, Cardinal's College, which he had founded at Oxford. Cooke had barely completed the work when Wolsey fell from power, and was in due course arrested for high treason. For a time it seemed as if his college at Oxford would be suppressed; but Henry decided to allow it to continue after ordering Cooke to remove Wolsey's coat-of-arms which had been fixed above every gate. The name of the college was then changed from Cardinal's College to "King Henry VIII's College". It later became known as "Christ Church".

In carrying out these great building projects for the King and the Cardinal and other important patrons, Cooke was dealing in brick and stone as well as wood. He was far more than just a carpenter; he was, in modern language, both architect and builder. In dealing in stone and other materials, Cooke was transgressing against the ordinances of the Carpenters' Company and of the City Corporation and the demarcation agreements with the other Livery Companies; but, like other successful men of his period, he did not allow his hands to be fettered by a slavish compliance with the letter of the law, and was influential enough to be able to adopt this attitude with impunity.

In 1531 Cooke was succeeded as King's Carpenter by James Nedeham. He was a Derbyshire man who became a carpenter and moved to London. He became a liveryman of the Carpenters' Company. He obtained employment in the King's service at the Tower of London at a wage of sixpence a day. In 1522, only two years after the meeting at the Field of Cloth-of-Gold, Henry VIII declared war on Francis I in alliance with Charles V, and in 1523 he sent an army to invade France. Nedeham went with the army to carry out any necessary work on bridges and on the army encampments. His wages were twelvepence a day. The English advanced to within sixty miles of Paris, but then had to retreat to Calais because their supply carts became bogged down in the November mud after an early onset of winter.

After leaving the army, Nedeham worked for several important patrons, doing building work for Cardinal Wolsey; but he was in a predicament when Wolsey was dismissed from office in the autumn of 1529. Henry waited for a year before ordering Wolsey's arrest on a charge of high treason; but the Cardinal's property was immediately forfeited to the King. This meant that his creditors could not sue him for the money that he owed them; but Henry allotted £1,000 of Wolsey's forfeited property for the payment of his debts. Nedeham put in a claim for the money owing to him for building work. The King's officials looked at all the creditors' claims with suspicion, and tried to avoid paying them; but Nedeham was so persistent that Henry decided to intervene personally, and in May 1530 he summoned Nedeham to an audience with him.

Henry questioned Nedeham closely about all the items in his account. Nedeham must have made a good impression, for Henry ordered that his claim should be paid in full. In March 1531 Nedeham was appointed to succeed Cooke as Chief Carpenter of the King's Works in England. His area of operations extended all over England, including Berwick, the English garrison town across the Tweed facing the Scots, but not the Marches of Calais or the English Pale in Ireland.

It was not long before Nedeham was promoted to higher office. In October 1532 he was appointed Clerk and Surveyor of the King's Works in England. He was to be paid two shillings a day for himself and a further sixpence a day for his clerk. When he travelled on the King's business he was to have "riding costs" of four shillings a day, and expenses of twenty pence a day when he travelled by water from London either to Westminster or to Greenwich.

The King's Controller, whose duty was to prevent the King's servants and contractors from cheating him with false claims, became suspicious of Nedeham, and in the summer of 1534 he confided his suspicions to the King. Henry behaved as he often did when one of the Privy councillors denounced another Privy councillor as a traitor or a heretic; he led his informant to think that he believed his allegations, and then came down on the side of the accused man. This served as a warning to his underlings to behave themselves, and by sowing suspicion between them made it difficult for them to conspire together against him. He told the Controller that he suspected that some of his servants were paying themselves double wages, and that he thought that Nedeham was one of them; he also thought that Nedeham was falsifying his accounts regarding the quantity of bricks, lime and timber which had been purchased. Henry ordered the Controller to look into this carefully. He added that Nedeham ought not to pay a penny to himself or to any other person without authorisation from the Controller.

But Nedeham persuaded Sir Henry Norris, who was one of the King's favourite courtiers, to intervene on his behalf. Norris assured Nedeham that he need not submit his accounts to the Controller; and when the Controller questioned him, Nedeham refused to give him any information. He told the Controller that he should question those to whom the King had paid money, and not him, as he had not received the money that was owing to him.

Nedeham's victory over the Controller encouraged him to insist that he should be paid for the work that he was carrying out in repairing and strengthening the Tower of London. On 26 July 1534 he wrote to Thomas Cromwell, who was now the King's Secretary and all-powerful, and complained that he was not being paid quickly enough. He explained that it would be necessary to do a great deal of work at the Tower; the gates and bridges would have to be completely replaced, and extensive repairs would have to be carried out to the Lieutenant's lodgings and to the roof of the White Tower. He demanded that he be paid the

12. Reconstruction of Cromwell's house, c.1540: built by Nedeham for Thomas Cromwell, the house was acquired by the Drapers' Company in 1543. Although no drawings have survived to show the original details of the mansion, this reconstruction (1993), by architect Robert Chitham, is based upon a detailed ground plan of c.1620 and a description in the Drapers Court minutes.

money in advance, for he did not like to be behind-hand with the wages. Only a very influential person could have written to Cromwell in the way that Nedeham wrote, which was very different from the cringing and sycophantic language of most of Cromwell's correspondents.

After Nedeham was appointed King's Surveyor he no longer engaged chiefly in military projects, but was in charge of repairing the King's palaces at Greenwich, Eltham, Windsor, Ampthill, Woking, The Moor in Hertfordshire and Leeds Castle in Kent, as well as working on the fortifications at the Tower and Dover Castle. Henry VIII not only engaged in many building projects, but also acquired many palaces and houses by virtually forcing his ministers and courtiers to make "exchanges" with him whereby they gave their house to him in exchange for some royal estate which was nearly always of lesser value than the one they gave to the King. Henry's pliant Archbishop of Canterbury, Thomas Cranmer, suffered particularly from the exchanges; he was forced to surrender to Henry seven of the Archbishop's eleven palaces.

On one occasion, when Cranmer was entertaining Henry at Knole near Sevenoaks in Kent, Henry asked Cranmer to give him Knole. Cranmer, who was very fond of Knole, tried to persuade Henry to take another of his palaces, Otford, instead of Knole. After Cranmer had stressed the advantages to Henry of having Otford, Henry said that he would have both Otford and Knole, and Cranmer was forced to give them to him. Henry decided to enlarge and embellish both houses, and he employed Nedeham to do the work.

Nedeham also worked privately for Cromwell, who employed Nedeham to build a house for him in the City of London, about 150 yards to the south of Carpenters' Hall. Cromwell's

13. The Lord Mayor's Show, c.1650: river processions frequently took place on the Thames. These were primarily royal pageants but also included the Lord Mayor's Show up to 1856. This picture depicts a 17th Century Master of the Carpenters' Company embarking on a barge to participate in the Lord Mayor's Show. The picture was commissioned in 1912 by the Master, William Cobay. The artist, Frank Brangwyn (1867–1956), was paid £200 for his work.

house was in what is now Throgmorton Street, and today Drapers' Hall stands on the site. Nedeham began building the house for Cromwell at the end of 1535, when important political developments were about to occur. Henry had divorced Catherine of Aragon, repudiated Papal supremacy, and quarrelled with Catherine's nephew, the Emperor Charles V, because of his infatuation for Anne Boleyn; but now he was getting tired of Anne Boleyn, who had failed to give him a son, and he was falling in love with Jane Seymour. When Catherine of Aragon died in January 1536, Cromwell thought that this was a good opportunity to improve relations with the Emperor. If Henry got rid of Anne Boleyn, Charles V should not object, now that Catherine was dead, if Henry married a third wife.

43

Cromwell decided to discuss the matter with the Emperor's ambassador, Eustace Chapuys; but he wished his approach to Chapuys to be kept very secret. He contacted Chapuys, and suggested that they should meet in the new house that was being built for him. He knew that Nedeham's men would not be working there on 23 February, because it was the eve of St. Matthias's Day, a holy day; so he arranged that he and Chapuys should enter the half-built house from opposite sides through different entrances. They stood and talked together for nearly an hour among Nedeham's building materials without anyone seeing them. The ambassador's response was encouraging, and he and Cromwell had other meetings elsewhere at which the fate of Anne Boleyn was sealed.

Three months later, in May 1536, Anne was arrested and accused of adultery with five men, one of whom was her own brother. Another was Norris, who had helped Nedeham when he was denounced by the King's Controller. Norris was said to be Anne's favourite lover, and he and she were accused of plotting together to murder Henry so that they could marry each other. Anne and the five men were executed.

Henry waited for only eleven days after Anne's execution before marrying Jane Seymour. She bore him the son whom he so eagerly desired, but died in childbirth. Henry's ministers then advised him to marry a fourth wife. Cromwell urged him to make an alliance with the Protestant German Princes by marrying Anne, the sister of the Duke of Cleves, and Henry agreed to do so after his court painter, Holbein, went to Cleves and returned with a very flattering portrait of Anne.

Cromwell made great preparations to welcome Anne of Cleves. She was to travel to Calais, where she would be welcomed to English territory by the Lord Deputy of Calais, and then cross to Dover. Archbishop Cranmer would meet her on Barham Down and would escort her to Canterbury, and she would then proceed in slow and dignified stages towards London, staying the night at the usual stopping places of Faversham, Sittingbourne and Rochester. Henry would greet her at Shooters Hill and escort her to Greenwich, surrounded by his nobles and dignitaries and watched by a large crowd of the common people.

The Mayor of London and the Livery Companies were ordered to take part in the proceedings, and the Master and Wardens and members of the Court of the Carpenters' Company went with the others. They were told to come to Greenwich by water; when they arrived, the King's Marshal would direct them where they were to moor their barge. They were not to set foot on land at Greenwich, but to remain on their barges. They were to be dressed in their liveries, and to bring musicians with them who would welcome the Lady Anne of Cleves, when she arrived, with as many different kinds of music as possible.

Henry, Anne and their escort were to ride through the park at Greenwich and then through the town to the great gate of the palace on the waterside. The streets were to be gravelled, and paving stones were to be laid down; at certain places on the route, where the streets were very narrow, buildings were to be demolished to widen the road. Nedeham was put in charge of all the paving and demolition work. He was also instructed to erect barriers along the side of the Thames so "that no man be in danger of drowning by press of people".

Anne arrived in Calais in the middle of December 1539, but had to remain there for a fortnight until the weather was good enough for her to cross the Channel. She duly reached Rochester. Henry was so impatient to see her that he rode secretly with a small escort to

Rochester on New Year's Day; he told her who he was, and had dinner with her and her ladies. He was bitterly disappointed, for he found her physically repulsive. He received her with every propriety when she arrived at Shooter's Hill, and the arrival ceremony at Greenwich on 3 January went off as planned; but he told his Privy Council that he would not marry her, and only agreed to do so very reluctantly when Cromwell pointed out the diplomatic embarrassment which would be caused if he broke off the engagement at this stage.

Five months later Cromwell was arrested at a meeting of the Council on a charge of high treason against the King, and Convocation was persuaded to find a far-fetched reason for divorcing Henry from Anne. On 28 July 1540 Cromwell was beheaded. All his property was forfeited to the King, who granted the house that Nedeham had built for Cromwell to the Drapers' Company. They converted it into their Hall. It was burned down in the Great Fire of London in 1666. The present Drapers' Hall was afterwards built on the same site.

Nedeham survived the fall of Cromwell as he had survived the fall of Norris, and soon afterwards was put in charge of another of Henry's building projects. He demolished the fourteenth century priory at Dartford and built a new manor house for Henry on the site. He was engaged on this project for three years; between 1541 and 1544 he arranged with a supplier to sell him nearly a million bricks and a comparable quantity of lime.

Like all Henry's officials, Nedeham was able to derive various benefits from his position which more than compensated for his comparatively low salary. He no longer had to solicit favours from influential people and send them gifts; he was himself solicited and received gifts from men who wanted a job in the King's service or to be selected by Nedeham to supply building materials for the King's houses. There was also the chance to acquire the monastic lands and the lands forfeited by traitors.

Henry had dissolved all the smaller monasteries and convents in 1536, and three years later followed this up by suppressing the greater monasteries. He then granted the lands of the monasteries, including the house itself with the valuable lead on the roofs, to his ministers and favourites and to anyone else who had sufficient influence or good luck to obtain a larger or smaller part of the spoils. They then sold the lands to speculators or direct to the local gentry. Nedeham had a better claim on the King's gratitude than many of the grantees who obtained monastic lands, and he was not disappointed. Henry granted him the house and lands of monasteries in Cambridgeshire and Nottinghamshire. Nedeham sold them to local gentlemen, but he himself bought monastic land near Baldock in Hertfordshire from another of the King's servants who had obtained it from Henry.

Nedeham was also able to obtain various benefits from being appointed receiver for the King of the lands in Yorkshire of the leaders of the revolt that was known as the Pilgrimage of Grace. Lord Darcy, Sir Robert Constable and Sir John Bulmer were executed in 1537 for their part in the revolt, and Lady Bulmer was burned alive for high treason. The Abbot of Jervaulx and the Prior of Bridlington were hanged, drawn and quartered for having supported the Pilgrimage of Grace. Nedeham was appointed receiver of their forfeited lands.

Henry ended his reign as he had begun it by going to war with France, and led his army in person to the siege of Boulogne. His officials drew up a list of "such noble men, knights, gentlemen and others as be appointed to go in person with the King's Majesty in His Grace's battle, with the numbers and sorts of horsemen which each of them bringeth with them". The Duke of Suffolk headed the list, being required to bring 300 horsemen. Nedeham was told to come with six horsemen. He took part in the siege of Boulogne, and died there on 22 September 1544, eight days after Henry captured the town.

In 1534 Nedeham had been elected Master of the Carpenters' Company. When his year of office ended he was re-elected Master for a second year, and six years later became Master for the third time in 1542. We do not know if he played an active part in running the Company, for during the years whilst he was on the Court the names of the members attending the meetings were usually not recorded in the minutes. But the Company was obviously pleased to have such an important personage as their Master, although he left nothing to the Company in his will.

Nedeham had gone far since the days when, as a young carpenter from Derbyshire, he had earned sixpence a day; but he was determined that his sons should have a better start in life than he himself had had. He arranged for one of his sons to become, by redemption, a liveryman of the Grocers' Company.

4
Dangerous Times

The Carpenters' Company's attitude to the religious changes and persecutions in the sixteenth century – the Carpenters' Company supports the Lords of the Council's coup d'état against Protector Somerset in 1549 – The Carpenters' Company forced to pay for new charters – The Dutch Church in London, and the Dutchmen's relations with the Carpenters' Company – The Carpenters' Charter and Ordinances of 1607 – The Carpenters refuse to help colonize Virginia, but acquire land in Ulster – Richard Wyatt founds the almshouses in Godalming in 1619.

When Nedeham was promoted to be Surveyor of the King's Works, he was succeeded as King's Carpenter by Humphrey Cooke's son-in-law, John Russell, who was partly responsible for designing the roof of the hall of Trinity College, Cambridge. Russell was a Warden of the Carpenters' Company in 1538, 1539 and 1540, and was then elected Master in 1541. He was again Master in 1549 and 1557, and for the fourth time in 1565, but he died during his year of office. After Nedeham died, Lawrence Bradshaw succeeded him as Clerk and Surveyor of the King's Works. Bradshaw was Master of the Carpenters' Company eight times between 1551 and 1580 – a record which has not been equalled by any other Master in the Company's history.

Nedeham, Russell and Bradshaw lived in dangerous times, when a Princess might be sent to the Tower as a prisoner one day and a few years later go there as Queen; when all-powerful ministers were suddenly arrested and beheaded for high treason; when an Archbishop of Canterbury was burned as a heretic. But the liverymen and freemen of the Carpenters' Company and the other Livery Companies, like most of the people of England, submitted to every King and government who gained power and changed their religion and their political allegiance when the King ordered them to do so. As in all other periods of revolutionary turmoil, a few ambitious men were prepared to run any risk to gain political power. Another small minority were prepared to be martyrs and suffer torture and death for their faith. But the great majority wished only to preserve their lives and property in what Cranmer's secretary, Ralph Morice, called "a most dangerous world".

They could justify their unheroic conduct by claiming to be obeying the King and the law. Everyone except the zealots and martyrs agreed that it was for the King to decide which religion his subjects should adopt, and that it was the subject's duty to obey the King. If the King ordered them to be heretics, the King would have to account for it to God on the Day of Judgment; but they would not be condemned to everlasting damnation if they pleaded on that awful day that they had been heretics only because they were obeying the King.

When Henry VIII died, the Carpenters joined with the other Livery Companies in saluting the nine-year-old King Edward VI when he rode through London from the Tower to Westminster in the traditional way on the eve of his coronation on 19 February 1547. Edward's regent was his uncle, Edward Seymour, Duke of Somerset, who worked closely

47

with Archbishop Cranmer to carry the Protestant Reformation much further than Henry VIII had allowed it to go. When the Carpenters went to the church of All Hallows-on-the-Wall before electing their new Master and Wardens on 10 August 1549, they found that instead of the Latin Mass which they had attended in the previous year there was a service in English composed by Cranmer which contained words that by subtle interpretation could be held to deny that the Body and Blood of Christ were really present in the consecrated bread and wine. The Carpenters, as usual, adapted themselves to the new circumstances and obeyed "the Prince" and "the magistrates"; but the service in English aroused great resentment in the country, and led to a serious revolt in Devon and Cornwall, while at the same time resentment against the enclosures of common land by the landlords caused another formidable revolt in Norfolk.

Both the revolts were suppressed; but the wealthier classes blamed Somerset for having encouraged the discontent among the people. The majority of the lords of his Privy Council decided to overthrow him. Somerset called on the people to join him and the young King at Hampton Court; the lords of the Council hurried to London and relied on the support of the City against the demagogic Lord Protector Somerset and the popular forces who supported him.

For the only time during the Tudor era, the Carpenters' Company supported a rebellion against the established government. When the City Corporation agreed to furnish 400 footmen and 100 horsemen to support the rebellious lords, the Carpenters voted to pay for the equipment of four of the infantrymen – for four swords, four daggers, four girdles, four coats with red cloth for crosses, four caps and other equipment, and for their wages for five days, as well as for the riding boots, saddle and harness and travelling expenses of one cavalryman, at a total cost of £4.12s.5d. Somerset capitulated after a few days, and fifteen months later he was beheaded on Tower Hill.

England continued to be a Protestant state after the fall of Somerset, and many foreign Protestants came to London. Most of them came from the Netherlands, where the Emperor Charles V began a savage persecution of heretics in 1550. They were welcomed by Archbishop Cranmer, and thanks largely to him they were permitted to establish their own Protestant church in London, in the old Augustinian friary (now Austin Friars), within 200 yards of Carpenters' Hall. Their form of service differed in some respects from the services of the Protestant Church of England, being rather more Protestant. Some English Protestants, including the Bishop of London, Nicholas Ridley, believed that the foreign Protestants should be compelled to attend the services of the Church of England; but Cranmer's influence prevailed. All the foreign Protestants were placed under the control of the Polish Protestant, John à Lasco, who could be trusted to ensure that no Anabaptist or other extremist Protestant heresy was allowed to develop in the "strangers' church". The Carpenters' Company developed ties with the congregation in Austin Friars.

More than 5,000 foreign Protestants settled in London; they amounted to nearly ten per cent of the total population of the City. The Londoners, who were famous throughout Europe for their hatred of foreigners, did not like them. Many people complained that England had become "a harbour of all infidelity".

Edward VI died before his sixteenth birthday. John Dudley, Duke of Northumberland, who had led the revolt of the lords against Somerset, persuaded Edward before he died to bequeath the crown in his will to the Protestant Lady Jane Grey, excluding his Roman Catholic sister Mary; but Mary called on the people to join her in Norfolk and rise against Jane and Northumberland, and they flocked to her support. When Northumberland raised an army and marched against Mary, London rose against him behind his back. On 19 July 1553, at the cross in Cheapside, the Lord Mayor proclaimed Mary as Queen and the Carpenters joined the other Livery Companies and nearly all the people of London in celebrating and cheering the triumph of their lawful sovereign Queen Mary. The church bells rang and the fountains and conduits in the streets flowed with wine, as was usual on occasions of great rejoicing.

By the time that the Carpenters held their Election Day service in All-Hallows in 1554, the Catholic Latin Mass had been restored and all Protestant services were illegal. The burning of the Protestant martyrs at Smithfield began in February 1555, and the Carpenters and most Londoners accepted it, as they had done in the days of Henry VIII, although there were more Protestants in London and Kent than elsewhere in England.

The foreign Protestants in England were not burned, but were deported, and their church in Austin Friars was closed. Mary told the Emperor's ambassador when they were leaving, so that he could warn Charles V and have them arrested when they landed in the Netherlands and burned there as heretics; but most of them managed to escape to the Protestant city state of Emden in North Germany.

Mary married Charles V's son, Philip of Spain, in 1554 and they ruled jointly as King and Queen of England. The people of London disliked the Catholic Spaniards as much as they had disliked the Protestant Dutch a few years earlier; the English hatred of foreigners, which had turned the people of London against the Protestants under Edward VI, turned them against the Catholics under Philip and Mary. They did not like the heavy taxes which they had to pay to finance Philip's wars against the French, especially when it resulted in the loss of Calais, which the French captured after the English had held it for 211 years; and they did not like the rise in prices which caused an annual inflation of 10 per cent and doubled prices in the ten years between 1545 and 1555.

One of the ways in which Philip and Mary raised money for the wars in France was by forcing the Livery Companies to pay for new charters. On 1 November 1558 they issued a new charter to the Carpenters' Company in precisely the same terms as the charter which the Carpenters had been granted by Edward IV. It cost the Company, including all extras and incidental expenses, a total of £8.19s.7d., about £2,250 in terms of present-day prices. For the Carpenters' Company, it was money paid for nothing.

Sixteen days later Mary died, and her sister Elizabeth became Queen. Elizabeth had saved her life by going to Mass during Mary's reign, but she had always secretly been a Protestant. When the Carpenters' Company came out as usual to greet the Queen as she rode through London on 14 January 1559 on the eve of her coronation, they found that they were witnessing a great Protestant demonstration organised by the London Protestant zealots who had survived the persecution of the last four years. The Carpenters' Election Day service on 10 August 1559 was once again the Protestant service of the Book of Common Prayer.

49

14. Austin Friars, 1919: the interior of Austin Friars by A. Van Anrooy. The church was completely destroyed during an air raid in October 1940. Rebuilding started in 1950. The picture was presented to the Company by the Consistory of the Dutch Reformed Church on 31 May 1960.

During Elizabeth's reign, London became staunchly Protestant, thanks largely to that great propaganda work, John Foxe's Book of Martyrs, which described the sufferings of the Protestants in Mary's reign; a copy of the book was required by law to be placed in every cathedral and in most parish churches, and it was read in many households. The Dutch Protestants returned to England, and took back their church in Austin Friars. They were now much more welcome than they had been in Edward VI's reign. In 1568 the people in the Netherlands rose in revolt against the Catholic tyranny of their sovereign, Philip II of Spain. The people of London felt great sympathy for the Dutch Protestants, and the Carpenters' Company established a close friendship with their neighbours in the Dutch Church. They shared their grief at the capture of Haarlem by the Spaniards, their joy at the heroic and successful defence of Leyden, and their rage at the assassination of the great Dutch leader, William of Orange, by a Catholic fanatic. When the Spanish soldiers sacked Antwerp, looting and raping, the Carpenters agreed with the writers of the many broadsheets

50

and pamphlets which warned the citizens of London that the horrors of Antwerp would be repeated if the Spanish soldiers invaded England and captured London.

The danger became very real in 1588 when the Spanish Armada sailed up the Channel past Plymouth to Calais; and the Carpenters willingly contributed £3.14s.3d. towards the cost of equipping ships to resist the Spaniards. The Armada was scattered by Drake's fireships and the gales, and on 24 November Elizabeth came in state to St. Paul's Cathedral to attend the thanksgiving service. The Carpenters built a stand near the Cathedral from where they watched the Queen's arrival, and spent £3.2s.0d. in decorating their stand and the rails with long blue cloth.

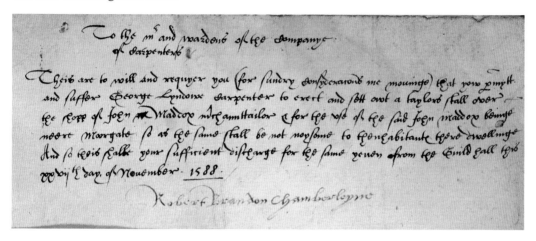

15. *Building licence, 1588: a licence issued by Robert Brandon, Chamberlain of London, and sent to the Master and Wardens of the Carpenters' Company. The licence, dated 27th November 1588, requests that George Lyndowe, carpenter, be permitted to build a stall near Moorgate for John Maddox, merchant tailor. Noise from the stall must not disturb the neighbouring residents.*

Elizabeth, like Philip and Mary, insisted on granting a new charter to the Carpenters, and they had to pay her for their charter of November 1560; but the Company prospered during her reign. It was a century of great development in London. The City's population of 50,000 in 1500 doubled during the next fifty years, and doubled again to reach 200,000 by 1600. People came into London from the provinces; some of them were carpenters, despite the eagerness of the London carpenters to keep them out. Many of them came from distant parts of England; in 1583 only 13 per cent of carpenters' apprentices in London had been born in the City, or the surrounding counties of Middlesex, Surrey, Kent or Essex.

The membership of the Carpenters' Company was growing, but they were still a small select group among the carpenters. By the end of Elizabeth's reign there were probably about 1,500 carpenters in London. There were only 300 freemen in the Carpenters' Company, and only 40 of these were liverymen.

The Carpenters still could not compete with the great merchant Companies, who in 1528 had been granted by the City Corporation the privilege of being described as the "Great

51

16. *Royal Charter, 1607: the total cost of the new charter and the ordinances was £95.3s.0d. In return for the money, James I extended the Company's jurisdiction to two miles beyond the City walls.*

Twelve" among the City Livery Companies, with their own order of precedence, from the first Company, the Mercers, to the twelfth, the Clothworkers. The order of precedence among the Livery Companies and among the Twelve was not determined, as is often stated, by the date at which they were formed but by money and influence. Some of the Twelve had an income which was about eighteen times greater than the income of the Carpenters' Company; but the Carpenters were becoming wealthier. In 1591, in the list of 55 Livery Companies who were taxed, the Carpenters were twenty-eighth in order of wealth, and they established the position which they hold today of being twenty-sixth in precedence among the 100 Livery Companies of 1995.

The old Queen died on 24 March 1603, and the Carpenters came out to welcome the new King, James VI of Scotland and I of England, when he arrived in London from Edinburgh on 7 May. They spent 9s.5d. on wages and drinks for their servants who went to greet him in the fields between Camden and Islington. The Carpenters joined in the coronation celebrations on 25 July; but by now the plague was raging. In the week of the coronation 857 people died of the plague in London; and when the Company held their Election Day on Monday 15 August, they reduced the number of people attending the dinner in order to lessen the risk from the plague. Only the members of the Livery were invited, with no women except the wives of the Wardens, no children and no guests; and it was to be a "small dinner", with only roast beef, leg of mutton and capon served.

Like his predecessors Elizabeth and Mary, James I made the Carpenters pay for the expense of obtaining a new charter confirming their privileges; but at least this time the Company got something for their money, for they obtained more extensive powers over the trade of carpentry. Hitherto their jurisdiction had applied only in the City; the charter and ordinances of 1607 extended it to two miles beyond the City walls, which meant that it included the populated areas of Southwark, Westminster and Holborn. The Company had always claimed to exercise jurisdiction over all carpenters working in London, even those who were not liverymen or freemen. Now it was expressly stated to apply to "every person . . . occupying the occupation of carpentry" within the City and the two-mile radius. The Master and Wardens had power to make regulations about the quality of materials and the standard of work, and to enter the homes or premises of any carpenter to make sure that their regulations were complied with.

The Company ordinances also laid down that no one was to carry on the trade of carpentry in the City and two miles therefrom unless he had been apprenticed, and no one could become an apprentice without the consent of the Master and Wardens of the Carpenters' Company. Every carpenter was "to be of good and honest behaviour, as well in their words as deeds, towards the Master and Wardens and such as had been Master or Warden, and tractable, conformable and obedient to the ordinances", on pain of imprisonment for ten days in the King's prison.

The ordinances made some changes and additions to the rules for the internal government of the Company. The regulations of 1455 had stated that the Court should consist of the Master and Wardens and those who had been Master or Warden or were otherwise "most honest persons". This reference to "most honest persons" was now omitted, implying that only former Masters and Wardens could be members of the Court, which was no longer limited to eight persons. The Ordinances of 1607 directed that a General Court of all the members of the Livery must be held at least four times a year. The date of the annual election was changed from St. Lawrence's Day (10 August) to the second Monday in August. The Court was to put forward the names of the candidates for the offices of Master and the three Wardens, and the liverymen were entitled to vote for any of the persons nominated by the Court. They were not entitled to vote for any candidate who had not been nominated by the Court. This regulation and the provision that only Past Masters and Past Wardens could be members of the Court caused arguments on several occasions during the next four centuries.

The Ordinances were issued on 7 December 1607 by Lord Ellesmere (The Lord Chancellor), the Earl of Dorset (the Lord Treasurer), Sir Thomas Fleming (Chief Justice of the Court of King's Bench), and the famous Sir Edward Coke, who was then Chief Justice of the Court of Common Pleas. The charter and the ordinances cost the Company £95.3s.0d.

A few months later, the City Corporation put forward a plan to encourage paupers in London to emigrate to America and colonise Virginia, where they would be granted 100

17. Richard Wyatt: Master 1604, 1605 and 1616. Wyatt's bequest of £500 provided for the building of almshouses in Godalming. This portrait of Wyatt was given to the Company by Margaret Metcalfe (née Wyatt) in 1969. The artist is not known.

acres of land. The Lord Mayor asked the Livery Companies to contribute. The Merchant Taylors gave £200, and several other Companies contributed; the Carpenters' Company refused. Throughout all their seven hundred years' history the Carpenters have always been cautious and have thought at least twice before embarking on any new venture. They had no wish to get involved in emigration to Virginia. They did, however, agree in 1619 to give four shillings and some gifts "towards the poor that went to Virginia".

The Carpenters did not escape so easily from another colonization project. When James I in 1609 decided to send English and Scots Protestants to live in Ulster, this was largely a security measure in the most ardently Catholic and rebellious province in Ireland. He had therefore no compunction in forcing the City of London to take part in the scheme. His plan was that the City should pay money to him and be granted land in Ulster in return. The City Corporation had no choice but to agree and pay him £60,000 and the Lord Mayor called on all the Livery Companies to send four representatives to dicuss how to implement the scheme. The Carpenters' Company sent the Master (George Isack), the Upper Warden (John Reeve), and two Past Masters, William Allen and Richard Wyatt. Allen and Wyatt had both been Master twice, Allen in 1594 and 1595, and Wyatt in 1604 and 1605.

It was agreed that the Carpenters should contribute £100 as their share. This was a heavy burden for the Company; they decided to pay £50 from the Company's funds and called on the liverymen to raise the other £50 by their personal contributions. But the 131 members who were prepared to contribute only managed to raise a total of £44.2s.8d. The Company told the Lord Mayor that they would pay the balance later.

After the Carpenters had sent Past Master Cobb and another liveryman to Ireland to

54

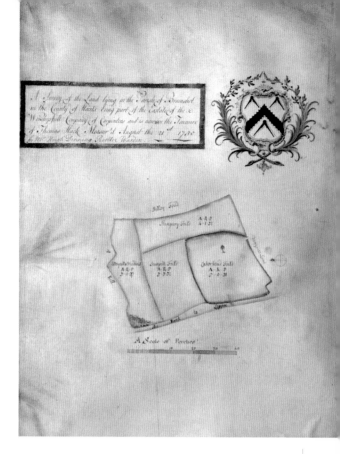

18. Plan of Bramshott, Hampshire, 1750: Wyatt intended the rents from the land to cover the expense of the annual Court visit to Godalming. The land was exchanged for property on Fulham Road, London in the 1850s.

inspect the land that was being offered to them, they entered into an arrangement with the Ironmongers and five other Companies to raise £5,000. The Ironmongers were to play the leading part in the scheme. They paid £2,300; the Brewers £700; the Scriveners £570; the Coopers £240; the Pewterers £360; the Barbers £350; and the Carpenters £300. Most of the Carpenters' share was contributed by individual members.

The Carpenters were duly allotted their share of the land in Ulster. This was to involve them and the other six Companies in lengthy and not very satisfactory negotiations 270 years later, when the Irish Land Acts gave tenants in Ireland the right to purchase the freehold of their land.

Richard Wyatt was another enterprising business man who had begun life as a carpenter and became a very wealthy architect and merchant. He was born in the village of Slindon near Arundel in Sussex, and came to London to be apprenticed to the prosperous carpenter, Roger Sheres, who in 1575, while Wyatt was his apprentice, became Youngest Warden of the Carpenters' Company and was afterwards Master in 1587 and 1592. Wyatt, like the traditional apprentice, married Sheres's daughter, and soon became a thriving master carpenter and architect. He then bought up building materials and resold them to other carpenters, and also acquired a wharf on the Thames in the City, where he could charge landing fees to carpenters and other tradesmen who unloaded their supplies there.

He became a leading timber merchant. This was a useful and profitable business in view

55

19. Godalming almshouses: front view of the almshouses which continue to be occupied by beneficiaries of Wyatt's charity.

of the shortage of timber. The large-scale felling of trees in the Weald of Sussex and Kent to supply fuel for iron-foundries there, and for house building and shipbuilding, was worrying the government, and Parliament was continually passing statutes to restrict the felling of timber.

It is not surprising that a forceful entrepreneur like Wyatt made enemies, and he became engaged in litigation with the Woodmongers' Company; but, like many other successful men of the period, he gave generously to charity. He made his will in 1619, eighteen months after he finished his third term as Master and a year before he died. He left several properties to the Carpenters' Company in trust for various charitable purposes. The rents of a property near Henley-on-Thames were to be used in paying a pension of ten shillings a year to thirteen poor widows. He left £500 to be used in building almshouses at Godalming in Surrey, and the rent of his nearby farm at Shackleford was to be applied in maintaining ten poor men in the almshouses. Five of them were to come from the parish of Godalming, and the other five from adjoining parishes – two from Puttenham and one each from Hambledon, Compton and Dunsfold. The rent from Wyatt's land at Bramshott in Hampshire was to pay for an annual visit to the almshouses at Godalming by the Master and Wardens of the Carpenters'

56

20. Godalming almshouses: back view of the almshouses.

Company and members of the Court. The almshouses still stand today, and are still occupied by almsmen selected by the Carpenters' Company.

The almshouses, known as Richard Wyatt's Oyspital, opened in 1622, and the Master and Wardens and Court paid their first annual visit there next year. They left London on Tuesday 26 August 1623. There were seven members in the party; the Master (A. Messenger) and the Upper Warden (Edward Baker), who were performing their last duty before ending their year of office; the Master Elect (Thomas Rushall), who would take office a week later at the September Court; the aged William Allen, who had been Master nearly thirty years before, and George Isack, a much younger Past Master; the Clerk, Thomas Turner; and a clergyman, Mr Parker, who came to preach the sermon at the church service.

Godalming is 35 miles from London. In 1623, this was a day's journey for a rider on horseback; only King's messengers and other travellers who had arranged for relays of fresh horses to be ready at the post-stages on the great highways, could go much further than 40 miles a day. The Master and his colleagues had dinner at Cobham, which cost 7s.4d. for the seven of them, and rode on in the afternoon to Godalming, where they arrived in time for supper that night. Next day they attended the meeting in the almshouse chapel, the service

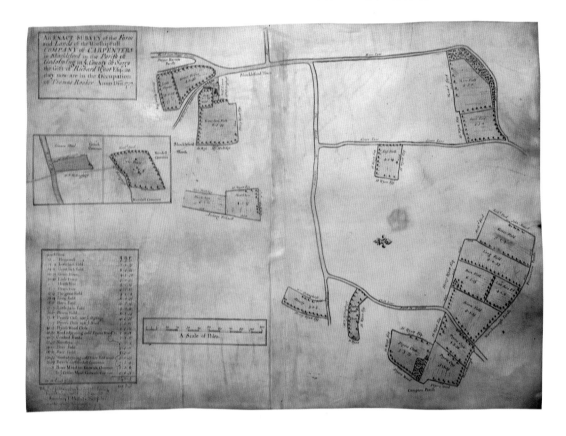

21. Plan of Shackleford, Surrey, 1727: the Godalming almshouses were to be maintained by the rents collected from this farm. The land was sold in 1891 and the money reinvested.

in the parish church, and a dinner in Godalming; the dinner, the supper the previous evening, and the night's lodging cost them £2.8s.6d. It was now too late in the day for them to get back to London that night, so they spent the night of 27 August at Kingston, where their supper cost 13s.6d. They reached London on 28 August. The total cost of the visit, including the hire of the horses and their fodder at Godalming and Kingston, was £7.4s.6d.

The Court of the Carpenters' Company, and sometimes the Livery too, have been going to Godalming every summer, with some exceptions, for the last 372 years. Until 1748 they usually rode to Godalming on horseback, staying the night at Kingston on the return journey. In 1749 some members of the Court began to travel by coach, though others continued to ride on horseback. After 1767 they went in postchaises. In the nineteenth century they went by train and could go to Godalming and return to London on the same day. In the twentieth century some members go by train from London and others drive there in their cars in order to carry out the annual inspection.

58

5
Civil War

The plague of 1625 – The City, and the Carpenters' Company, fined for the murder of Dr. Lamb – demarcation disputes between the Carpenters' Company and the Joiners' Company – Charles I welcomed by the City on his return from Scotland in 1641 – The Civil War – the Carpenters contribute money repeatedly to the Roundhead cause – the Carpenters support the Presbyterians against the Independents in the Second Civil War – The Carpenters prevent Carpenters' Hall from being requisitioned by Cromwell's troops when the Army occupies London in December 1648 – the Carpenters accept the Commonwealth and Cromwell as Lord Protector – the Carpenters welcome Charles II at his Restoration in 1660.

James I died on 27 March 1625. The coronation normally took place within two months of the new sovereign's accession; but the coronation of Charles I was postponed for nearly a year because of plague. It was the most severe outbreak within living memory; 41,000 people are said to have died of plague in the City and neighbourhood. The Carpenters cancelled all meetings of the Livery and all entertainments except for the General Court on Election Day; the election had to be held, but without the usual dinner.

Every house where there was plague was marked by a red cross on the door to keep visitors away; no one called there except for the carts that went around collecting the dead. "What slaughter, what lamentation, what horror was there in the streets of our mother city!" said Joseph Hall when he was at last able to preach before the King at the "public thanksgiving for the wonderful mitigation of the late mortality" on 29 January 1626. "Danger made men wisely and unwillingly inhospital. The cousin, the brother, forgets his own blood; and the father looks slyly upon his own child, and welcomes him with frowns . . . . The Arms of London are the Red Cross and the Sword; what house almost wanted these? Here was the Red Cross upon the door, the Sword of God's Judgment within doors; and the Motto was, Lord, have mercy upon us." Next year, Hall was appointed Bishop of Exeter, and was afterwards Bishop of Norwich.

Before his death James I had begun to quarrel with his Parliaments and the City of London. Matters became worse under Charles I. The Puritans and Presbyterians condemned the retention of "dregs of Popery" in the doctrine and ceremonies of the Church of England and the failure of the Government to intervene on the Protestant side against the Catholics in the Thirty Years War in Europe. The common lawyers resented the arbitrary powers of the Crown and the Court of Star Chamber, which they claimed violated the English common law. The traders and merchants resented the monopolies in salt, tobacco and other commodities granted by the King to his favourites at court. They had been prepared to accept these things from the great Queen Elizabeth, but not from King James or King Charles.

London was the centre of the opposition to the King's policy, and the City apprentices

were an unruly revolutionary element. The Livery Companies were much more cautious and respectable, but they did not entirely disapprove of the apprentices' activities.

The King's Minister, the Duke of Buckingham, was particularly unpopular. When the House of Commons tried to impeach Buckingham in 1626, Charles dissolved Parliament and arrested some prominent members of the Opposition. As Parliament would not vote him money, he tried to raise money from his subjects by other means. In 1627 he demanded that the City of London make him a loan of £120,000. The City Corporation told the Carpenters' Company that they must contribute £300, and as they could not raise enough from private contributions by the Livery, the Court was forced to sell some of the Company's plate.

A London physician, Dr. Lamb, was a favourite of Buckingham's; it was rumoured that he had committed several crimes, but had been protected from prosecution by Buckingham. In June 1628 Lamb was attacked by a mob in the streets of London, and died of his injuries. Buckingham himself was assassinated by a zealous Puritan in August. All over the country and in London the people celebrated, lighting bonfires, and drinking the assassin's health in the taverns.

The City authorities were unable to discover who had killed Dr. Lamb. The King thought that they were conniving at the murder, and imposed a collective fine of £6,000 on the City of London; he threatened to revoke the Corporation's charter if the fine was not paid. The Corporation protested their innocence and pleaded for mercy, and Charles agreed to reduce the fine to 1,500 marks (£1,000). The Corporation ordered the Carpenters' Company to contribute £5 towards the payment of the fine.

In 1629 the King again dissolved Parliament and ruled without a Parliament for eleven years. He raised money by imposing various taxes, though the Parliamentary party's lawyers disputed their legality. The Carpenters' Company were duly required to pay £7 a year under the Shipmoney tax.

But the Company had greater worries than the arbitrary exactions of the King. The carpenters in London, like the workmen in the other crafts, resented the control exercised over them by their Livery Company. Carpenters were increasingly breaking the Company's regulations about the quality of timber and the hours of work in the trade.

The Livery Companies were also involved in demarcation disputes with each other. By 1621 the Carpenters' Company was engaged in a serious dispute with the Joiners' Company, which was becoming wealthier and was now nearly as rich as the Carpenters. The Carpenters objected to joiners, not carpenters, making windows and doing other work which should be done by carpenters. The Carpenters' Company appointed three Past Masters, Isack, Allen and Pedley, and a former Warden, Thornton, to meet the representatives of the Joiners to negotiate a settlement. For seven years they met the Joiners at fairly regular intervals over dinner in some tavern; but in 1628 the Carpenters broke off the talks and complained to the City Corporation about the Joiners' conduct.

◀ *22. Master and Wardens' cups: these silver gilt steeple cups were presented to the Company as follows* (left to right) *Warden's cup by John Ansell, 1611; Master's cup by John Reeves, 1611; Warden's cup by Thomas Edmones, 1612. There is a third Warden's cup* (not shown) *which was presented to the Company by Anthony Jarman, 1628.*

61

23. Royal Charter, 1640: illuminated initial and border portraying Charles I. This Charter cost the Company £117.17s.0d. and extended the Company's jurisdiction to four miles outside the City walls.

The Corporation appointed a committee of arbitrators which took three years to complete its work, but in 1632 imposed a compromise settlement. Joiners were to make most kinds of bedsteads, chairs, tables made of walnut, chests, cabinets, wainscots, shop windows "which cannot be made without glue", pews, and most kinds of coffins. Carpenters were to make tables for drapers, taverns and counting-houses, tables made of oak, elm or beech "or other wood nailed together without glue", washing stools and bucking stools, unpanelled shelves, uncarved signboards, galleries in churches and floors for pews in churches, and kitchen shelves; they were to lay all floors in buildings, except groved floors, which was the work of joiners; and they were to make partitions in rooms and warehouses. Pillars for lights and a number of other things could be made by both joiners and carpenters. In general the fine work was to be done by joiners and general building work by carpenters. The committee ordered the Carpenters' Company to pay £4 damages to one joiner and ten shillings each to four others, for having trespassed on their area of work on several occasions.

In 1636 there was another outbreak of plague, and the Carpenters took the usual precaution of meeting as few people as possible. When they went to Godalming in August they hired a coach and took food and wine with them, so that they could sleep and dine in the coach and avoid entering the inns at Godalming and Kingston.

The resentment of the London Puritans increased during Charles I's eleven-year rule without a Parliament. Several Puritan pamphleteers were sentenced to stand in the pillory, to be whipped through the streets from Temple Bar to the Palace of Westminster, to be branded on the face, and to have their ears cut off. Charles was trying to raise money by offering various favours, such as knighthoods or charters to individuals and corporations, and making them pay well for these honours and benefits. Many people who opposed his policies and sympathised with his victims refused to accept his offers; but the Carpenters' Company decided on 14 December 1637 to approach the Attorney-General and intimate

24. Wyatt's tankards: these tankards have a London hall-mark for 1621–2 and appear to commemorate Wyatt's death. Engraved are the words "Richard Wyatt Citizen and Carpenter of London in the Yeare 1619" accompanied by the Wyatt coat-of-arms. The tankards were bequeathed to the Company by Stewart C. Wyatt in 1946.

that they would be very happy to be granted a new charter which re-emphasized and extended their control over the craft of carpentry.

By the time that their negotiations with the Attorney-General had been completed, Charles had been faced with a rebellion in Scotland, after he had tried to force the Scottish Presbyterians to accept a new order of service which was closer to the High Church service of the Church of England. The Scots defeated the royal army and invaded England, forcing Charles to accept peace terms under which he not only agreed to allow the Scots to remain Presbyterians but also to pay a war indemnity to the Scots.

Charles was now desperately in need of money, and resorted to every expedient to raise it. On 17 July 1640 he gave the Carpenters' Company a new charter which extended the area of their jurisdiction from two to four miles beyond the boundaries of the City, and forbade anyone to build a house in this area unless he had either been apprenticed or had worked as a carpenter for at least seven years. It gave power to the Court of the Carpenters' Company to make ordinances for the control of the trade. The charter cost the Carpenters' Company, with all incidental expenses, a total of £117.17s.0d., including ten shillings to the Attorney-General's doorkeeper and one shilling to the Lord Mayor's gentleman's man.

Charles's need for money eventually forced him to summon Parliament and to grant all their demands for the limitations on his arbitrary powers and the execution of his hated minister, the Earl of Strafford, after the London apprentices had marched to Westminster and threatened to storm the Palace of Whitehall if the King did not consent to Strafford's death. It was the presence of the London apprentices, with their short hair, at the anti-royalist demonstrations in 1641 which led the King's supporters to call the Parliament supporters "Roundheads".

Charles seemed to have capitulated and turned over a new leaf. When he visited his Scottish kingdom he asked the leading Parliamentarians to accompany him, and on his return to London on 25 November 1641 the City turned out to welcome him in a great display of loyalty. The Lord Mayor, escorted by the Master and Wardens of every Livery

Company and 500 horsemen, rode out to Kingsland, two miles beyond the City limits. There they waited while the Sheriffs, escorted by 72 armed men and four trumpeters, rode on another three miles to meet the King at Stamford Hill. The Sheriffs escorted him to Kingsland where he was welcomed by the Lord Mayor and the Master and Wardens, and the whole party rode into London, entering the City at Moorgate and going by London Wall past Carpenters' Hall to Bishopsgate and by Cornhill and Cheapside to a banquet at the Guildhall. The Masters and Wardens of all the Livery Companies were invited to the banquet. As usual on these ceremonial occasions the conduits in the street ran with wine. The Carpenters' Company paid 10s.10d. for the wine in the conduit at Moorgate, and a total of £11.3s.2d. for their part in the day's celebrations.

Charles was biding his time. Six weeks later he marched with his bodyguard to the House of Commons and entered the chamber, intending to arrest the five leading members of the Parliamentary party. They had been warned by their spies in the King's household, and had fled to the City. When Charles marched on into the City to find them, the apprentices and the people came out into the streets and erected barricades which completely blocked his path. He was forced to retreat to Westminster. As he passed through Temple Bar someone threw a piece of paper into his carriage containing the words "To your tents, O Israel!". It was the declaration of war.

Parliament decided to leave Westminster and to continue the Parliamentary session in Merchant Taylor's Hall in the safety of the City. Charles left Whitehall and assembled his army at Nottingham and in August 1642 the Civil War began.

The first battle of the war was fought at Edgehill in Warwickshire on 23 October. It was indecisive, but King Charles's nephew Prince Rupert, the most successful and daring of his generals, led his cavalry on a dash for London, hoping to capture the rebellious City and crush the centre of the revolution. There was great anxiety in London; but the Parliamentary leaders quickly organised the defences of the City, and the Puritan preachers aroused the people to fight to the death against the "Papist" Cavaliers in the King's army who threatened them. On 7 November Thomas King, the Master of the Carpenters' Company, attended a meeting in the Guildhall when a committee of Parliament appealed to the City Corporation and the Livery Companies to send men and give money immediately to bar Prince Rupert's road to London.

The City trainbands marched to Turnham Green, some thirteen miles west of London, in such strength that when Rupert arrived there on 13 November he did not venture to attack them and retreated to Brentford. London and the Roundhead cause were saved, and both sides settled down to a long war. Charles established his capital at Oxford, and from Westminster a committee appointed by Parliament governed the territory under Roundhead control.

The Roundhead cause suffered several reverses, and Parliament's financial demands upon the citizens of London became more pressing. In November 1642 they ordered the City to raise £30,000 to carry on the war; by March 1643 they were demanding £10,000 a week. In order to placate the waverers, the Parliamentary leaders denied that they were rebelling against the King, and stated that they were fighting only against the King's evil advisers who were forcing him to make war on his loyal Parliament; and they imprisoned a few extremists who demanded the establishment of a republic. While the Cavaliers fought for the King, the Parliamentary leaders claimed to be fighting for "King and Parliament". This has misled some writers into stating that during the Civil War the Carpenters' Company sent money to both sides; but in fact their donations to "the King and Parliament" were to the Roundhead cause.

There were a few supporters of King Charles in the City. "The King hath his martyrs in London", wrote one of them on 5 August 1643 to a friend in Cavalier Oxford, sending the letter "secretly, as much as the close obstruction of the ways of conveyance will permit", though he admitted that they were only "a handful of faithful subjects" compared to the "Rebels, the Puritans, Brownists and Anabaptists". Who was it who "would have pulled the crown from the King's head? .... 'twas the proud, unthankful, schismatical, rebellious, bloody City of London". It was particularly shameful that the Masters and Wardens of the Livery Companies, who were not the owners but the trustees of their Companies' property, should use their assets to finance rebellion against the King. To see Aldermen "with their beards put into a feasting posture, not a hair awry" and with their best ruffs carefully arranged, anyone would think that they were on their way to dine with the Masters of their Livery Companies; but in fact they were going to a meeting to plot treason against the King. He called on the country people to join "with their gracious Sovereign in chastising these rebellious insolencies and reducing this stubborn city either to obedience or ashes", although he realised that he himself, like the bellows which fan the flames, might perish in the fire.

In May 1643 the Carpenters' Company decided, after long discussions at the Court meetings, that they could not hope to raise the money that Parliament demanded unless they sold some of the Company's plate. This raised £95.5s.0d., but this would only "pay several weeks' assessment imposed upon the Hall". In August they had to sell more plate to raise another £250 which the Lord Mayor had ordered them to contribute. In view of all this expenditure they decided to economise by cancelling all their dinners, including the Election Day dinner.

They also cancelled the annual visit to Godalming in August "by reason of these troublesome times and the great danger in travelling". Godalming and all the country between there and London was in Roundhead territory, but there was always the danger of a raid by Cavalier bands. So the Company sent the Superintendent of the almshouses, Mr Launder, to carry out the necessary duties at Godalming while the Master and Wardens and members of the Court remained in London.

The Civil War ended with the capture of King Charles's capital at Oxford in June 1646. On 21 July the Master and Wardens of the Carpenters' Company attended the thanksgiving service in St. Paul's, and then invited the Livery to the Bear Tavern in Bread Street to celebrate, at a cost of £1.6s.5d. But it was not long before the victorious Roundheads began to quarrel amongst themselves. The Presbyterians were challenged by some extreme Protestants whom they denounced as Anabaptists or Independents. The Independents demanded religious toleration for all protestant sects, which the Presbyterians refused to concede. The City of London and the apprentices supported the Presbyterians; but the Roundhead army was on the side of the Independents. Sir Thomas Fairfax was Commander-in-Chief of the Army, but he was merely a figurehead; his second-in-command, Oliver Cromwell, decided Army policy.

25. Plate sold, 20 May 1643: inventory from the Company's Abstract and Memorandum Book listing the provenance and weight (ounces and penny weight) for each item sold.

The disagreements between the Presbyterians and the Independents was King Charles's opportunity. He was a prisoner in the hands of the Army, but he succeeded in entering into secret communication with the Presbyterian leaders. In May 1648 the Second Civil War broke out. The Scottish Presbyterians invaded England, some English Cavaliers seized Colchester, and Presbyterian soldiers in the army captured Pembroke. Cromwell and the Army marched against them. When the news reached London that the Presbyterian soldiers had captured Pembroke, a thanksgiving service was held in St. Paul's, which the Master and Wardens of the Carpenters' Company attended; they spent 5s.9d. on the decorations. But Cromwell and the Army recaptured Colchester and Pembroke, defeated the Scots at Preston, and won the Second Civil War.

The City and the Livery Companies had backed the losing side in the Second Civil War, and now had to bear the consequences. Cromwell decided to seize power. On 2 December 1648 the Army occupied London and Westminster. Four days later, Colonel Pride and his soldiers prevented all except 80 of the 500 MPs from entering the House of Commons. After 30 of them had withdrawn in protest, the 50 Independent MPs who remained proclaimed themselves to be the only lawful representatives of the people of England. They abolished the monarchy and the House of Lords and set up a High Court of Justice to try "Charles Stuart" for high treason against the people of England. He was condemned to death and beheaded on 30 January 1649 on a scaffold outside his palace of Whitehall.

When it was known in the last week of November 1648 that the Army was about to occupy London, there was great anxiety in the City. Did it mean that the soldiers would be quartered on the population, living in private houses, where the householders would have to feed them at their own expense? But on 30 November the Lord Mayor received a letter signed by Lieutenant General Sir Thomas Fairfax. He informed the Lord Mayor that if the City paid a contribution of £40,000 towards the cost of the Army's operations, he would try as far as possible to avoid quartering the troops in private houses in London; the soldiers would be lodged in "great and void houses". The City Corporation agreed to comply with this demand, and the Carpenters' Company, at the request of the Lord Mayor, agreed on 2 December to pay £6.11s.0d. immediately. The Lord Mayor then received another message from Fairfax explaining that the "great and void houses" that he had in mind were the Halls of the Livery Companies, which would be requisitioned as lodgings for the soldiers.

The Army promptly occupied most of the Halls of the Livery Companies, but a few Halls were not taken. One of these was Carpenters' Hall. The Court of the Carpenters' Company was expecting the worst, and on 15 December decided to sell all their plate at once. The only exceptions were plate which were the gifts of members of the Court, including the four silver-gilt cups that the Company had acquired in about 1614. These are still owned by the Company today.

The sale of the plate raised £60.1s.0d. The Court obviously thought that if the soldiers came into the Hall they would steal the plate, whereas the money obtained from the sale of the plate could be hidden. The few remaining pieces of plate and the Company's title deeds and other valuables were entrusted to Thomas Birkett, who had been Master in 1639. He agreed to hide them in his own house in the City.

But the soldiers did not come to Carpenters' Hall. Cromwell and the zealous Puritans in the Army were incorruptible, but some of the quartermaster-sergeants were not. The Carpenters' Clerk had useful contacts who used their influence in the right place. Two entries in the Company records tell the whole story. "11th April 1649. Whereas there were soldiers appointed to be quartered in the Hall of this Company, and the Clerk of this Company was enforced to use many friends of his, for the getting them off, for not to be quartered there. It is this day ordered that the Master and Wardens shall present the Clerk's friends with what presents they shall think fitting for their favour and assistance in preventing that the soldiers should not be quartered in the Hall of said Company".

The Wardens had already hastened to make the payments before being authorised to do so by the Court. There is an entry for 21 March 1649: "Given away in gratuities to several men of quality for keeping of the soldiers for not to be quartered in the Hall of this Company, and spent upon the same occasion, £13.2s.6d."

On 31 January 1649, the day after the King's execution, the Council of State issued a proclamation that anyone who recognised Charles Stuart's son as King Charles II would be guilty of high treason against the people of England. The Lord Mayor refused to read out the proclamation in the City, so the Council of State dismissed him from office and appointed a new Lord Mayor who was prepared to comply. The Carpenters' Company collaborated with the new regime, and joined in removing the royal arms wherever they were displayed in London.

At this time, John Read was a Warden of the Company. He became Master in 1650, but died during his year of office. In his will he left money to the Company to be used for buying a pair of gloves every year for each member of the Court, and for educating a scholar at Oxford and Cambridge Universities. The gift of gloves has been changed into a Christmas present of £1.50 to the members of the Court – it has not been increased to keep up with inflation – but the Carpenters today still send scholars to Oxford and Cambridge under the terms of the Read's Trust.

In 1653 Cromwell dispersed the Rump Parliament, and in December he was proclaimed Lord Protector. The City was quite pleased at this development. Cromwell had crushed the Levellers and the extremists of the Barebones Parliament, and now seemed the best hope of establishing some kind of order in the country. Two months after he became Lord Protector the Lord Mayor entertained him on 8 February 1654 at a great banquet in Grocers' Hall. All the Livery Companies turned out to decorate their stalls and receive Cromwell when he entered the City, and all the Masters and Wardens were invited to the banquet. After the dinner, Cromwell knighted the Lord Mayor before he left Grocers' Hall. While the Master and Wardens of the Carpenters' Company were at the banquet for Cromwell, the other members of the Court and the Livery were enjoying their own dinner in Carpenters' Hall to celebrate "the Lord Protector's show", at a cost of £27.10s.10d.

It was a different story six years later, after Cromwell had died and General Monck had marched from Coldstream on the Tweed to London, intending to restore Charles II to the throne. There was an outburst of royalist sentiment throughout the country and especially in London; for the Presbyterians, who had always been strong in the City, were as bitter as the Cavaliers and High Church Anglicans against their former allies, the Independents, and as enthusiastic for restoring the King. While Charles II waited at Breda in Holland and prepared to sail to Dover, the City Corporation proved their loyalty by giving him £12,000, and called on the Carpenters' Company to contribute £60.

At a meeting of the Court of the Carpenters' Company on 5 May 1660 a resolution was duly passed that "for as much as it hath pleased Almighty God wonderfully to preserve from many imminent dangers His most gracious Majesty Charles II...and by wonderful instruments to bring about the sudden return of the King's Majesty to the exercise of his kingly office" of which he had been unjustly deprived "from and after the martyrdom of his father our late sovereign King Charles I of happy and blessed memory", the £60 demanded of the Carpenters' Company would "be freely given and advanced".

When Charles entered London on his birthday, 29 May, the Carpenters went with the other Livery Companies to welcome him in St. George's Fields in Southwark; and on 5 July their Master and Wardens attended the great banquet which the Lord Mayor gave to the King and his brother, the Duke of York (afterwards James II) at the Guildhall. The banquet cost the City £3,000, and the Carpenters paid their share of £15.

26. *The Great Fire of London, 1666: an eastern view of the Fire showing the flames reaching old St Pauls Cathedral while the inhabitants leave the City. This picture was painted from a boat near Tower Wharf but the artist is not known.*

6
Plague, Fire and Quo Warranto

The numbers on the Court of Assistants are greatly reduced because of deaths from the Great Plague of 1665 – new members co-opted to the Court – Carpenters' Hall escapes the Great Fire of London in 1666 – the Carpenters offer the use of their Hall to the Lord Mayor – Charles II crushes the Whig Opposition in London by confiscating the charters of the City and of the Livery Companies – the Quo Warranto proceedings and Judge Jeffreys – The Revolution of 1688 restores the old charters to the City and to the Carpenters' Company.

It was not long before Charles II's ministers, and the "Cavalier Parliament" which was elected on the wave of monarchist enthusiasm, turned against their Presbyterian and Nonconformist allies. All religious services except those of the Church of England were banned; Nonconformist ministers were ejected from their churches and forbidden to live within five miles of any city or borough or of any parish where they had been ministers; and only men who attended the services of the Church of England were allowed to be members of city or borough corporations. Soon the City of London and the Livery Companies were once again in opposition to the King's policy.

Charles II's war against the Dutch went badly. The King asked the City to pay £100,000 towards the cost of the war, and the Carpenters had to contribute £300; but this did not prevent the Company from making an important addition to the Hall. In 1664 they built a new wing on the west side of the Hall containing an office for the Clerk and a meeting room for the Court. It was an expensive project, costing more than £1,500, and the Company had to borrow part of the money.

The war was still in progress when the Great Plague broke out in London during the very hot weather in June 1665. It was more devastating than any plague since the Black Death three hundred years earlier. The recorded deaths were over 70,000; but as many of the deaths among Jews, Quakers and other sects outside the official Church were unrecorded, the true figure is probably nearer 100,000 – one in five of the population of the City, which had again more than doubled in fifty years and was now approaching half a million. The City Corporation tried to stop the spread of plague by sealing the doors of houses where a case of plague had been reported; the inmates, who were unable to escape from the house, were left to die without any medical help, though occasionally a few survived and recovered.

On 27 July 1665 the Court of the Carpenters' Company decided to cancel the service in All Hallows Church and the dinner on Election Day "in regard of the great increase of the plague", and to hold the election "without a sermon, dinner, music and other ceremonies, only a cup of wine and Naples biscuit". They did not cancel the visit to Godalming in August, but decided that only three members of the Court should go. They could not stop all contact with each other, for they had to meet to conduct their business; but only four members of the Court attended the Audit Court in September.

They decided to reduce the risk of catching the plague by smoking. The smoking of

71

27. The Great Plague, 1665: contemporary woodcut of nine scenes drawn by John Dunstall (d.1693).

1. A sick room in an infected house.
2. London street scene. Doors are marked with red crosses, a dog-killer slaughters stray dogs, searchers look for plague victims and bearers carry a victim to the pest-house.

3. The flight from London by river.

4. The flight from London by road. Country guards stop the travellers to inspect their certificates of health.
5. Bearers carry the bodies of plague victims.
6. Open and hooded dead-carts make their way to the graveyards.
7. Burial of the dead in a churchyard outside the City walls.

8. Mourners follow a coffin in spite of prohibitions against such processions.
9. Londoners return to the City as the threat from Plague recedes.

tobacco in clay pipes had started in England in the 1590s and rapidly became very popular, and though some doctors condemned it as being bad for the smoker's health, others said that it lessened the chance of catching infectious diseases. The members of the Carpenters' Company probably started smoking at the beginning of the seventeenth century; but in 1665 they decided that pipes and tobacco should be provided for members of the Court to smoke during the Court meetings.

In September the Beadle, Thomas Heake, died of the plague, and by December several members of the Court had also caught it and died. On 5 December the Court decided to appoint four members of the Livery to be members of the Court although they had not been Master or Warden, and that every year for the next four years one other liveryman, apart from the Youngest Warden, should be brought on to the Court.

The Corporation's ban on public gatherings and feastings was still in force in July 1666 "for avoiding of the infection and in regard to the commotions at sea" (with the Dutch). Again in August 1666 there was no sermon, dinner or music on Election Day.

Within three weeks the City faced another disaster. At one o'clock in the morning of Sunday 2 September a fire broke out in a bakery in Pudding Lane near London Bridge, for a baker's apprentice had gone to bed leaving a candle burning. No one noticed the fire until it had set the whole house alight, and even then it did not cause much alarm, for it was a common occurrence for a wooden house to be burned. But a strong east wind drove the flames westward through the narrow streets with their wooden houses and along the river, where they set fire to the wooden wharves. By Sunday evening the whole of the southern part of the City between London Bridge and the Fleet river beyond Ludgate was burning; but no one took any measures to fight the fire.

It was only on Monday morning, after the fire had been burning for more than twenty-four hours, that the Lord Mayor and the Corporation bestirred themselves and appointed a committee to consider what could be done to save the City. By midday on Monday the King himself had arrived with his brother the Duke of York and several of his ministers, and Charles directed the firefighting operations, calling on the people to blow up their houses in order to clear a space to stop the flames and to clear away the debris before the fire reached it. He distributed golden sovereigns to the most energetic workers, and lent a hand himself, working to clear the rubble; his face became black from the smoke. The fire had now spread to the northern part of the City and was approaching London Wall; but the position of Carpenters' Hall gave it a good chance of escaping. To the north was the City Wall and beyond it was the open space of Moor Fields; on the southern side it was separated from Drapers' Hall by the gardens of the two Companies, some 100 yards long.

The people fled from their homes and out of the City, some of them carrying a few of their belongings. Most of them streamed through Moorgate and waited in Moor Fields, where the King came and spoke words of sympathy to them. The fire was still burning strongly on the Tuesday; but the wind had now subsided, and it seemed that it might be possible to contain the flames. By Wednesday 5 September only the barristers' chambers in the Temple at the western edge of the City were still burning. The fires in the Temple were finally extinguished on Thursday 6 September.

Considering the scale of the disaster, there was surprisingly little loss of life. Only six people died, but the damage to property was enormous. The fire destroyed 436 acres of buildings covering 400 streets and lanes, three of the City gates, 13,200 houses, St. Paul's Cathedral and 86 parish churches, the Guildhall, the Royal Exchange, many hospitals, and the Halls of 52 Livery Companies. Drapers' Hall, the house that Nedeham had built for Thomas Cromwell 130 years before, was burned; but the flames did not cross the Carpenters' garden, and Carpenters' Hall was saved. The Company's property in Lime Street was threatened, but the fire was checked two-thirds of the way along the street after one of the Carpenters' houses had been burned. This was the only property of the Company which was lost.

The Carpenters' Company found that its Hall was in great demand by the other Livery Companies who had lost their own Halls. At a meeting of the Court on 18 September, it was decided to let the Hall to any Livery Company, but to no one else, so as to keep it available for the Livery Companies. Their neighbours the Drapers were the first to apply, and were granted the use of the Hall for a year on several days in the week for their Court meetings. The Carpenters also granted the use of the Hall to the Goldsmiths, the Feltworkers and the Weavers. The Haberdashers' Company also applied for the use of Carpenters' Hall; but before their application could be granted the Lord Mayor elect had asked the Carpenters' to lease their Hall to him for the meetings of the Common Council, as the Guildhall had been destroyed, and as a residence for himself.

The Lord Mayor did not then have an official residence – the Mansion House was built between 1737 and 1755 – because all Lord Mayors were residents of London, and continued to live during their mayoralty at their own private houses in the City. But Sir William Bolton's house had been burned in the fire. The Carpenters' Company therefore let him have the larger part of the garden, as well as the Hall, for a year from 29 October 1666 at a rent of £100 per annum, retaining for themselves only two rooms and the use of the Hall on their Election Day. The Lord Mayor was to indemnify them against claims for damages for breach of contract by the Drapers', Goldsmiths', Weavers' or Feltworkers' Companies to whom the Carpenters had agreed to let it.

The Carpenters' Company granted a similar lease of the Hall for a year to Bolton's three successors as Lord Mayor, but asked and received an increased rent of £150 per annum. At first the relations between the Carpenters and the Lord Mayor were very friendly. Bolton invited all the members of the Court and their wives to dinner with him in Carpenters' Hall in July 1667; his successor, Sir William Peake, asked them all to dinner twice during his year of office, in January and in May 1668; and the two following Lord Mayors invited them in July 1669 and July 1670. But there was some difficulty in October 1670; although the Company again let the Hall to the new Lord Mayor for a year, they insisted that he should pay the rent of £150 in advance. This may have been because they knew that the repairs to the Guildhall would soon be completed and that the Lord Mayor would then return there, for he did in fact leave Carpenters' Hall in December 1670. It may also have been because his four predecessors had not carried out any repairs to the Hall and had left the property in a bad state, for after regaining possession the Carpenters' Company had to spend money in redecorating, repairing and improving the Hall.

London was quickly rebuilt after the fire. The King appointed three commissioners –

28. Reversal of Quo Warranto, 1690: the first page from an annotated copy of the Act for reversing the Quo Warranto decision. Contemporary definitions of "Quo Warranto" and "Franchise" have been written.

Christopher Wren, John Evelyn and Robert Hooke – to supervise the rebuilding of London. They drew up a plan to build wide streets up to 90 feet wide and great squares as a precaution against fire; but this town-planners' dream was thwarted by the conservatism of the traditionalists, who insisted on rebuilding the same streets with the houses, churches and Halls in the same places that they had occupied before the fire. But one precaution against fire was taken: houses were no longer to be built of wood. The Act for Rebuildng the City of London of 1667, after stating that "building with brick was not only more comely and durable but also more safe against future perils of fire" than building in wood, enacted "that all the outsides of all buildings in and about the City should be made of brick or stone, except doorcases and window frames and other parts of the first storey to the front between the piers", where stout oak could be used "for the conveniency of shops".

It was a blow to the London carpenters, especially as the only woodwork which was allowed was work which by the award of 1632 was in most cases to be performed by joiners, not carpenters. Unemployment increased among carpenters. The Carpenters' Company tried to help them by sending petitions and appeals on their behalf to the Government and City authorities, and by asking Christopher Wren and his wife to their Election Day dinner; but they could not prevent the continued unemployment, and a general fall in carpenters' wages during the thirty years after the Great Fire. In the days of Henry VII and Henry VIII enterprising carpenters like Cooke, Nedeham and Russell had made their fortune by building in brick; but no London carpenter with their drive and adaptability succeeded in doing likewise after the Act for the Rebuilding of the City of London was passed.

Not for the first or last time, the interests and fortunes of the London carpenters and the Carpenters' Company diverged. While the Great Fire reduced work for carpenters, it made the Carpenters' Company realise that they could make money by letting property. When the Lord Mayor no longer needed to rent Carpenters' Hall, the Company decided to look for other tenants. They could not find anyone who was prepared to pay a rent of £150 per annum; but after letting the Hall for a year to one of the Sheriffs at £100 per annum, they let it in 1673 to Mr. Gabriel Roberts, a merchant who traded with Smyrna and the Turkish Empire. Roberts took a lease for seven years which he later renewed, though the Company had to agree to a lower rent now that the building shortage had largely passed. Roberts (now Sir Gabriel) remained the tenant of the Hall for 42 years till his death in 1715.

The death of so many members of the Court during the plague had made it difficult to transact business, and this had not been remedied by the decision in 1665 to bring on to the Court liverymen who had never been Master or Warden. In December 1670 two more members of the Livery who had not been Master or Warden were brought on to the Court; four more in September 1671; and seven more in February 1677. Apparently no one suggested that these nominations to the Court violated the Ordinances of 1607, and they were completely overlooked during the arguments about the legality of such nominations which took place in 1846, 1930, 1938 and 1993.

While the City recovered from the effects of the fire, new political conflicts were looming. After the euphoria of the Restoration had passed, opposition to royal absolutism was renewed, and there was fear of what would happen when the Duke of York became King, because it was known that he was a Roman Catholic. An opposition party began to form under the leadership of the Earl of Shaftesbury. His party became known as the Whigs and the King's supporters as the Tories. Shaftesbury succeeded in uniting the Dissenters and many members of the Church of England against the King. He had a following throughout the country, but London was his power base. His brand of constitutional Protestantism appealed to the City far more than the revolutionary Puritanism of Cromwell's Army. His allegations about the existence of a "Popish Plot" in 1678 won great support, especially in London.

Shaftesbury was a skilful and unscrupulous political operator, but he met his match in Charles II. The King played for time, pretending to believe in the existence of a Popish plot and to acquiesce in the exclusion of his brother from the throne. Having made a secret agreement with King Louis XIV of France that Louis would send him money if he pursued a pro-French and pro-Catholic policy, he summoned a Parliament to meet at Oxford, away from the influence of the London apprentices, and dissolved it in March 1681 and ruled without Parliament. Shaftesbury was arrested and put on trial in London on a charge of sedition; but the jury returned a verdict of "Not Guilty". The Carpenters' Company thereupon found themselves in trouble because of political controversies. Shaftesbury had been acquitted by a London jury; London juries were chosen by the City Sheriff; and the Sheriffs were elected by the Livery Companies.

Charles II and his brother James, who was now acting as the King's chief adviser, were determined to gain control of London by controlling the City Officers. The King would not interfere with the rights and privileges of the Corporation and the Livery Companies provided that the Corporation and the Companies elected the Lord Mayor, the Sheriffs and the Masters of whom he approved, and provided that they recognised that the King might remove the Lord Mayor, Sheriffs and Masters from office if they did not do what he wished. He asked the City to surrender its charter, and he would then grant a new charter in which his power to appoint and remove officers was clearly recognised.

As the City Corporation was reluctant to comply, the King began quo warranto proceedings in the Court of King's Bench, requiring the City to show cause why its charter should not be revoked for misconduct. Charles and James had found an able agent to carry out their policy. George Jeffreys was a skilful lawyer who had realised that his career would best be advanced by loyal service to the King and the Tory party. In 1683 he was appointed Lord Chief Justice of the King's Bench at the age of 38. Other judges in the eighteenth and early nineteenth centuries were as harsh as he and as biassed in favour of the Government in political cases; but as he and his party were overthrown by a successful revolution, he is remembered in history as the infamous "Judge Jeffreys".

He gave judgment for the King in the quo warranto case, and declared that the City of London had forfeited its charter. He then dealt with the Livery Companies, who had been well frightened by the fate of the City Corporation. They all surrendered their charters and humbly petitioned the King to grant them new charters on any terms which he chose. All over the country the charters of Whig boroughs were forfeited.

While the Carpenters' Company waited for Jeffreys to begin proceedings against them, several members of the Court died. This was perhaps because of the bitterly cold winter of 1683–4, when the Thames froze for four weeks in December and fairs were held on the frozen river; oxen were roasted over fires which had been lit on the ice, which was eleven inches thick. On 1 January 1684 the Court again brought on to the Court some liverymen who had never been Master or Warden.

The Carpenters decided to forestall Jeffreys, and surrender their charter before they were ordered to do so. A special General Court of the Livery was held at Carpenters' Hall on 11 June 1684, and it was agreed nem. con. (but apparently not unanimously) "that His Sacred Majesty should be presented with a petition in order to the delivering up into the hands of his most gracious Majesty the governing part" of the Company. The phrase "Sacred Majesty" had come into use at the Restoration in 1660 to emphasise the crime of the regicides who

29. "Judge Jeffreys", 1684: a Victorian engraving of a contemporary portrait of Sir George Jeffreys in his post of Lord Chief Justice of England and de facto ruler of London.

had spilt the "sacred blood" of Charles I. The surrender of the charter did not apply to the Company's property, but only to the "governing part" of the Company. The liverymen did not mind so much about the government of the Company, and they knew that it was this that the King wished to have.

The Livery at the General Court approved the wording of the petition. It reminded the King that the Carpenters had been granted charters by Edward IV, by other Kings and Queens, "and more especially by Your Majesty since your happy Restoration. Nevertheless Your Sacred Majesty, having lately in your princely wisdom thought fit to order several quo warrantos to be brought against several Companies within London for that they have some ways offended Your Majesty; and albeit there is none as yet brought against your petitioners, yet fearing they may be likewise in Your Majesty's displeasure whom in duty and allegiance they ought to obey, your petitioners earnestly beg that Your Majesty will be graciously pleased to pardon what is past and accept of their humble submission to Your Sacred Majesty's good will and pleasure".

Two days later, the Court sent the petition to the King and informed him that they surrendered the right that had been granted to them by earlier charters to elect, nominate or appoint their Master, Wardens and Clerk, or to hold meetings of the Court. They asked the King to grant once again to their Master, Wardens and liverymen the right to choose "such officers who shall manage the government of the said Company under such restrictions and regulations as Your Majesty in your great wisdom shall think fit".

The Company's submission was complete, though they did not go quite as far as their neighbours the Drapers, who invited Jeffreys to dinner and made him an Honorary Freeman of the Drapers' Company. He did not trouble to subject the Carpenters' Company to the strict control that he established over the more powerful Companies; he forced every member of the Court of the Grocers to make a declaration that he had never signed the Covenant of the Scottish Presbyterian Whigs. Jeffreys had done his work well. He boasted that "the King of England is now likewise King of London". Under the King, it was Jeffreys himself who governed London. The Lord Mayor felt powerless. He told a friend that "he had the title of Lord Mayor, but my Lord Chief Justice Jeffreys usurped that power .... that himself and the Aldermen were looked upon as his instruments, and that upon all occasions his lordship used them contemptibly and not according to the dignity of the City".

Jeffreys allowed the Carpenters' Company to hold their election day in August 1684 and approved their choice of Master and Wardens; but he removed their Clerk, John Smalley, and appointed in his place Jeffreys's nominee, James Stone, though the Company had never heard of Stone. The Court duly dismissed Smalley, and accepted Stone; but Smalley refused to hand over to Stone the Company's minute book and other documents. Smalley was in due course arrested at Jeffreys's orders, and forced to surrender the Company's documents, in March 1685. Charles II had died a month before and James II had succeeded him.

When the Carpenters' Company held their Election Day in August 1685, the Duke of Monmouth's rebellion against James II had been defeated at Sedgmoor, Monmouth had been beheaded, and Jeffreys was on the point of leaving on the Western Circuit to try the rebels at the "Bloody Assizes". James II ordered the Carpenters to re-elect the same Master and Wardens whom he had approved the year before.

On 19 March 1686 the King granted the Carpenters' Company its new charter. It confirmed and indeed extended the Company's privileges, giving them control over carpentry for an area of twelve miles around the City; but it laid down that the Master, Wardens and all members of the Court must be approved by the King, and must have taken communion in the Church of England during the six months before their election. They were to obey all orders issued to them by the Lord Mayor, and would be removable (like the Lord Mayor himself) at any time without cause at the King's pleasure. The charter also placed restrictions on who might be admitted to the Livery. All liverymen must be approved by the Lord Mayor; they must be members of the Church of England, must take the oath of allegiance to the King as Supreme Governor of the Church of England (although it was known that the King himself was a Roman Catholic) and must sign a declaration that they had never attended and never would attend any Nonconformist prayer-meeting.

At the elections in August 1686, 1687 and 1688, the Carpenters duly chose the Master and Wardens approved by the King; they were very largely the same men as those who had been Master and Wardens before the quo warranto proceedings and the surrender of the old charter. By Election Day in 1688, James II had issued his Declaration of Indulgence granting religious toleration to both Roman Catholics and Protestant Nonconformists, and had ordered it to be read out to the congregation in every church in London and the country. His order was obeyed in only four of the hundred City churches. When the Archbishop of Canterbury and six other bishops protested against the Declaration, they were prosecuted for sedition.

Anglican Tories and Nonconformist Whigs united against the King. On 30 June the seven bishops were acquitted by a London jury, and that same evening, seven of the leading dignitaries of the realm wrote to James's son-in-law, William, Prince of Orange, asking him to invade England with an army from the Netherlands and succeed James as King. On 5 November 1688 William landed at Torbay. A fortnight later James issued a proclamation revoking the quo warranto proceedings and the new charters that had subsequently been granted. He restored to all the Livery Companies their old charters and released them from the obligation to submit to the royal authority and to be members of the Church of England. It was much too late. His own generals were already preparing to desert to William.

After William reached London and James had fled to France, the citizens of London welcomed the Glorious Revolution and the proclamation of William and his wife, James's daughter Mary, as joint King and Queen. An Act of Parliament of 1690 revoked all the charters which had been granted under the quo warranto proceedings, which were declared to have been illegal, and restored the old charters which had been surrendered. But the Carpenters' Company retained the Clerk who had been imposed upon them in 1684. Stone may have been unknown to them when they were forced to appoint him; but four years later they had come to value his services as Clerk. He was one of the many second-rank men who was able to change sides and survive while his superiors had to suffer the consequences of their policies and their defeat.

On 5 February 1689, after William had reached London and when Jeffreys was a prisoner in the Tower, Smalley applied to the Carpenters to reinstate him as Clerk in Stone's place. But the Company felt no gratitude to Smalley for having tried to prevent their records and documents from falling into the hands of Jeffreys's nominee. Perhaps they felt that his resistance to Jeffreys and his imprisonment in 1685 had risked bringing the Company into bad odour with the men who had then been in power and that it was safer to have a more compliant Clerk. So Stone, like all the members of the Court, swore allegiance to William and Mary, and continued to be the Clerk to the Carpenters' Company.

30. Carpenters' Hall: this engraving is one in a series of pictures of Livery Companies drawn by Thomas H Shepherd in the 1830s. It shows the façade of the "new" wing which was built, in 1664, on the west side of the Hall. The wing contained an office for the Clerk and a meeting room for the Court. The building was altered several times in the eighteenth century. It was pulled down in 1876 to make way for the creation of Throgmorton Avenue.

7
The Eighteenth Century

The Carpenters erect Carpenters' Buildings in 1737 – Carpenters' Hall leased permanently to tenants – The Carpenters do well in the South Sea Bubble, selling out before the shares become valueless – The Carpenters' Company purchase lands at Stratford in East London – Changing attitudes towards charitable giving – the Carpenters' hold their dinners at the London Tavern and elsewhere – Sir William Staines becomes the first Carpenter Lord Mayor in 1801

William III had restored the freedom and privileges of the City, but he made them pay for his wars in the Netherlands against Louis XIV of France. The Land Tax of 1691 required the Carpenters' Company to pay £20 in tax on Carpenters' Hall, or 20 per cent of the annual rent of £100 that they received from Sir Gabriel Roberts. By 1699 they were paying a total of £110 in land tax on their total annual income of £500. In 1689 the Carpenters decided to insure the Hall against damage by fire and other causes. This was a novel step to take, for insurance had only just been introduced into England. The Hall was valued for a total capital value of £1,000, and the Company paid a premium of £16 per annum.

Stone remained Clerk for twenty-five years. His successor Joseph Knapp, who was appointed in 1709, held the office for a much shorter time. The circumstances of Knapp's departure in 1712 are mysterious, for it was obviously decided to write very little about them in the Court minutes; but it would seem that he incurred personal debts which he could not repay. This was obviously an embarrassment for the Company. Knapp's salary as Clerk was £8 per annum, but he also received a gift of £10 every Christmas and rent-free accommodation at the Hall, where he lived even though the rest of the Hall was let to Roberts. On 4 November 1712 Knapp wrote to the Court, referring to his "unhappy misfortunes" which he "would not enlarge upon", but added: "My intention is to seek my fortunes abroad, and with what your Worships please to allow me, I design to buy up necessaries proper for my intended voyage". On 2 December the Court decided to pay him his usual £10 Christmas gift and a further £10 with which to pay off his debts. They also paid the £11.11s.0d. that he owed to the Beadle.

The Court had miscalculated when they added to their number by bringing on to the Court liverymen who had never been Master or Warden. The Court was now too large, not too small. On 8 August 1710 the Court decided not to bring any member of the Livery on to the Court as Youngest Warden until the number of members of the Court had fallen to 20; but in 1713 there were still 25 members of the Court, including the Master and Wardens. Of the 21 other members, only 9 were Past Masters and 5 had never been either Master or Warden.

The Carpenters' Company's control over carpenters was weakening, at a time when ideas about economic freedom and free trade were becoming fashionable. This development, combined with the rise in unemployment among carpenters and the fall in their wages and the regulations against housebuilding in wood in the City, encouraged the Carpenters' Company to search for a new and more profitable line of activity. Two avenues looked promising: to buy land and lease it to tenants, and to make profits from investments in stocks and shares. They decided to continue leasing their Hall, keeping only a few rooms for the Court meetings, a residence for the Clerk, and the use of the dining hall for Election Day on the second Tuesday in August every year. After 1666 they were never again in possession of the whole of their old Hall. When Sir Gabriel Roberts died in 1715, and his executors relinquished his lease two years later, the Company granted a lease for 41 years to James Fordham, a member of the Skinners' Company, though they had to agree to a much lower rent of £52 per annum.

Soon after Fordham acquired his lease he asked the Company to enlarge the Hall. They agreed to build an additional storey at the top of the 1664 building and to raise the height of the roof by 9 feet. Fordham agreed to contribute 30 guineas towards the cost of the improvements and for the remainder of his lease to pay an increased rent of £67 per annum. The Company thought that they could obtain higher rents by erecting other buildings near the Hall. They began building there in 1736, and the work was completed by 5 July 1737 when they decided to call the buildings, "Carpenters' Buildings". The Buildings were let to various tenants, and by 1740 were bringing in rents of £110 per annum, considerably more than the £67 per annum that Fordham paid for the Hall itself. By 1800 the rents of Carpenters' Buildings were £191 per annum, which was £51 more than the rents of all the Company's other properties in London Wall, including the Hall.

The Company could afford to carry out these building works because they had done very well in their investments in the South Sea Company. This Company was formed by a group of wealthy merchants who had spread stories about the vast wealth that was to be found in the Pacific islands in the South Sea, and claimed to have acquired a monopoly of the very profitable slave trade between the west coast of Africa and South America. They offered to pay the whole of the National Debt on condition that the holders of annuities payable by the Government were allotted shares in the South Sea Company instead of their annuities. When the Act of Parliament which authorised this was passed in April 1720, the value of South Sea shares, which had been at $128\frac{1}{2}$ in January, rose to 330. By May they were at 550, by June 890, and by July at nearly 1000.

Then the news arrived that a similar scheme in Paris had been a fraud and that thousands of French investors had lost a great deal of money. In August shareholders began to sell, and by September the price had fallen to 175. By November it was 135. When it was known that the directors of the South Sea Company had sold their shares in April, there was a public outcry, and some of the directors, several of whom were MPs, were arrested and prosecuted for fraud. An Act was passed confiscating the property of the directors for the benefit of the defrauded shareholders; but many investors were ruined.

The Carpenters' Company did well in the South Sea Bubble. They bought shares in 1719 for £700, and sold them at the same time as the directors, in April 1720, for £2,408. They would have done even better if they had waited till June or July before selling, but they got out before the rapid price fall in August.

It was at the beginning of the eighteenth century, in the reign of Queen Anne, that the

31. Sir John Cass, 1710: Master of the Company in 1711, Cass was the founder of a charity school situated next to St Botolph Aldgate, London. This contemporary drawing shows the statue of Cass which used to stand in a niche above the school entrance.

Carpenters first produced a liveryman who played an important part in the civic and political life of the City. John Cass was the son of a carpenter, but went into business as a general merchant, and made a fortune. In 1710 he was elected as a Tory MP for the City, and in 1711 he became one of the City Sheriffs. In this same year, in July, he was appointed to the Court of the Carpenters' Company, though he had never been a Master or Warden, and on Election Day in August he was elected Master. He was knighted in June 1712, when the City Corporation presented a petition to Queen Anne in favour of the Tory policy of making peace with France; but he never became Lord Mayor. In 1713 he decided to join the Skinners' Company, with the full consent of the Carpenters' Company, who sent six members of the Court to join six members of the Skinners to consent to the transfer before the Court of Aldermen.

But Cass was an exceptional case; for the next eighty years no member of the Carpenters' Company became prominent in City politics. The Carpenters' Company was an association of carpenters. Indeed, in 1727 the Court decided that no one could be admitted as a freeman by redemption unless he was a carpenter by trade; and after the Company in 1736 limited the number of liverymen to 100, it was decided in 1737 and again in 1738 that only carpenters by trade could be admitted to the Livery by patrimony.

This was the first time in the history of the Company that a complete ban had been imposed on the admission of non-carpenters to the Freedom and Livery, and it was not

85

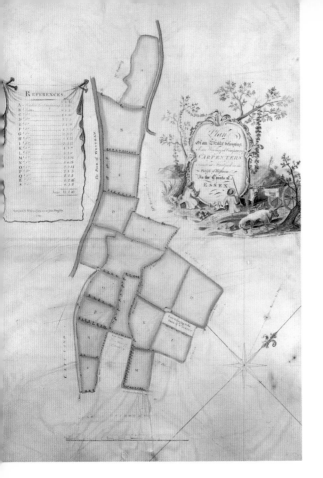

32. *Plan of Stratford estate, 1769: this freehold farm in West Ham, Stratford, consisted of 63 acres and cost £3150. Much of the land is still owned by the Company.*
◄

33. *Plan of Carpenters' Hall and buildings, 1727: a general survey of Company property was ordered by the Court in February 1725.*
►

maintained for long; but in the middle of the eighteenth century the great majority of liverymen were carpenters by trade. In 1746 of the 100 liverymen in the Company (26 of them were on the Court) 70 were carpenters, 13 were timber merchants, 3 were described as "gentlemen", and one each was a brewer, a goldsmith, a button seller, a bedsteadmaker, a broker, an attorney-at-law, a woollen draper, a coal merchant, a merchant, a corn factor, a painter, a mason, an apothecary and a proctor.

The Carpenters' Company was conscious that London was expanding far beyond the City itself. By 1720 the built-up area stretched beyond Aldgate as far east as Whitechapel, and to the west beyond Westminster to Hyde Park. The Carpenters thought that it would be a good investment to buy land on the edge of London. They were already discussing this in 1721, but it was not until 1767 that a decision was actually made. Richard Mount, who had been Master in 1762, drew the attention of the Court to a property near Stratford to the east of London. It was "a freehold farm consisting of 63 acres of marsh land title free lying in the parish of West Ham"; the rents paid for tenancies on the land came to £126 per annum. A special meeting of the Court was held to discuss the matter on 20 October 1767, and it was decided to buy the property for 3,000 guineas (£3,150). The Carpenters' Company still holds much of the original Stratford Estate today.

The Company became wealthier during the eighteenth century; in a period in which there

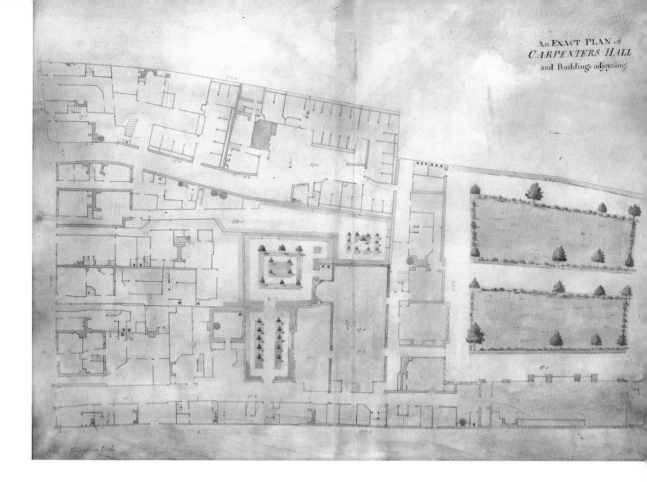

was very little inflation, its annual income rose from £750 in 1700 to £1,300 in 1788. This had been achieved by sound investments in purchasing the farmland at Stratford, in building development around Carpenters' Hall, in increased rents and in the shrewd and fortunate buying and selling of stocks and shares. The Company could afford to pay for these investments only by saving money in some way. It occasionally economised on dinners and entertainments, and in payments to members of the Court.

Until 1741, the members of the Court were not paid for attending meetings, but were given breakfast before the meeting and dinner afterwards, at the Company's expense. They had originally met, like the House of Commons and most other bodies, at 8.00 a.m. By the beginning of the eighteenth century they were meeting at 10.00 a.m. and by 1740 at 11.00 a.m. On 6 January 1741 the Court decided that, in order to reduce expenditure, breakfast and dinner would no longer be served, but that 5 shillings would be paid at every Court meeting to the first twelve members to arrive, provided that they had arrived at the Hall by 11 o'clock. In September 1751 a further economy was made when the fee was reduced from 5s. to 1s., still paid only to the first twelve to arrive by 11 o'clock.

But the greatest economies were made, not in reducing entertainments and dinners and payments to the Court, but in grants to charity. When Sir John Cass died in 1718 he left money for building twenty almshouses in Portsoken Ward for the poor, to be administered by the Carpenters' Company. His next-of-kin challenged the validity of the bequest because they wanted the money for themselves. The Carpenters' Company at first contested this claim, and the case dragged on interminably, as litigation often did in the eighteenth century. When the case at last reached the Court of Chancery in 1734, judgment was given for the Carpenters; but the next-of-kin appealed, and the Carpenters decided in 1742 not to oppose the appeal, on the grounds that Cass's bequest did not bring any financial benefit to the Company, but only the burden of choosing the almsmen. So no almshouses were built.

In 1722 there was trouble at the almshouses in Godalming. Some of the almsmen petitioned the Company for an increase in their pensions. They said that the pensions were not enough to live on, and if they applied to the Justices of the Peace for aid under the poor law, they would have to go into the workhouse. The Company told them to go into the workhouse. In 1744 the Company stopped paying the Christmas gifts to their pensioners.

In 1752 the Clerk drew the Court's attention to an oversight which had gone unnoticed for over a hundred years. The Company paid their pensions once a quarter to their own pensioners, and they had therefore also paid quarterly the payments left by Richard Wyatt and other benefactors in their wills to the almsmen and other poor men and women. The Clerk had now noticed that by the terms of the wills the sums were payable annually. This was a good way to economise. The Court decided that in future it would pay the sums annually, not quarterly, with the result that the almsmen were informed that they would only receive a quarter of what they had been paid hitherto.

The Court's attitude to charitable gifts was typical of the period in which they lived. In 1333 the Catholic Church had taught, and the people believed, that if a man gave generously to "religious uses", or charities, this was the best way to ensure that he went to Heaven; it was the "salvation by works" of Roman Catholic teaching. The charitable donations usually took the form of gifts to monasteries or other ecclesiastical bodies. The Reformation in the sixteenth century did not discourage gifts to charity, for although the Protestants believed that salvation would be obtained by faith, not by works, one of the manifestations of that faith was to give to charity. This should consist, not of gifts to corrupt immoral monks in return for prayers for the donor's soul, but of bequests to found schools, hospitals and almshouses. The charitable gifts by Richard Wyatt in 1619 are a good example of post-Reformation Protestant charity, with the prohibition on drunkenness and the insistence on attendance at chapel which he imposed on the recipients of his charity.

But by the eighteenth century public opinion had changed. People now believed in freedom, personal responsibility, reward for initiative, and free trade, though the phrase "free market economy" had not yet come into use. Charitable gifts to the poor would upset the free play of the laws of supply and demand, which would solve all problems if they were allowed to operate. The poor would be unable to buy commodities, the demand would therefore fall, the sellers would then be forced to reduce their prices, and as the prices fell the poor would once again be able to buy. If some of them had meanwhile died of starvation, this too was beneficial, as it was a necessary if painful way of preventing too rapid a growth of the population. As sinful man refused to check the growth of population by abstaining from sexual intercourse, it was God's will that it should be limited by death from starvation.

Charitable gifts did not entirely cease. In the villages, the aristocratic lady and the squire's wife, the "Lady Bountiful" of legend and caricature, gave gifts at Christmas and other times to the "deserving poor". But this attitude was not so common among the successful entrepreneurs, the men who made their fortunes in the eighteenth century and especially during the Industrial Revolution after 1770. They were usually men who had been born poor, had risen in society, and had become rich by their own exertions. They had no sympathy, only contempt, for their fellow-workmen who had lacked their virtues of thrift and hard work, and had therefore remained poor. To give them charitable grants would only encourage their vices and idleness.

By the end of the century, the Carpenters' Company's gifts to charities had been substantially reduced, and economies had also been made on the dinners. In 1739 the Company spent £417 on dinners and £357 on charities; by 1799 they were spending £333 on dinners and £252 on charities.

As the Hall was permanently let after 1666, the Company had to make other arrangements for their dinners. Only the Election Day dinner was still held in the Hall. The Court dinners, and any other dinner that was given to the Livery, were usually held in the private houses of a member of the Court. They were sometimes held in the Master's house, but usually in the house of the Company cook. Occasionally they held a dinner in a tavern in the City.

At the beginning of the eighteenth century, an "Audit dinner" was held every year in July to which the members of the Court could bring their wives. In 1725 it began to be called the "Ladies dinner", and was held at the George Inn in Ironmonger Lane. In 1770 the Court decided that in future the Ladies' dinner should be held at some place outside London, the decision as to the place and the arrangements for the dinner being left to a committee of the Court. The committee usually decided to hold the Ladies' dinner at either the Castle Inn or the Star and Garter at Richmond, which was a fashionable hotel, or at the Bull tavern at Shooter's Hill near Blackheath. A coach was hired to take each member of the Court and his guests to the hotel where the dinner was to take place.

A Livery dinner for all the liverymen was held four times a year, on Midsummer Day, on Election Day in August, after the election of the Lord Mayor at Michaelmas on 29 September, and on 9 November. By the end of the eighteenth century the Election Day dinner was no longer held at the Hall, but, like the other dinners, at various taverns and hotels. They met at the Albion Hotel, the Star and Garter at Richmond, the Brunswick Tavern at Blackwall, the Ship Tavern at Greenwich, and after 1850 at the Crystal Palace, the Ship and Turtle in Leadenhall Street, Radley's Hotel in New Bridge Street, or more often at the Cannon Street Hotel. But the favourite place for dinners was the London Tavern, Bishopsgate, one of the most select eating places in London. The London Tavern had been given an impressive new entrance in 1770. The architect was William Jupp. He was a prominent member of the Carpenters' Company, and was the architect when additions were made to Carpenters' Hall in 1779; but, unlike his father and brother, he never became Master of the Company.

By the end of the eighteenth century the Company had abandoned the attempt in the 1730's to ensure that every liveryman should be a carpenter by trade. Many members of other trades were now being admitted, both by patrimony and by redemption. In 1823, when the number of liverymen had risen to 125, only about 20 per cent of them were carpenters. Many of the others were connected with the building trade, being builders,

34. Sir William Staines, 1804: the Lord Mayor of London engraved by William Say (1768–1834), after the oil painting by Sir William Beechey (1753–1839).

architects, masons, bricklayers and timber merchants; but 65 per cent had no connection with the building industry. These included a banker, two brokers, a jeweller and a surgeon, and artisans in various occupations.

In the eighteenth century several new members joined the Company by servitude or redemption whose descendants were to play a prominent part in the Company's affairs for the next two hundred years. The Carpenters, unlike some other Livery Companies, have no members today whose ancestors first joined in the thirteenth or fourteenth centuries; but several of them can claim a connection with the Company as far back as the eighteenth century. The names Jacob, Stuckey, Pocock, Evelegh and Preston all appear in the eighteenth-century Livery lists.

There had been a recent development in the building industry. The design for a new building was thought out by an architect, a member of a new profession which was officially recognised when the Architects Club was formed in 1791. Several of the leading architects joined the Carpenters' Company. They included William Jupp, the architect of the London Tavern, and his brother Richard; their father, Richard Jupp, had been Master of the Carpenters' Company in 1768. The younger Richard Jupp was for many years the Surveyor in London of the East India Company, the great trading organisation which officially governed India for the King. He sometimes did other work, and was the architect who designed a new wing of Guy's Hospital. He was one of the founder members of the Architects Club, and Master of the Carpenters' Company in 1779.

These architects and builders were prosperous and successful men, but they never claimed to be gentlemen by rank or gave themselves airs above their station. In 1805 the Court of the Carpenters' Company was displeased to find that one liveryman had been described as "Esquire" in the Livery list. The title was still used only by men who were entitled to be called "Esquire" – the sons of noblemen, MPs, JPs, barristers and those holding certain official positions. The Court ordered that the designation "Esquire" should be deleted in the Livery list, "being convinced that he had no right to it and that many gentlemen of the Company who did not claim the title had had a greater right to it". The members of the Carpenters' Company were not pushing parvenus who tried to get into Almack's, the aristocratic club in St. James's Street, which rigidly excluded them and was said to be "the ambition and despair of the middle classes".

The typical liveryman in the Carpenters' Company was an artisan, often but not always connected with the building trade, who had become wealthy by taking advantage of the opportunities which the Industrial Revolution and the great economic growth had opened up at the end of the eighteenth century. When for the first time in the history of the City a member of the Carpenters' Company became Lord Mayor, he was a much more typical liveryman than Sir John Cass had been nearly a hundred years before. Sir William Staines had started as a stonemason, and became a successful builder. He was Middle Warden of the Carpenters' Company in 1791, Upper Warden in 1792, and Master in 1793. He was again Master for four months in 1799 after two Masters had died in office during the year. In 1796 he was elected a City Sheriff, and in 1801 Lord Mayor. In the next 160 years the Carpenters would provide six more Lord Mayors – an unusually high number for one of the minor Companies.

35. *Interior of Carpenters' Hall, 1877: illustration from* The Graphic *(3 March 1877) showing the medieval Hall in the course of demolition. The top picture shows the detail of the ornate ceiling while the bottom picture shows the interior. The inset picture* (bottom left) *is of the façade of the Hall.*

8
Mr. Simmons and Captain Yallowley

Radical influence in the City of London – Matthew Wood as Lord Mayor leads the Radicals – The country is split by the matrimonial disputes between King George IV and Queen Caroline – the issue splits the Carpenters' Company – on the Court of the Carpenters' Company, John Simmons denounces Joseph Yallowley as a Nonconformist and a supporter of Queen Caroline – Simmons expelled from the Carpenters' Company.

In 1789 the French Revolution broke out. The original instigators of the Revolution had been inspired by the example of the English Revolution of 1688 and the society which had been established in eighteenth-century Britain; the Jacobins who had come to power in Paris had gone much further, and had aroused great hatred and fear in Britain. In February 1791 the French revolutionary government suppressed all the French guilds and confiscated their property. When the French armies conquered the Spanish Netherlands and Holland, the flourishing guilds of Antwerp and Amsterdam were also suppressed. They were not revived after the overthrow of Napoleon and the restoration of the old régime in France and the Netherlands, and by the middle of the nineteenth century the guilds had ceased to exist in Germany, Austria, Italy, Spain and Portugal. The guilds survived only in Britain; but here they were saved by Nelson and the Royal Navy, along with all the other institutions, both good and bad, of eighteenth-century Britain.

The City of London and its Livery Companies were becoming richer every year. The early nineteenth century was a period of great economic growth, particularly in the building industry. By 1820 the built-up area of London stretched from Mile End in the east to Chelsea and Paddington in the west, and from Somers Town and Islington in the north to Kennington and Walworth in the south, and had a population of over 1,500,000. But poverty among the lower classes increased during the Napoleonic Wars and in the years after 1815. A vociferous Radical movement was developing. Trades unions were being formed, though they were illegal. Poets like Shelley and Byron attacked the injustices and oppression from which the poor suffered under Lord Liverpool's Tory government. Radical pamphlets and newspapers, some legal and some illegal, attacked the King, the aristocracy, the Church of England and the most cherished religious doctrines. The Government reacted with increased repression.

The Carpenters' Company felt the impact of the political unrest. It was inevitable that some reformers should attack the City of London and its Livery Companies. They were denounced as bastions of privilege and oppressors of the poor. The electoral system in the City was criticised. The Common Council was elected by the City ratepayers, but the Sheriffs were elected by the Livery Companies before they could be elected by the Court of Aldermen; and at Parliamentary elections all liverymen, as well as ratepayers, had the vote. But the Whigs, and even the Radicals, were strong in the City. The liverymen had not forgotten how the Tory Judge Jeffreys had oppressed them in the 1680s, and how in the

1760s John Wilkes, who became Lord Mayor, had defied the King and rallied the people behind him with the cry "Wilkes and Liberty!" The Fishmongers' Company was a Whig stronghold, and had the reputation of being as Radical as the Merchant Taylors were Tory.

Matthew Wood was a member of a Nonconformist family in Exeter. He came to London as a young man, opened a pharmacy in the City, and became a liveryman of the Fishmongers' Company. He became a close friend of Sir Williams Staines and other members of the Carpenters' Company, and when Staines died in 1807 he succeeded him on the Court of Aldermen. He became Lord Mayor in 1815. Next year he was re-elected for a second term; he was the first Lord Mayor for over a century to serve for two years in succession. The liverymen nominated him for a third term in 1817, but the Court of Aldermen vetoed this. Wood was the leader of the Radicals in the City; but the City elected him as their MP, and named the City barge "The Maria Wood" after his daughter.

By this time, the matrimonial disagreements between the Prince and Princess of Wales were arousing widespread interest. The Prince of Wales was regent for his old father, George III, and as Prince Regent had become identified with the repressive policies of his Tory government. It was well known that he had had many mistresses. His wife, Caroline of Brunswick, the Princess of Wales, had gone to live in Milan, where she became very intimate with Bartolommeo Pergami, a rough-and-ready former soldier of Napoleon's army. No one had any doubt that Pergami was her lover.

In January 1820 George III died, and the Prince Regent became King George IV. He refused to recognise Caroline as his Queen, and offered her £50,000 per annum if she promised never to set foot in England. She was on the point of accepting this offer when Wood arrived in Milan and persuaded her to refuse and to return to England with him. They entered London sitting side by side in an open carriage amid the cheers of the people. The Whigs and the Radicals took up the Queen's cause. When God Save the King was played, the Radicals shouted it down and demanded that instead they should play "God Save the Queen".

A bill divorcing the King from the Queen was introduced in the House of Lords; but after it had passed with a majority of only 9, it was withdrawn, as the Government knew that it would never pass the House of Commons. When George IV was crowned, he gave orders that Caroline was not to be admitted to Westminster Abbey. She tried to enter, and was ejected by force. Soon afterwards, in 1821, she died.

The quarrel between the King and Queen divided the Nation, and it divided the Carpenters' Company. John Simmons was an ardent Tory and a supporter of the King and the Church of England. He was a surveyor and became a liveryman of the Carpenters' Company in 1795. He also joined the Honourable Artillery Company and several other organisations, including the Society for the Encouragement of Arts, Manufactures and Commerce.

Joseph Yallowley was also a liveryman in the Carpenters' Company; he had joined in 1796, a year after Simmons, and three years before his father, the elder Joseph Yallowley, was Master. Like Simmons, Joseph Yallowley junior was a member of the Honourable Artillery Company, where he held the rank of captain; but he was a Whig, a Nonconformist and a supporter of Queen Caroline.

The Yallowley family, who had originally come from Durham, were all devout Con-

36. London Wall, 1811: watercolour by George Sidney Shepherd (1784–1862) showing Luck and Kent's carpet warehouse at Carpenters' Hall.

gregationalists, and worshipped at the Countess of Huntingdon's Tabernacle in Tottenham Court Road. When Simmons discovered this, he smelt sedition. He agreed with the Bishop of London that any form of religious teaching "which does not conform, in every particular of religious innovation, to the principles of the Church of England or admit the super-intendence of the regular clergyman of the parish" would "multiply dissension and error, already too numerous among the people".

There was one matter on which Mr. Simmons felt particularly strongly. He thought that whenever the King's health was drunk it should be accompanied by "noise" – by loud cheering, by the traditional "three times three", with "Hip hip hip hurrah!" repeated three times and then repeated three times again on two more occasions. To drink the loyal toast in silence was an insult to "our most princely-minded and gracious Sovereign", to "the best of Kings".

Simmons attended a dinner of the Arts Society at which the King's brother, His Royal Highness the Duke of Sussex, presided. The Duke of Sussex was a Whig supporter. When it was time to drink the loyal toast, the Duke proposed the King's health, but added: "No cheers". As the diners drank the toast, Simmons shouted out indignantly: "What? No cheering?" "No cheering", replied the Duke.

Simmons wrote an indignant letter to the press. He was invited to attend a meeting of the Committee of the Arts Society to explain his conduct. He did not come, but wrote in reply that if he believed that the Society wished to discourage their members' loyalty to "a beloved King", he would resign. The committee treated his letter as his resignation from the society, and accepted it. When he subsequently attended a meeting of the Society, he was informed that he was no longer a member.

It was just at the time of his brush with the Duke of Sussex at the Arts Society dinner that the Court of the Carpenters' Company nominated Simmons as their chosen candidate for election as Renter Warden, as the youngest Warden was now called. He had reached this position by seniority after nearly thirty years on the Livery, and he was duly elected at the General Court of the Livery in August 1823. But before his year of office had expired, he had published a pamphlet A Letter to His Grace the Duke of Northumberland (a member of the Arts Society) describing his confrontation with the Duke of Sussex and his expulsion from the Society; and the Court of the Carpenters' Company had realised that he might be a nuisance in the Carpenters too. He was not nominated for Middle Warden in 1824; but Captain Joseph Yallowley was nominated Renter Warden, and elected at the General Court on Election Day. Simmons remained on the Court as a Past Warden.

During the next year Simmons became increasingly unpopular with his colleagues on the Court. He quarrelled with the Clerk, Richard Webb Jupp, and continued to be on bad terms with Yallowley. Neither Simmons nor Yallowley were nominated for further office in 1825, but both remained on the Court as Past Wardens.

A week after Election Day, on 16 August 1825, the Court paid their annual visit to Godalming. As they were waiting to go in to dinner at Godalming, Simmons became involved in a heated argument with three other members of the Court. Yallowley came into the room and joined the group, and intervened in the discussion against Simmons. "Yallowley", said Simmons, "you are a fool to interfere in what you do not understand". According to Simmons, Yallowley then clenched his fist, leaned over the table towards Simmons, and threatened to knock him down unless he withdrew this remark. At this point Yallowley's aged father, who was still on the Court twentysix years after he had been Master, put his hand on his son's arm to restrain him from assaulting Simmons.

At the next meeting of the Court on 6 September, Yallowley proposed that the words of the Lord's Prayer, the Creed and the Ten Commandments be written on the wall of the chapel at Godalming, and he offered to pay for the expense of doing this. The Court gratefully accepted his offer, and the words are still there on the chapel wall today; but this was not enough to convince Simmons that Yallowley was a good Christian of the right denomination.

Simmons now wrote to the Colonel and all the higher officers of the regiment of the Honourable Artillery Company in which he and Yallowley served, and complained about Yallowley's conduct. He explained that he and Yallowley were both "members of the Court of Assistants of an incorporated Company", and that at a meeting of this Company at Godalming on 16 August Captain Yallowley had tried to assault him, a brother officer.

"Whatever superiority the Captain holds in the Corps, by virtue of his commission, I do assert myself to be his superior in years, in religion and also in loyalty to His Sacred Majesty, our Captain-General. First, I am aged enough to have been the father of such as the Captain. Secondly, *I* am not an Arian dissenter but an Episcopalian, adoring the Trinity in Unity. Lastly, *my* loyalty has never been questioned, nor did I pay homage to the greatest personal enemy (Caroline) our Sovereign ever had".

The Carpenters were losing all patience with Simmons. He found that none of the other members of the Court would speak to him; he complained that at the instigation of the Master (Thomas Lett), he had been "sent … to what the vulgar call Coventry". After the Livery Dinner at the London Tavern on 9 November 1825 he went home to his house at The Pavilion, Euston Square, and that same evening wrote a Letter to the Liverymen of the Worshipful Company of Carpenters, which he published as a pamphlet. He sent a copy of the pamphlet to the Upper Warden and to the Master's son.

At the meeting of the Court on 6 December 1825 the Master raised the question of the pamphlet, and a committee of the Master, Wardens and all past Masters was appointed to consider it. They had drafted their report by February. They were "compelled by a sense of duty, painful as it may be", to report that "your committee most sincerely regret that any member of the Carpenters' Company, and particularly one of the Court, by the indulgence of private pique … and by behaviour contrary to the usages of civilised society should assiduously endeavour to create dissension in a fellowship that has for so long a period acted together with uniform harmony and cordiality." As for Simmons's action in sending to the Master's son the pamphlet which criticised his father's conduct, "we are at a loss for words to express our sentiments on conduct so abhorrent to the good feelings of human nature but particularly to the 'hallowed principles of Christianity' to which he makes such claims". The other members of the Court had treated Simmons with every civility and had left him to "the enjoyment of his own farcical superiority in 'Religion and Loyalty' ". If they had recently sent him, in his own words, "to Coventry", this was not at the instigation of the Master but from their own spontaneous annoyance at Simmons's refusal to apologise for his conduct.

At the meeting of the Court on 7 March 1826 the committee's report was accepted and a resolution was passed expelling Simmons from the Company. The Renter Warden, W. Woodyer, went over to Simmons, who was sitting in his place at the Court table, and handed him £21, the money that he had paid on joining the Livery, thirty-one years before. Simmons refused to accept it. The Master directed that the £21 should be held in the Clerk's office and that Simmons could come and collect it whenever he wished. The Court then passed a resolution that after the meetings of the Court the Master could invite any member of the Court whom he pleased to attend the Court dinner. At the end of the meeting the Master invited all the members to dinner except Simmons.

At a General Court of the Livery on Midsummer Day, the liverymen passed a resolution congratulating the Court on the "not unmerited severity" with which they had dealt with Simmons. At the General Court on Election Day in August, Yallowley was elected Middle Warden, and in 1827 Upper Warden. In 1828 he was elected Master, but died three weeks after taking office on 25 September 1828.

Surprisingly, Simmons's name was not deleted from the Livery List, but remained among

37. Twickenham almshouses, 1842: design for almshouses by William Fuller Pocock, architect and Master in 1840. By 1842, the ten central almshouses were occupied but, due to lack of funds, the houses on either side were never constructed.

the list of members of the Court until his death in 1835. He apparently never collected his admission money from the Clerk's office, for there is no record of the repayment of the money in the appropriate column in the records.

At the Court meeting in September 1829 it was decided that "for the information of the new members of the Court" the resolution condemning and expelling Simmons should be read out at this meeting and at the September meeting of the Court every year until the Court decided otherwise. There is no record of any further resolution of the Court on this matter, but the practice of reading out the resolution denouncing Simmons had undoubtedly lapsed long before the September meeting of the Court was abolished in 1873.

9

The Nineteenth Century

Increased wealth of the Carpenters' Company – the Carpenters sell land to the Great Eastern Railway – the Company opens almshouses for its freemen at Twickenham in 1841 – increased wealth and higher social standing of the liverymen of the Carpenters' Company – Richard Webb Jupp and Edward Basil Jupp as Clerks of the Carpenters' Company for seventy-nine years – Sir William and Sir James Clarke Lawrence as Lord Mayors and Masters of the Carpenters' Company – the origin of the Lord Mayor's attendance at the Carpenters' Company's annual dinner in November.

The Carpenters' Company was prospering. Between 1800 and 1830 its annual income rose by more than 35 per cent, from £2,000 to £2,700. But this was only the beginning; the great expansion began with the railways. The first railway train ran from Darlington to Stockton in 1825, and the railway from Liverpool to Manchester opened in 1830. By 1840 there were 1,331 miles of railway tracks in Britain; by 1850, 6,635 miles; by 1860, 10,410 miles; by 1870, 15,310 miles. It was a bad development for the Innholders' Company, for travellers from London to Edinburgh or Plymouth, instead of going on horseback or in carriages and spending several nights in an inn on the journey, now reached their destination in one day without staying at an inn; but it was a good thing for the Carpenters' Company, who in 1834 and 1836 sold land in Bermondsey to the London and Greenwich Railway and land in Stratford in 1837 to the Eastern Counties Railway.

The Carpenters owned land in the Manor of Norton Folgate to the north of Carpenters' Hall; they had bought it in 1631 when it was in the fields just outside the City walls. Between 1862 and 1872 they sold the land to the Great Eastern Railway, the North London Railway and the London and North-Western Railway. The railway companies paid good prices for land. Legislation had been passed to prevent a recalcitrant landowner from holding up the development of railways; it gave the railway companies the right to acquire land by compulsory purchase, but as the idea of compulsory purchase offended the prevailing belief in economic freedom, the Act provided that when land was acquired by compulsory purchase, the railway companies must pay 10 per cent above the value of the land to compensate the landowner for the compulsion. The result was that landowners refused to sell to railway companies by agreement in order to force the companies to resort to their compulsory powers.

The sale to the Great Eastern Railway caused the Carpenters' Company some worry. The Great Eastern got into financial difficulties, and it seemed as if it was about to go into liquidation; but it survived, and was able to build a link line to its terminus of Liverpool Street on the land that it had bought from the Carpenters' Company. After waiting four years for their money, the Carpenters' received £8,000 for the sale.

The Carpenters' increased wealth enabled them to launch a new charitable venture and build almshouses for poor liverymen and freemen and their widows. In 1840 the Company bought six acres of land at Twickenham which had been part of Pope's Villa Estate, and in 1841 erected ten almshouses on the land. The Master of the Company that year, William Fuller Pocock, was a well-known architect, and he designed and supervised the building of the almshouses without fee. The cost of purchasing the land was paid out of the Company's funds but the members of the Court and the Livery contributed towards the cost of endowing the Almshouses; one benefactor gave £500.

The Company seems always to have regarded the almsmen and almswomen at Twickenham in a rather different light from those at Godalming. The almsmen at Godalming were poor people of Godalming and the surrounding parishes for whom the Company was caring out of the assets left to them by Richard Wyatt in trust for this purpose; the almsfolk at Twickenham were their own people, their freemen and liverymen, who might have had the misfortune to have fallen on hard times but were considered to be socially superior to the paupers of the Surrey villages.

The Twickenham almshouses were placed under the supervision of the Middle Warden; the Godalming almshouses were dealt with by the Upper Warden, whose name was changed to "Senior Warden" in 1845. The two Wardens visited their respective almshouses regularly, usually once a month. The Court went to both almshouses once a year; they visited Godalming in August, and Twickenham in the last week of June. After inspecting the Twickenham almshouses and talking to the almsfolk, the Court finished their day's outing by having dinner at the Star and Garter Inn in Richmond. The Lord Mayor was often the guest of honour at these dinners in Richmond.

As the Carpenters' Company's wealth increased, the social status of its leading members also rose. The grandsons and great-grandsons of the builders, timber merchants and architects of the late eighteenth century, who did not presume to add the title "Esquire" after their names, were themselves still in many cases the leading partners in building, timber and architectural firms; but they had often been educated at the best public schools, and many of them owned a gentleman's country estate in South-East England, as well as a town house in Greater London. In 1895 the Court postponed the date of their visit to Twickenham so that their members could attend the Ascot race meeting.

The Carpenters were becoming increasingly a family affair, with a few families providing many liverymen and many Masters of the Company. In 1883 there were four Pococks, four Jacobs, five Roshers and seven Prestons on the Livery; in 1914, four Pococks, four Jacobs, eight Roshers and nine Prestons, one-sixth of all the liverymen being members of these four families.

In 1798 Richard Webb Jupp, who was a thirty-one year old solicitor and the Master's son, was appointed Clerk. He remained Clerk for fifty-four years till he died at the age of eighty-five in 1852; but for the last nine years of his service as Clerk he was helped by his son, Edward Basil Jupp, who was appointed joint Clerk with his father in 1843. When Richard Webb Jupp died, Edward Basil Jupp was appointed the sole Clerk at a salary of £300 per annum, and served for twenty-five years till his death in 1877. Edward Basil Jupp wrote the first History of the Company, which was also the first history of any City Livery Company; it was published in 1848.

In the 1860s the Carpenters provided their second and third Lord Mayor with William

38. Twickenham almshouses, c.1890: the Company considered the almsmen to be more genteel than their fellow beneficiaries at Godalming.

Lawrence and James Clarke Lawrence. Their father, William Lawrence, was a Cornishman who came to London as a young man and established the very successful building firm of William Lawrence and Sons. He was elected Master of the Carpenters' Company in 1848 without having served as a Warden, and was Sheriff of London in 1849. One of his sons, Sir William Lawrence, was Master in 1856 and Lord Mayor in 1863.

His other son, James Clarke Lawrence, became Master in unusual circumstances. On Election Day in August 1860 Thomas Smith was elected Master but he died in December after having been Master for less than four months. A special General Court of the Livery was held on 10 January 1861 at which Thomas Finden was elected Master; but he died within three weeks before he could take office at the February meeting of the Court. Strictly speaking, he was never Master, and the Court minutes recording his death refer to him as the Master Elect; but in later records he is duly listed as having been Master. Another special General Court of the Livery was held in February at which Alderman James Clarke Lawrence was elected Master. He served as Master for the remaining six months before the Senior Warden, George Faith, a prominent ship owner of the time, took office after having been elected Master in August 1861. Sir James Clarke Lawrence was Lord Mayor in 1868.

It was equally important for the Carpenters that William and James Clarke Lawrence

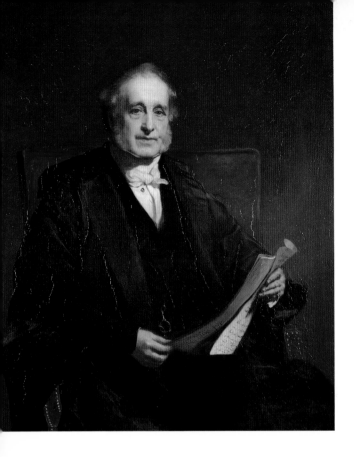

39. Richard Webb Jupp: Clerk to the Company from 1798–1852 when he died aged eighty-five. Artist unknown.
◄

carried on the Liberal political tradition of the Company. William was a Liberal MP for the City from 1863 to 1874, and after losing his seat in Disraeli's Conservative victory in 1874 he was again one of the City MPs during Gladstone's government from 1880 to 1885. James Clarke was Liberal MP for Lambeth in 1865 and from 1868 to 1885. They were able to use their position in the Liberal Party to oppose the attacks on the City and the Livery Companies that were being launched by some of their Liberal parliamentary colleagues.

Sir William and Sir James Clarke Lawrence were probably also responsible for starting the custom, which has become so greatly valued by the Carpenters, that their November Livery dinner is the first Livery dinner that the new Lord Mayor attends during his year of office; for though he dines first with the Mercers at the Gresham Dinner, this is not a Livery dinner. From time to time it has been suggested that the Lord Mayor should dine with the Grocers' Company in November before he comes to the Carpenters; but the Carpenters have always fought hard for their privilege of being the first to entertain the Lord Mayor at a Livery dinner, and the Grocers have always generously agreed to this.

There is a tradition in the Carpenters' Company that the Lord Mayor has been dining first with them, before attending any other Livery dinner, ever since the Great Fire, and has done so out of gratitude for having been allowed the use of Carpenters' Hall after the Guildhall and his own house were destroyed in the Fire; but like so many cherished traditions in other organisations, this is a myth. The Lord Mayor often dined with the Livery

102

40. *Sir William Lawrence: Master in 1856, Lord Mayor in 1863 and Liberal MP for the City, 1863–1874 and 1880–1885. Artist: John Prescott Knight (1803–1881).*
◄

41. *Sir James Clarke Lawrence, 1869: Master in 1861, Lord Mayor in 1868 and Liberal MP for Lambeth, 1865, 1868–1885. Artist: George Richmond (1809–1896).* ►

43. The Master's chair: the carved mahogeny chair is used by the Master at Court meetings. Its origins are not known but in 1887 the Clerk, E.B. Jupp, suggested that the lower part of the chair dated from 1713 while the more ornate upper portion had been added on at a later stage, c.1740.

▶

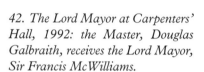

42. The Lord Mayor at Carpenters' Hall, 1992: the Master, Douglas Galbraith, receives the Lord Mayor, Sir Francis McWilliams.

◀

Companies, and invited their Masters to dine with him, in the Middle Ages and in the seventeenth and eighteenth centuries; but the practice for the Lord Mayor to dine in turn with the Livery Companies on approximately the same date every year is a much later development, dating only from the middle of the nineteenth century. One of the earliest of these regular dining dates to be established was the Livery dinner with the Carpenters' Company.

Although on several occasions after 1841 the Lord Mayor came to the Carpenters' dinner at Richmond when they visited the Twickenham almshouses at the end of June, he could not come to their November dinner as long as it was held on 9 November while the Lord Mayor was attending a function at the Mansion House after his Show. But after 1847 the Carpenters' dinner was held a few days later in November; and in 1862, when William Lawrence was Sheriff, the Lord Mayor with the Sheriffs came to the Carpenters' dinner at the London Tavern on 13 November. Next year they came again when William Lawrence was Lord Mayor. The Lord Mayor did not attend in 1864 nor 1865, but he did in 1866 when Sir James Clarke Lawrence was Sheriff, and he has attended every year since with a few exceptions which included the two World Wars and 1947, when the dinner was cancelled because of the rationing restrictions. In 1973 and 1979 he had to attend a state banquet on the evening of the Carpenters' dinner. No doubt Sir James Clarke Lawrence, who was particularly strong on the Company's history, used the Carpenters' hospitality to the Lord

44. Some of Mr George Faith's Fleet, 1806: *painted by Thomas Luny (1759–1837), the shipowner is believed to be the grandfather of George Faith, Master in 1861. The Company received the picture from a bequest of Robert Howard Denholm in 1992.*

Mayor in 1666 as the justification for establishing the tradition, and this is probably why the Carpenters have associated the Lord Mayor's presence at the November dinner with the Great Fire, although Edward Basil Jupp, of course, made no reference to the Lord Mayor's presence at the November Dinner in his History of the Carpenters' Company of 1848.

The Carpenters should not be too distressed to discover that the tradition dates not from 1666 but only 1862, as it is old enough to override all other Livery Companies' claims. It began sixty-five years before the Lord Mayor first came to a November Livery dinner at the Grocers in 1927; he had previously dined there in July. The Carpenters should recognise the truth and give the credit to where it belongs, to Sir William and Sir James Clarke Lawrence, to whom they are also indebted for their part in preserving the City Corporation and the Livery Companies.

106

10
The Attack on the Livery Companies

The Radicals' demand for a reform of the government of the City of London after 1832 – the leading role played by Sir James Clarke Lawrence of the Carpenters' Company in defending the City institutions from the Radical attack – the arrival of Princess Alexandra of Denmark in London in 1863 – J. F. B. Firth's attack on the Livery Companies – the appointment of a Royal Commission to inquire into the Livery Companies in 1882 – the failure to take any action to reform the City from 1882 to 1995 shows the lack of public support for the attacks on the City – Under Disraeli, the Conservatives gain the political support of the City of London.

The Radicals were on the attack, and their target was the City of London. In 1830 the long years of Tory government ended, and the Whigs returned to power; and in 1832 the Great Reform Bill was passed at last, abolishing the rotten boroughs and giving seats in the House of Commons to the great manufacturing towns in the North. A leading part in the victory had been played by Francis Place, the Radical tailor of Charing Cross. He had brought down the Duke of Wellington's Tory government which was resisting the Reform Bill by launching the slogan: "To stop the Duke, go for gold!". The run on the banks that followed forced Wellington to resign.

Place next turned his attention to local government. The electoral system must be changed so as to give the vote to residents and ratepayers, not to members of Livery Companies and other privileged bodies. He denounced "our corrupt, rotting, robbing, infamous corporation of London", which was "a burlesque on the human understanding, more contemptible than the most paltry farce played in a booth at Bartholomew's Fair". He wanted a new, more democratically elected council for the City, with "no shows, no parade, no feasts, no fooleries". He was supported by James Acland's City of London Municipal Reform Association, which had a membership of 1,200 shopkeepers who could not afford to pay the fee to become a freeman of a Livery Company, and were therefore deprived of the vote; and *The Times*, which was then a Radical newspaper, supported the campaign. Even the City Solicitor, Charles Pearson, wished to abolish the Lord Mayor's Show: "The time has arrived when the civic exhibition with the Mayor as chief performer can no longer be tolerated".

The City Corporation survived the attack. In 1835 Lord Grey's Whig government passed the Municipal Corporations Act which reformed local government and the municipal franchise in the cities throughout Britain; but the Act did not apply to the City of London. This appears to have been the result of a political compromise between the supporters and the opponents of municipal reform; the opponents gave way about the other towns and cities of Britain in return for the reformers keeping their hands off London. It was probably also because of the long-standing connection of the City with the Whig Party. Lord John Russell, who was one of the most Radical members of Lord Grey's government, was MP for the City, and probably played his part in saving the City Corporation.

Twenty years later, the Radicals tried again. Lord Palmerston's government introduced a bill to set up the Metropolitan Board of Works which had powers to control local government throughout the London metropolitan area, except the City. The Metropolitan Board of Works aroused the hostility of many Conservatives, who disliked it as much as Lord Salisbury in 1894, and Margaret Thatcher in 1986, disliked the London County Council and the Greater London Council; they believed that the Metropolitan Board of Works threatened the independence of the City. The Liberal supporters of the City favoured the idea of an authority for London provided that its jurisdiction did not extend to the City. While many Livery Companies denounced the Metropolitan Board of Works, the Carpenters' Company invited the chairman of the Board to their Election Day Livery dinner in 1860.

A Royal Commission was set up to consider reforming the electoral system and local government in the City. In 1854 Fraser's Magazine reported that the Radicals rejoiced that "this gigantic anomaly, the Corporation of London, is at length to totter to its fall ... it cannot survive the year; the last Lord Mayor's Show has been given; the state coach is bespoken by Madam Tussaud; Gog and Magog, doing duty as humble firewood, will frown no more over turtle and champagne ... it's existence now merely negatives the doing of good". Two years later the Government introduced a bill to reform the City administration.

The Corporation organised opposition to the bill. They asked the Livery Companies to petition Parliament against the bill, and obtained the signatures of 2,130 individual liverymen from all the Companies protesting against it. But the Livery Companies were not over-enthusiastic in their support of the City. Many of them took the line that it was for the City, not the Livery Companies, to oppose the bill, and that the intervention of the Livery Companies might cause the Radicals to attack the Companies as well as the Corporation. Of the 69 Livery Companies, only 29 agreed to petition Parliament against the bill.

The Carpenters' Company was one of the twenty-nine, and played a prominent part in the campaign. This was because of the zeal of the Lawrence family. On 15 April 1856 a meeting was held at Common Hall to protest against the bill. James Clarke Lawrence made a powerful speech. "The bill has been called a moderate measure", he said, "That moderation was the moderation of the border plunderer, who took away as much as he could in one foray, leaving the remainder for a future incursion". His speech was received with loud cheers, and the press hailed him as "the City Demosthenes", who was rousing the City to the defence of its freedom against the Radicals in Parliament as Demosthenes had inspired the resistance of the Athenians to Philip of Macedon twenty-two centuries earlier.

The reformers were defeated again. There were influential MPs who supported the City, and the Government did not give Parliamentary time for the bill to go through. The Prime Minister, Palmerston, was not enthusiastic for reform; Disraeli called him "the Tory Chief of a Radical Cabinet". There were more urgent problems confronting the nation than the limitations on the powers of the City of London; there was above all the greatly-exaggerated danger of a French invasion by the new steamships of the Emperor Napoleon III. The Government called on the people to enlist in rifle brigades to defend the country if the French came. The Carpenters' Company duly gave a donation of £10.10s.0d. in October 1859 to the City of London Rifle Brigade; and Alfred Tennyson, in his poem Riflemen Form, urged his readers to enlist and to forget about electoral reform:

45. The expansion of London: a section from
J.H.Bank's balloon view of London, seen from
the north. The view was published in May 1851
with potential sales at the Great Exhibition in mind.

◄

"Let your reforms for a moment go!
Look to your butts, and take good aims!
Better a rotten borough or so
Than a rotten fleet and a city in flames!"

In March 1863 Princess Alexandra of Denmark arrived in London to marry the Prince of Wales. The Carpenters' Company celebrated the marriage by a gift of five guineas to every almsman and almswoman in their Twickenham almshouses and £2.10s.0d. to every almsman at Godalming; the distinction between the two classes of almsfolk was observed. Princess Alexandra's entry into London was a great occasion. The Master and Wardens of the Carpenters' Company were asked to join the procession and to follow behind the Princess in their carriages. They dressed the postilions in jackets of cream-coloured cloth with cuffs and collars in black, representing the Company's colours, their jackets were braided with red, the national colour of Denmark; and they wore black velvet capes with silver tassles. The Company was offered a hundred seats within the railings in St. Paul's Churchyard to watch the procession, on condition that they paid their share of the expenses; but as nearly every liveryman wished to attend, the Clerk persuaded the City to allot them another forty seats. Every liveryman was entitled to bring a lady, but the invitation insisted that "no lady can be admitted unless upon the personal introduction of the gentleman whose name will appear upon the ticket". The Carpenters' Company had to preserve its reputation for respectability.

Unfortunately the happy occasion was marred by an incident in which the crowds trying to see the Princess started a stampede, and several people were trampled on and killed. The press blamed the City of London Police for the mismanagement of the crowd control, and the Radicals began a campaign for the abolition of the City's police force and its incorporation into the Metropolitan Police. But again the Government did not find time for legislation about the City. There was much greater public interest in a new Reform Bill which gave the vote in Parliamentary elections for the first time to the working class in the towns. The bill, which became law in 1867, also went a little way towards satisfying the Radical criticism of the Livery franchise in London by enacting that no one could vote more than three times in the same Parliamentary election.

When the Radicals renewed the attack a few years later, it was directed not against the City Corporation but against the Livery Companies. In 1876 J.F.B. Firth published his book Municipal London. Firth was a Yorkshire Quaker. In his very long and rather dull book he put the case against the Livery Companies in moderate language; but his conclusions were drastic, for he proposed that Parliament should suppress the Livery Companies and confiscate their assets.

He argued that the Livery Companies had outlived their usefulness. They had originally been formed to be "State departments" to regulate their trades and thus help in procuring good government in the City; but all these functions had now been taken over by new government bodies. A considerable amount of property had been given to the Livery Companies in trust to pay stipulated sums to charities; but although, over the years, the values of the property had greatly increased, the Companies still paid only the stipulated sums to charity and spent the rest of the income of the property on themselves. They did not show their accounts even to the members of the Livery, and certainly did not subject

46. Dining Hall, 1927: Firth commented, "No one who has partaken of those gorgeous banquets could find it in his heart to treat his hosts hardly". The picture was given to the Company by Humphrey Morris in 1943, the year in which he was Master. Artist: John Lavery (1856–1951).

111

48. The Fatal Effects of Gluttony, 1830: *attacks on Livery Companies were not new, especially satirical comment upon appetites! The turtle represented the unreformed City, primarily because turtle soup frequently appeared on Livery Company dinner menus.*

▶

47. *J.F. Bottomley Firth, 1889: Firth was a fervant campaigner against the Livery Companies and their privileges. Later he became an MP and the Deputy Chairman of London County Council. This engraving appeared in the* Illustrated London News.

◀

them to public scrutiny; and many of the liverymen had no connection at all with the trade which the Company was supposed to represent. They now existed merely to give dinners to the liverymen, and greater benefits to the members of the Court. "The responsibility of a seat on the Court carries with it a salary; the meetings of the committees are duly paid for; some Companies have dinners of some kind as often as once a week, and lucky are the committeemen of such Companies, for in addition to their salaries they sometimes find a bank-note delicately secreted under their plates, and sometimes find huge boxes of bon-bons upon them. It is indeed a good thing to be on the Court of a City Company".

Why had the Livery Companies been able for so long to resist the demands for their abolition? It was because they invited members of the Government and Judges to their dinners. "No one who has partaken of those gorgeous banquets could find it in his heart to treat his hosts hardly. The source of the funds and their misappropriation seem matters of small moment after a dinner representing the perfected skill of four hundred years of continuous dining. No one who has quaffed rich wines from the chased goblets of the Skinners' Company is inclined to be over inquisitive as to their charters; and no one who has sat at table with the Merchant Taylors troubles himself to ask how many tailors there are on the Livery".

There were a number of MPs who agreed with Firth, and in May 1876 W.H. James, the Liberal MP for Gateshead, moved in the House of Commons that a commission should be

FATAL EFFECTS OF GLUTTONY

A LORD MAYOR'S DAY NIGHT MARE.
Dedicated to all the City Gourmands, — to be had at all the Taverns in the United Kingdom.
Published by Tho.ˢ M.ᶜ Lean 26 Haymarket, Nov.⁴ 1830.

set up to obtain a full return of the Livery Companies' income and property. The Prime Minister, Disraeli, and the Conservative majority in the House of Commons were opposed to any interference with the government of the City or Livery Companies; but it was alarming that the former Prime Minister, Gladstone, gave cautious support to James's motion. Next year James moved his motion again, and a debate took place in the House of Commons on 10 April 1877. James criticised the Skinners, the Goldsmiths, the Joiners and the Innholders for the amount they spent on dinners and their neglect of the poor.

His motion was seconded by Mr Pease, the MP for South Durham, who attacked the Clothworkers and the Drapers for their extravagant dinners. "Then there are the Carpenters, whose income is £2,000 a year, much of which goes in dinners, a little to the poor, and the rest in salaries and fees for the attendance of gentlemen at the Court".

The supporters of the Livery Companies rejected the whole basis of the arguments of Firth and James. They maintained that the Livery Companies had not originally been "State departments"; they had not been formed to regulate their trades or to play any part in the government of the City. They were organisations of private individuals who had come together and formed a Livery Company, and had provided it with funds from their admission

113

fees, in order to help each other in hard times by paying pensions to the members, and to provide the members with other benefits, including dinners. They admitted that during a comparatively short period in their history, the Livery Companies had helped regulate their trades; but though they had agreed to do this at the request of the City Corporation, they had not been formed for this purpose.

Nor had they come into existence in order to make charitable grants to the poor. Some benefactors had left them money in trust for the poor, and the Companies had then acted as good trustees and carried out the terms of these trusts; but a distinction must be made between this property, which they held as trustees, and their own private property which they were entitled to use in any way they pleased, including expenditure on dinners. In fact, however, the Livery Companies often made payments to charity out of their own private funds, though they were under no legal obligation to do so. The supporters of the Livery Companies ridiculed James's statement that the Fishmongers' Company gave dinners to their liverymen at a cost of ten guineas a head; for how could any dinner, however lavish and extravagant, cost as much as ten guineas a head? But if any Livery Company wished to spend ten guineas a head on a dinner, they were perfectly entitled so to do.

Alderman Cotton, the MP for the City, who had been Lord Mayor in 1875 and was a member of the Haberdashers' Company, said that none of the leading Livery Companies spent more than 30 per cent of its income on dinners. He quoted from an old song: "Though the rich we entertain, we don't forget the poor". Sir James Clarke Lawrence spoke against the motion. The Solicitor-General, Sir Hardinge Giffard, replied to the debate; he later became Lord Chancellor with the title of Lord Halsbury. He called on the House to reject James's motion, "because it appears to me that it is one of a most mischievous example; it is a sort of general Communistic inquiry". To set up a commission "would establish the principle that you have only to point out a large quantity of property and that should be a sufficient justification for the interference of a reformer in search of a victim". It would "unsettle the feeling in this Country that private property is sacred". The motion was defeated by 168 votes against 72.

But in 1880 the Liberals won the general election, and Gladstone became Prime Minister. A month after the Government came to power, they appointed a Royal Commission of inquiry into the City Livery Companies. The Earl of Derby, who afterwards became a minister in the Liberal government, was the chairman of the commission, which included the Lord Chief Justice, Lord Coleridge, and other eminent public figures. Both James and Firth, who had just been elected as a Liberal MP for Chelsea at the general election, were appointed members of the commission; so was the great champion of the City and the Livery Companies, Alderman Cotton. The Liberals and critics of the Livery Companies had a clear majority on the twelve-man commission.

The commission did not begin their hearings until 1882, when the Commissioners heard evidence from many sources. One of the witnesses who supported the position of the Livery Companies was the Liberal Lord Chancellor, Lord Selborne, who was a Past Master of the Mercers' Company. The Court of the Carpenters' Company held several meetings to discuss what evidence they should submit to the commission, and decided to present a full statement of their income and expenditure.

The commission presented its report in April 1884. In view of the composition of the commission, it was naturally not unanimous. The majority report, signed by nine of the twelve commissioners, stated that "it appears to us obvious that the State has a right at any time to disestablish and disendow the Companies of London, provided the just claims of existing members to compensation be allowed". But they did not recommend this course; they proposed only that legislation be introduced to ensure that a considerable part of the Companies' income was applied to useful purposes. Three members of the commission issued a minority dissenting report, saying that the Livery Companies were private bodies who were entitled to use their money in any way they pleased. Although Firth signed the majority report, he also issued his own dissenting report recommending that the Companies be suppressed and that their property should be confiscated and applied to useful purposes, such as improving secondary education, hospitals, art galleries and libraries in London. The members of the Livery Companies should be paid fair compensation.

The Liberal government fell before any legislation could be passed to implement the commission's recommendation. When Lord Salisbury's Conservative government returned to power, the City was safe; but it was this government that in 1888 introduced legislation to grant the reformers' long-standing demand to have a central body for the government of London in succession to the Metropolitan Board of Works. The Act of 1888 established the London County Council, but excluded the City of London from its jurisdiction.

A hundred and seven years later the City of London, the Corporation and its Livery Companies are still there, though the London County Council has gone and has been replaced by the Greater London Council, which in its turn has also gone, at least for the time being. Radical politicians have threatened the City of London when in opposition, but have never attempted to carry out their threats when they were in a position to do so. The Liberals did nothing when Gladstone was Prime Minister for the fourth time in 1892, nor when they won a landslide majority in the general election of 1906. But the Representation of the People Act, passed under a coalition government in 1918, abolished the right of liverymen to vote in Parliamentary elections in the City. The bill passed without arousing any serious opposition.

It has been the same with the Labour Party, when it succeeded the Liberals as the main political opposition to the Conservatives. In 1917 Herbert Morrison, then secretary of the London Labour Party, asked the question: "Is it not time London faced up to the pretentious buffoonery of the City of London Corporation and wiped it off the municipal map?" But when he had led the Labour Party to victory in the London County Council elections in 1934 and had become the most important figure in London local government, he wrote much more cautiously about the City of London; and the Labour government of 1945–51, in which he was so important a figure, took no action against the City during its six years in office.

In the debates in the House of Commons in 1963 about the future of local government in London, the Labour opposition moved an amendment to include the City in the area under the Greater London Council. The amendment was duly defeated by the Conservative majority in the House; but again Harold Wilson's Labour government did nothing against the City in the six years between 1964 and 1970. During Wilson's last Labour government in 1977 the Labour-controlled Greater London Council passed a resolution urging the abolition of the City as a local government unit; but the Labour government did nothing. When a backbench Labour MP introduced a private member's bill to abolish the City Corporation, it was defeated in a House of Commons in which Labour had a majority. Geoffrey Finsberg, the Conservative MP for Hampstead, said during the debate that the City had "been a bastion of liberty in British history" and was "highly efficient in the financial world". He ended his speech: "The City should not be abolished to suit the jealous little men of the Far Left". It has not been abolished.

The enemies of the City, having failed to destroy it after 165 years' campaigning, regard their failure as proof of the nefarious influence of the City and the secret power which it exercises in high places; but the City and the Livery Companies are entitled to reply that their enemies' defeat shows that these enemies are not supported by public opinion; for if public opinion had been strongly opposed to the City, successive governments would have been forced to act against it.

But though Firth and his followers failed to abolish the City, they succeeded in driving the City of Wilkes and Matthew Wood, of William and James Clarke Lawrence, into the arms of the Conservatives. While the reformers were uttering their solemn denunciations, Disraeli was wooing the City. He told his confidante, Selina, Lady Bradford, with whom he carried on a platonic love affair, how bored he was at City dinners, talking to unattractive Lady Mayoresses; but he spoke very differently in his speeches after the dinners, and persuaded the City to support the Conservative Party for the next 120 years.

11
Victorian Philanthropy

The Carpenters' Company build a new Hall in 1876 – dinner in the new Hall in 1880 – Past Master Stanton Preston becomes Clerk – Alderman Nottage becomes Lord Mayor – Queen Victoria's Jubilees in 1887 and 1897 – The coronation of Edward VII in 1902 – The Carpenters' Trades Training School opened in 1893 – Henry Harben joins the Carpenters' Company – He buys land at Rustington to found the Carpenters' Convalescent Home there – the Honorary Freemen of the Carpenters' Company 1888–1910.

The Carpenters decided to spend part of the money they had received from the sale of land to the railway companies in building themselves a new Hall. The greater part of the old Hall had been let to tenants ever since the Great Fire. By the time that Fordham's 41-year lease had expired, in 1758, he had entered into partnership with Mr. Luck in a carpet importing business, and the firm of Luck and Kent continued to be the tenants of the Hall for another 92 years. They used it as a carpet warehouse. In 1850 the lease was assigned to Waterlow the printer.

The plan for the new Hall was part of a major building operation which the Carpenters undertook together with the Drapers' Company. A new road would be built connecting London Wall to the north with Throgmorton Street to the south; the northern part would be owned by the Carpenters' Company and the southern part by the Drapers' Company. The agreement with the Drapers was signed in 1876. It was surprisingly advantageous to the Drapers, as it gave them rights over the Carpenters' part of the new road without giving the Carpenters fully reciprocal rights over the Drapers' part, and it is difficult to see why the Carpenters made such a bad bargain, unless it was that they were prepared to pay any price in their eagerness to have their new Hall. The 1429 Hall was to be demolished, the Courtyard removed and the new Hall erected on the same site with the entrance going out into the new road.

When the new road was built, it was decided to call it "Throgmorton Avenue" because of its link with Throgmorton Street. Sir Nicholas Throckmorton had lived nearby in the sixteenth century. He was a zealous Protestant, who was sent to the Tower in Mary's reign and charged with high treason; but his life was saved because a London jury insisted on returning a verdict of Not Guilty. Mary imprisoned the jurymen for a year. Throckmorton afterwards became one of Elizabeth I's most important ambassadors, and conducted the negotiations with Mary, Queen of Scots, with great skill. Shortly before his death in 1571 he was invited to dinner by the Earl of Leicester, and the rumour spread that Leicester had put poison in his salad. The story was almost certainly untrue. Eleven years earlier, Throckmorton had warned the Queen that it would be politically disastrous if she married Leicester; but Leicester and Throckmorton later became firm allies in support of the Puritan faction against the more moderate Protestants in Elizabeth's government. Throgmorton Avenue is still today the private property of the Carpenters' and the Drapers' Companies.

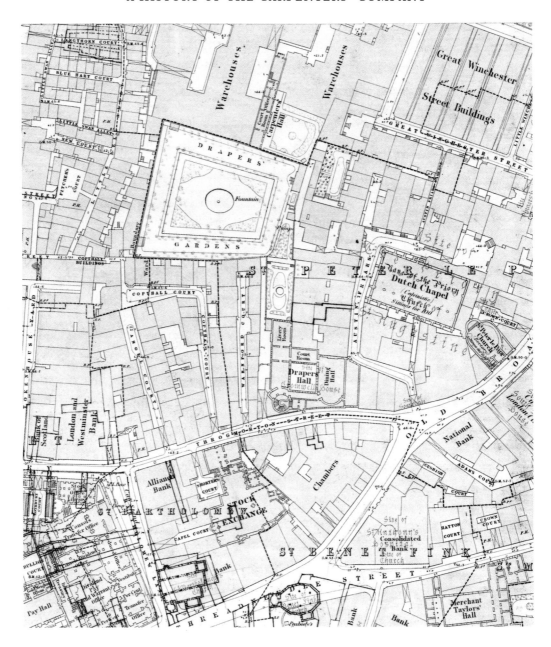

49. *Ordnance Survey map, 1874: layout of area surrounding Carpenters' Hall and Buildings shortly before the construction of Throgmorton Avenue.*

The Carpenters had no qualms about pulling down their old Hall which had stood for 450 years. In 1920 the newspaper The Builder wrote that the Hall had been "of no great architectural merit"; but it probably never occurred to anyone in 1876 even to consider the architectural merit of a fifteenth-century building, for the idea of preserving ancient monuments was only just beginning to take root. The people of the nineteenth century, like those in the fifteenth century itself, pulled down their forefathers' buildings without the least hesitation. The Victorians, with their unbounded pride in their own achievements, their confidence, and their optimism, looked to the present and the future, not to the past. Was not London the greatest city in the world? Was not Queen Victoria's realm the best society, politically, economically and socially, that had ever existed and as near to perfection as any merely human institution could ever be? Were they not approaching the dawn of a new century, the wonderful twentieth century, in which the last traces of despotism, with its summary executions and torture chambers, would be eradicated, and a world free from war and poverty would be created? "Ring out the old, ring in the new", wrote Tennyson, "Ring out the thousand wars of old, Ring in the thousand years of peace". Why should they preserve a Hall built in 1429?

The Court asked the eminent architect William Willmer Pocock to design a new Hall; he was a liveryman of the Company, and afterwards became Master in 1883. They invited tenders for the work, and at their meeting on 23 June 1876 considered the nine tenders which they had received, the highest from Ashby Brothers at £32,879, and the lowest from William Brass for £28,992. They decided to accept Brass's tender, though they had to borrow part of the money, and less than six weeks later the foundation stone was laid on 1 August. The liverymen were invited to be present and to come to a Livery dinner after the ceremony.

The proceedings began at 4 p.m. After Sir James Clarke Lawrence had made the opening speech, inviting the Master to lay the foundation stone, the Master, Stanton W. Preston, performed the ceremony. They deposited under the foundation stone a casket containing a copy of The Times, the Daily Telegraph, the Standard and the Daily News of 1 August 1876 and the City Press of 29 July 1876; a facsimile of the Grant of Arms to the Company in 1466; the Livery List of Christmas 1875; Jupp's History of the Carpenters' Company and his account of Wyatt's Almshouses at Godalming; an invitation to the ceremony of laying the foundation stone; the book of music to be played at the Livery dinner that evening; and a number of coins – an 1823 double sovereign, an 1876 sovereign and half-sovereign, an 1844 five shilling piece, an 1875 half a crown, florin, shilling, four penny piece, three penny piece, penny and farthing, an 1874 sixpence, and an 1876 halfpenny.

It took four years to complete the building of the Hall. There had been a delay because of a strike by the stonemasons and a dispute over questions of "light and air". When it was finished, it impressed the liverymen of the Carpenters and other Companies, the City press, and most of the other people who saw it as a splendid example of modern architecture. Fifty years later the grandsons of the liverymen of 1880 tended to criticise it as a glaring example of ostentatious and hideous Victorian Gothic; if it was still standing today it would probably once more be admired. The banqueting hall was one of the largest in the City; it was 76 feet long, 38 feet wide, and 36 feet high. The kitchen too was proudly shown by the Company to the press as an

50. Dining Hall, 1939: marbled and finely gilded, in 1880 this Hall, like the post-war Carpenters' Dining Hall, was considered to be an innovative and exciting example of modern architecture.

example of an up-to-date kitchen, and its size impressed them – 38 feet long, 26 feet wide and 20 feet high. The Court had decided that in future they would regularly hold their Court and Livery dinners in the Hall and no longer in fashionable restaurants.

The Court had dinner in the new Hall after their meeting on 20 April 1880, but the grand opening function was a Livery dinner on Thursday 25 November. The 153 guests included the Lord Mayor, Mr Justice Denman, and several MPs and City aldermen. The reply to the toast to "The House of Lords and the House of Commons" was made by Mr Henry Campbell-Bannerman, a Liberal MP and Financial Secretary to the War Office, who twenty-five years later became Prime Minister. Sir James Clarke Lawrence proposed the health of the Carpenters' Company and reviewed the history of the Company; the press reported that he spoke at "considerable length" and a speech of "considerable length" by 1880 standards must certainly have been long. After the Lord Mayor, Mr Justice Denman and the Prime Warden of the Fishmongers Company and other speakers had proposed and replied to

120

various toasts, the Prime Warden of the Goldsmiths Company replied to the toast to "The Visitors" in the nineteenth and last speech of the evening.

The Company had a new Clerk as well as a new Hall. When Edward Basil Jupp died in May 1877, he and his father between them had been Clerk for 79 years; but the Company now had to find a Clerk from another family. On 5 June 1877 the Court appointed Stanton William Preston, who nine months earlier had ended his year as Master, to be acting Clerk while a committee was appointed to consider the duties of the new Clerk and who should fill the post. Stanton Preston was a member of this committee. After considering the report of the committee, the Court passed a resolution on 12 February 1878 "that in the Opinion of the Court the Office of Clerk of the Company shall be filled by a Gentleman not a Solicitor"; and on 5 March they decided that "enquiry being made whether any Member of the Court would accept the Office of Clerk, Mr Stanton William Preston consented to do so and was thereupon unanimously Elected". During his term of office as Clerk he was not to be a member of the Court; but as Clerk, of course, he attended all the meetings. He was to have a salary of £400 per annum, which was retrospectively increased to £500 per annum in February 1881. His office was to be open from 10 a.m. to 4 p.m. every day from Monday to Friday, and from 10 a.m. to 2 p.m. on Saturdays.

After Edward Jupp's death, the Court decided to appoint a full-time solicitor. They again appointed a Past Master, George Hensman, who had been Master in 1869. He was to be paid two guineas whenever he attended a meeting of the Court and one guinea for each committee meeting. In 1887 the Court thought it necessary to provide the Clerk with the help of an assistant. George Hensman's son, Ernest Hensman, was appointed Assistant Clerk at a salary of £2.2s.0d. per week which was increased in 1889 to £2.10s.0d. When he died in 1891, the Court engaged Joseph Hutton Freeman to succeed him as Assistant Clerk at the same salary.

Stanton Preston was Clerk for twenty-four years, but resigned in 1902. As a Past Master he remained on the Court until his death in 1913; he had been a liveryman for seventy-one years. In appointing a new Clerk to succeed him, the Court decided to see first if any member of the Court would agree to be Clerk, or had some relation who would do so. If no member of the Court could be found, then they would invite members of the Livery to be Clerk or to recommend some member of their family. It was only if no member of either the Court or the Livery would undertake the office that they would look outside the Livery for a new Clerk. But no member of the Court or the Livery volunteered for the job; so the Assistant Clerk, Hutton Freeman, was appointed Clerk. When he retired after thirty-three years, he was elected Master in 1935.

In 1883 the Carpenters' Company set out to have their third Lord Mayor in just over twenty years. Alderman Nottage, who was a liveryman of the Spectacle Makers Company, was due to be Lord Mayor in 1884, and Sir James Clarke Lawrence proposed that he should be a liveryman of the Carpenters' Company and rapidly promoted to be Master in the same year he was Lord Mayor. Lawrence's proposal was adopted by the Court. Nottage was admitted as a freeman and liveryman in March 1883, elected Senior Warden five months later, and Master in August 1884. In November he took office as Lord Mayor, but died during his year of office as Lord Mayor and Master in April 1885.

The Carpenters' Company's wealth was continually increasing. By 1880 they had an income of £8,000 per annum, apart from the Great Twelve Companies, only the Leather-sellers, the Brewers and the Saddlers had higher incomes than the Carpenters. In June 1887 the nation celebrated Queen Victoria's Golden Jubilee, as she had reigned for fifty years. The Carpenters illuminated Carpenters' Hall, with gas lamps burning at every window facing London Wall, and the Court sent a suitable message to the Queen. "We most gratefully remember and humbly acknowledge the solicitude Your Majesty has always shown for the welfare of all classes of Your Majesty's subjects, and we pray that the Giver of all Good may continue to Your Majesty, the Royal Family and to the vast Empire beneath your sway those blessings which have been so mercifully bestowed under your Majesty's beneficent rule".

Ten years later the nation celebrated an even more glorious occasion on the occasion of the Queen's Diamond Jubilee. There was to be a thanksgiving service in St. Paul's Cathedral on the sixtieth anniversary of her accession, 20 June; but the highlight of the Diamond Jubilee celebrations was to come two days later, when the Queen would drive in state to St Paul's for another thanksgiving service on 22 June. The Carpenters asked the City Corporation if they could provide a stand in St Paul's Churchyard for the Carpenters to watch the Queen's arrival at the Cathedral on 22 June; but the Corporation could not find room for the Carpenters. The Court of the Carpenters' Company managed to make other arrangements for the Livery to watch the Queen's journey to St Paul's; but they seem to have been put out by their failure to obtain seats in St Paul's Churchyard. When they received from the Dean of St Paul's an offer of seats for the Carpenters in the Cathedral for the less glamorous thanksgiving service on 20 June, they sent a distinctly frosty reply. They did not thank him for the invitation, but curtly informed him that as the Company had made their own arrangements for 22 June, "the Court were not disposed to accept the invitation".

The next State occasion was even more unfortunate for the Carpenters' Company. When the aged Queen died at last, the country prepared for the coronation of Edward VII on 26 June 1902. The Carpenters had great difficulties in finding a stand from where they could watch the coronation procession, but eventually the Entertainments Committee arranged with the Polytechnic to hire a stand in St George's Churchyard in Southwark for £1,000, the Carpenters paying £500 of this £1,000 in advance. The stand would hold 400 people. When the Court, on 8 April, decided to hire the stand, they were confident that they would be able to recover a considerable part of the cost from the liverymen who would pay to take seats for themselves and their friends.

But on 24 June, two days before the coronation was due to take place, it was announced that the King was suffering from peritonitis and that an operation must be performed immediately. The coronation was therefore postponed. The King made a rapid recovery, and the coronation took place on 9 August; but the ceremonies were curtailed in order to spare the King too many exertions and to save further public expense. The coronation procession did not take place.

The people who had paid for seats in the stands to watch the coronation procession now

◄ *51. Stanton William Preston, 1900: Master in 1875 and Clerk to the Company, 1878–1902. Artist: Lance Calkin (1858–1936).*

52. *Rustington Convalescent Home, c.1920: the Home opened in 1897 and is still flourishing today.*
◀

53. *Rustington, c.1920: the Dining Hall was opened in September 1913. In 1920, the Carpenters' Company spent £1922.3s.9d. on food for the 864 patients visiting that year.*
▼

found that under their contracts with the standowners they had paid their money for the right to sit in these stands on 26 June whether or not the coronation procession took place on that day and even though there was nothing to see except the ordinary daily traffic going past. This led to litigation, and in a number of cases the Court of Appeal laid down the principles of the law of frustration of contract: as the contract to take seats in the stands on 26 June had been made on the assumption that the coronation procession would take place on that day, and as it did not take place, the contract had been frustrated. The Court of Appeal held that neither party could sue for money due under the contract or for damages for breach of contract, but that any money paid in advance, or due to be paid in advance, could not be recovered. This second part of the rule was overruled by the House of Lords in 1942; but under the law as laid down by the Court of Appeal in 1904 the Carpenters' Company could not recover the £500 that they had paid in advance for the 400 seats in the stand in St George's Churchyard, though they could not be compelled to pay the remaining £500 due under the contract. The Court nevertheless decided to refund the money they had received from the liverymen who had paid for the seats in the stand. The Court also decided to make a gift to King Edward on the occasion of his coronation; but when a resolution was moved that the cost of the gift should not exceed £200, an amendment was carried reducing this amount to £105.

The Company could afford to be generous, for it was prospering. In 1800 its income had been £2,000 per annum, by 1900 it had risen to £10,000 per annum. It was greatly expanding its charitable activities, especially in connection with the craft. This was partly a tribute to the pressure from Firth and the critics of the Livery Companies, but more to the general development of philanthropy during the mid-Victorian and later Victorian years in sharp contrast to the callous and fatalistic attitude towards the sufferings of the poor which had been adopted almost universally by the wealthier classes before 1845. At the suggestion of the Vicar of Stratford in East London, the Carpenters' Company opened a recreational centre and social club in the Church hall at Stratford for the Company's tenants in Carpenters Road, Jupp Road, and in other streets named after Past Masters of the Carpenters' Company.

Only once has there been any serious trouble at Stratford. In August 1873 the Court were informed "that assemblages of people take place in Lett Road on Sundays and that blasphemous and immoral addresses were delivered". The Court decided "that these meetings be put down" and their agent in Stratford was told that if they continued he was to prosecute the offenders in the Magistrate's Court.

People were also becoming conscious that British industry was being adversely affected by the lack of technical education, which was being encouraged in Germany. The Carpenters' Company was one of several Livery Companies who gave financial assistance to the City and Guilds of London Institute. One of the strongest supporters of technical education was Professor Banister Fletcher of King's College, London, an internationally famous writer and lecturer on architecture and building construction, and at one time Liberal MP for North-West Wiltshire. He became Master of the Carpenters' Company in 1889. When he was Middle Warden in 1888, he persuaded the Court to hold examinations in architecture at Carpenters' Hall. A number of students who had passed these examinations with distinction joined together in 1890 to form the Institute of Certified Carpenters (now the Institute of

54. Foundation ceremony, 1876: invitation to Benjamin Jacob to attend the laying of the foundation stone. The new Hall was not completed until 1880.

Carpenters), which has maintained close links with the Carpenters' Company for over a hundred years. In 1893 the Carpenters' Company founded a Trades Training School in Great Titchfield Street near Oxford Circus in the West End of London, where instruction in carpentry, stonemasonry and other building crafts was given to the students.

The most important development for the Company during the last years of the nineteenth century was the opening of the convalescent home at Rustington. The Company had acquired a new benefactor, Henry Harben. His grandfather had been a partner in the provision stores of Harben and Larkin of Whitechapel; and while his uncle continued to manage the stores, his father opened a wholesale trading business in the City. Henry Harben took a little time to settle down in an occupation. As a young man he worked first in his uncle's stores in Whitechapel. Then he was apprenticed to a surveyor, but changed his mind and became an accountant. In 1852, when he was aged 29, he became the accountant of the Prudential Mutual Assurance Investment and Loan Association, a small firm dealing in insurance which had started business in Blackfriars in 1848.

126

Harben suggested that the Prudential should embark on a new venture, and offer life assurance policies to the working classes. A similar scheme had been started a few years earlier by Richard Cobden, the Liberal MP; but Cobden's project had been financially unsound, and had been forced to close. Harben, who was a Conservative, thought he could do better, and succeed where the Liberal had failed. He suggested that the Prudential should collect two pence every week from the insured workmen, and pay their funeral expenses. It was a risky idea, because the death rate was higher among the working classes than in the wealthier sections of society, and there was the expense of collecting the twopence every week.

Harben did not find it easy to persuade the partners in the Prudential to adopt this scheme; but so many workmen were eager to participate that it soon became a thriving business. Harben became secretary of the Prudential in 1856, Resident Director in 1875, Deputy Chairman in 1878, Chairman in 1905, and President in 1907. In 1879 the offices moved to Holborn Bars. When Harben died in 1911, 2,000 clerks were employed in these offices, and the Prudential had an annual income of over £14,500,000 and assets of £77,000,000.

Harben was the cousin of Joseph Chamberlain, who, unlike Harben, began his political career as a Liberal, though he later became a Conservative. Chamberlain was still a Liberal, and President of the Board of Trade in Gladstone's government, when he was the principal speaker at the Livery dinner of the Carpenters' Company in November 1881. Harben, whose sister had married Stanton Preston, was admitted as a freeman of the Carpenters' Company on 5 March 1878, at the same meeting of the Court at which Stanton Preston was appointed Clerk, and he became a liveryman at the next meeting of the Court on 2 April. He was a busy man, not only running the Prudential but also becoming Mayor of Hampstead, where he lived, and representing Hampstead on the Metropolitan Board of Works and afterwards on its successor the London County Council. He also owned a house in Brighton, and Warnham Lodge near Horsham in Sussex with its 422 acres. He became High Sheriff of Sussex and Vice-Chairman of Sussex County Cricket Club, and twice stood unsuccessfully as Conservative candidate for Parliament, in Norwich in 1880 and in Cardiff in 1885. In 1893 he was elected Master of the Carpenters' Company ahead of his normal turn, only fifteen years after he had joined the Livery and without having served as Warden.

He had already begun to make valuable gifts to the Carpenters' Company. In July 1888 he offered £500 as prizes for competitions in woodwork organised by the Company. In the year after he was Master he gave £1,700 for the extension of the technical school at Stratford, and on several occasions he gave the Company some increasingly valuable shares in the Prudential.

His greatest benefaction to the Company was to buy 17 acres of land near the seafront at Rustington in Sussex and to build on the land a convalescent home for "persons of the working class and others". In 1896 the site was described as being "near Rustington", which was then a small village between Worthing and Littlehampton; in 1995 the town of Rustington surrounds the convalescent home. Harben spent over £50,000 in buying and building the convalescent home – a considerable sum of money at a time when the Clerk of the Carpenters' Company received a salary of £500 per annum and the employees looking after the almsfolk at Twickenham were paid eight shillings a week.

Harben invited the Carpenters' Company to become joint trustees with him of the convalescent home, intending ultimately to give the land and the house to the Company for them to run the home. When his offer was considered at a meeting of the Court on 7 July 1896, the Court, cautious as usual, decided "that whilst thanking Mr Harben for his generous offer, a special Committee should be summoned for Thursday the 16th to consider the scheme in detail". On this occasion the committee and the Court acted with unusual speed, and by 21 July the Court had agreed to accept the gift of the convalescent home at Rustington.

The Rustington Convalescent Home opened in March 1897. It immediately became very popular with the patients. Under its efficient matron, it was run on disciplinarian lines, and patients who turned up late for lunch were kindly but firmly rebuked when they went to make their humble apologies in the matron's office; but most of them appreciated the regulations and order which the regime introduced into their lives. One former patient, writing in about 1908, commented on the role played by the bell. "The bell is an institution at the Home. It rings you to bed and rings you up again. . . . It rings you to meals and it rings you to prayers". But he warmly praised the Home, in the flowery style of the period, for the relief which it gave him from his ordinary life in "this busy Metropolis". He remembered holidays spent at Cromer, Bournemouth, Liverpool, Hastings, Scotland, Jersey, and "cathedraled Chichester and casinoed Boulogne, pastoral Oxfordshire and fashionable Folkestone"; but "I honestly confess that, well or ill, if I had to choose now I should plump for my ideal home – Rustington".

In June 1898 Harben, who had been given a knighthood in the Diamond Jubilee Honours List, offered to give the Carpenters' Company a further eight acres of farm land adjoining the convalescent home at Rustington and to pay for the costs of the conveyance and all incidental expenses in connection with the transaction. This time the Court did not hesitate, and the gift of the additional land at Rustington from Sir Henry Harben had been sealed with the best thanks of the Court within a month.

In 1888 the Carpenters for the first time granted the Honorary Freedom of the Company to a distinguished public figure as a mark of recognition of his achievements. The honour was awarded to Sir John Lubbock. He was a most suitable choice. His father, a baronet and a City banker, was a friend of Charles Darwin. John Lubbock, as a boy, was encouraged by Darwin to take an interest in natural history. When he grew up he combined the successful management of his banking business with writing popular books on ants, wasps, bees and other insects. He also became a Liberal MP. In 1871 he introduced a private member's bill, which became law, creating a bank holiday on the first Monday in August. In 1882 he introduced the Act for the Protection of Ancient Monuments.

It was a wise move of the Carpenters' Company to confer the Honorary Freedom on Lubbock at a time when it seemed possible that if the Liberals returned to power they might introduce legislation to abolish the City corporation and the Livery Companies. Sir William Lawrence realised how important it was that both the two great political parties should contain leaders who did not hate, but loved, the City of London. It was William Lawrence who proposed that the Honorary Freedom should be offered to Lubbock, and who persuaded Lubbock to accept, though officially the honour was awarded to Lubbock only for "the eminent services rendered by him in the cause of technical education", which Lubbock had

55. *Building Crafts Training School, c.1950: initially called the Trades' Training School and now called Building Crafts College, the school opened in 1893 with Professor Banister Fletcher as Chairman (1893–1899). He was Master of the Company, 1889.*

supported as Chancellor of the recently-created London University.

The first elections for the London County Council returned a majority of Liberal and Radical councillors who called themselves "Progressives" and only a minority of their opponents, the Moderates (Conservatives). The Progressives promptly moved a resolution in the London County Council urging the Government to introduce legislation to implement the recommendations of the Royal Commission with regard to the Livery Companies. But Lubbock, who became Chairman of the London County Council, tried to restrain the anti-City zeal of his colleagues. In 1900 he was created Lord Avebury, and in 1904 he piloted through the House of Lords the Early Closing Act, which gave an afternoon's holiday to shop assistants on one day a week.

In 1894 the Carpenters' Company granted the Honorary Freedom to Sir Alfred Rollit, a Liberal MP who described himself as "a progressive Conservative"; to the Very Reverend Henry Wace, a writer of theological books who afterwards became Dean of Canterbury; to Professor William Smith of London University; and to Sir Joseph Fayrer, who had served as a doctor with the Army in the Burmese War of 1850 and the Indian Mutiny and later became Physician Extraordinary to Edward VII.

In 1901 the Honorary Freedom was granted to General Sir Redvers Buller, General Mackinnon, Colonel Cholmondeley and the Earl of Albemarle, all of whom had taken part in the Boer War. Albemarle afterwards became a Lord-in-Waiting to George V, and lived on until 1942, a year after Colonel Cholmondeley died.

Buller was by far the most famous and controversial of the four. After a military career of

129

56. Court Room, 1903: a Court meeting presided over by the Master, Percy Preston.

more than forty years, during which he served in China, Egypt and South Africa and won the Victoria Cross during the Zulu War in 1879, he was appointed Commander-in-Chief in South Africa at the outbreak of the Boer War. But he was attacked in the press, who held him responsible for the setbacks suffered in the first months of the war, and was superseded by Lord Roberts. He continued to serve in South Africa, but after he had led three attempts to relieve the siege of Ladysmith and had been defeated on each occasion, he was recalled to England and appointed General Officer Commanding in Aldershot in January 1901. This appointment was strongly criticised in the press.

The public outcry did not deter the Carpenters' Company from offering Buller the Freedom in April 1901. He said nothing indiscreet at the lunch to which the Court of the Carpenters' Company invited him on that occasion; but six months later, at another lunch in London, he answered his critics and defended himself in a manner which was held by the Government to be a breach of the King's Regulations, and he was summarily dismissed from his command at Aldershot. A vote of censure on the Government for dismissing him was moved in the House of Commons by the Liberal opposition, who had always favoured him; but the motion was defeated. He never held any other military appointment. But the Court of the Carpenters' Company, like the men who had served under him, continued to hold him in high regard, and when he died in 1908 the Court recorded their regret "at their loss of so distinguished a soldier".

In 1910 the Carpenters conferred the Honorary Freedom on Sir George Houston Reid, a former Australian Prime Minister who was then Australian High Commissioner in London. Despite opposition from some members of the Court, it was decided to invite journalists from *The Times*, the *Daily Telegraph* and the *Morning Post* to attend the lunch given to Reid after he had received the Freedom.

12

The First World War and the Inter-War Years

*The Carpenters' Company in the First World War – the Carpenters' Trades
Training School damaged in air raid by German Zeppelins in 1918 – Field
Marshal Haig made an Honorary Freeman of the Carpenters' Company –
The Carpenters' Company and the General Strike of 1926 – the Marquess of
Reading made an Honorary Freeman – the Prince of Wales at the six hundredth
anniversary dinner in 1933 – the Assistant Clerk's frauds involve the Car-
penters' Company in a leading legal case in the Court of Appeal – Henry Carl
Osborne becomes Clerk to the Company in 1935.*

At the General Court of the Livery on Election Day, 21 July 1914, the new Master and
Wardens were elected, and as usual a fortnight later, on the morning of Tuesday 4 August,
they took office in place of the retiring Master and Wardens. At midnight that evening Britain
declared war on Germany. On 8 September a meeting of what was called "a Committee of
the Whole Court" was held; these meetings of a Committee of the Whole Court to transact
special business between the ordinary Court meetings were held from time to time until
the end of the Second World War. It was the first time for forty-two years that the
Court had met in September. They decided unanimously that because of the outbreak of
war they would not hold the usual Court dinner in October or the Livery dinner in
November.

At the Court meeting in October the Clerk was instructed to send to the troops of the
British Expeditionary Force in France half a ton of tobacco, 1,000 pipes, 12,000 boxes of
matches, and 2,000 pairs of warm stockings, and 1,000 additional pairs of stockings to the
Navy at a total cost not exceeding £500. In November they sent another half ton of tobacco
and 500 warm cardigan jackets to the troops in France and 450 woollen jerseys to the Navy.
The Clerk reported "that a paragraph relating to the gifts had been sent to the London
press". In December they decided to cancel the usual Court dinner in February, and in
February 1915 resolved that all Livery dinners and Company entertainments should be
"given up until the election in July next or during the continuance of the war, which ever
occurred first". It was decided that the annual visit to Godalming in July should take place
as usual but that the dinner in the evening should be cancelled.

By July 1915 everyone realised that it would be a long war, and all Livery dinners were
cancelled until victory had been won and peace officially proclaimed. In July 1918 the
Court decided that all Court and committee lunches should be stopped and that instead
entertainments should be provided for wounded soldiers.

Eight liverymen died on active service during the First World War, including two sons of
members of the Court and members of the families most closely connected with the
Company – a Fletcher, a Lancaster, a Preston, a Rosher and a Stuckey. The Company
honoured its fallen liverymen by placing a memorial Roll of Honour in the Hall.

The Court strongly resented it when they were informed by the War Office in September

131

57. Mary Woodgate Wharrie: daughter of Sir Henry Harben and a generous benefactor to Rustington, Mrs Wharrie was the first woman to receive the Honorary Freedom. Given to the Company in 1969 by the artist, Liveryman Rodney Joseph Burn (1899–1984).

1917 that the large hall and the drawing room in Carpenters' Hall would be requisitioned under the provisions of the unpopular "DORA" – the Defence of the Realm Act – for use by the Records Department of the Territorial Force. The Court appointed a committee to deal with the first threat by the Army to take over Carpenters' Hall since the Roundhead army occupied London in 1648.

The committee reported back to a meeting of the Court on 2 October 1917. During the meeting the air raid warning sounded, for the German Zeppelins were making an air raid on London. People in the street came into the basement of Carpenters' Hall to shelter from the raid, but the meeting of the Court continued undisturbed. The meeting opened with the Master announcing the deaths in action of Major Stanley Preston and Private Robert Algernon Stuckey; Stuckey, who had enlisted when he was over age, had died of heat stroke while serving in the Middle East. After the Master had said "that no words of theirs could express the sympathy the Court felt for the relations and the pride they felt in the supreme sacrifice of their fellow liverymen", the Court decided to do all in their power to oppose the requisitioning of the Hall.

The Solicitor advised that it was doubtful whether the Government had power under DORA to requisition only part of a building, and recommended that they should take counsel's opinion on the point. But at the November meeting of the Court he reported that before counsel could be consulted, he had heard that more suitable premises had been found

132

for the Records Department of the Territorial Force, and that the authorities would not be requisitioning any part of Carpenters' Hall.

The Company also became involved in negotiations with the War Office about the convalescent home at Rustington. The home was flourishing. The Carpenters had received a further gift to help the Home in 1915 when Sir Henry Harben's daughter, Mrs Wharrie, who had inherited most of his fortune, gave another gift of Prudential shares for the maintenance of the Home. In gratitude the Court made Mrs Wharrie's husband an Honorary Freeman. When Wharrie died in 1917, Mrs. Wharrie became the first woman to receive the Honorary Freedom.

The idea of granting the Honorary Freedom to women did not appeal to many members of the Court. In May 1918 King George V's daughter, Princess Mary – later the Princess Royal – visited Carpenters' Hall for a function there of the London Girls Club Union, and she was received at the Hall by the Master. At the June meeting of the Court the Master suggested that the Princess's private secretary should be approached and asked whether the Princess would accept an offer of the Honorary Freedom; but "after discussion" it was moved, seconded and carried "that the matter should not be proceeded with". When Princess Mary married Viscount Lascelles in 1922 the Court sent her a message of congratulation and good wishes, assuring her that "the ancient City Guilds yield to none in their loyalty to and love for the Royal Family"; but no woman except Mrs Wharrie was granted the Honorary Freedom until it was given to Queen Juliana of the Netherlands in 1954.

The Company received further gifts of Prudential shares from Mrs Wharrie in later years, as well as £4,000 in cash; but they also raised money for the Home by inviting subscriptions from liverymen. Those liverymen who subscribed were entitled to nominate a patient for a place in the Convalescent Home.

The Home continued to function throughout the First World War, but in 1916 the War Office suggested to the Carpenters' Company that the Home might be taken by the Army as a convalescent home for wounded soldiers. The Court managed to persuade the War Office not to do this; but, to the Company's alarm, the matter was raised again by the War Office in the summer of 1918. The Chairman of the Rustington Home Committee "stated that the military authorities were again considering the taking over of the Rustington Home as a hospital. The Chairman assured the Court that he was taking every possible step to prevent this happening, and had pointed out the enormous amount which the War Office would have to pay should they decide to commandeer the Home. At present the Chairman hoped that the question was not serious".

The Company did not want beds at the Home to be occupied by convalescing soldiers at a time when they had just received an additional £200 in subscriptions to the Home by subscribers who hoped in return to be able to send patients there. But the Court offered to take a limited number of convalescent soldiers to avoid the requisitioning of the Home.

The soldiers did not stay there long. At the meeting of the Court on 14 January 1919 the Chairman of the Rustington Home Committee "explained that now that the Armistice was signed it had been found necessary in the interests of the new patients introduced by the subscribers and of the discipline and good report of the Home to give up receiving discharged soldiers who were sent there by the various War Pensions Committees". The Court unani-

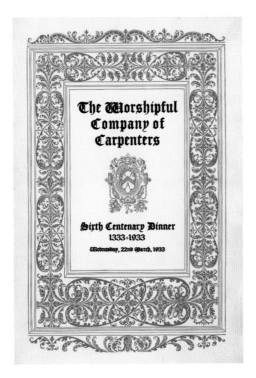

The Worshipful
Company of
Carpenters

Sixth Centenary Dinner
1333-1933
Wednesday, 22nd March, 1933

58. Menu, 1933: cover of menu for the dinner held to celebrate the Company's Sixth Centenary.

mously approved the action of the Committee. Soldiers everywhere were behaving in a rather unruly and undisciplined way in the weeks that followed the Armistice in November 1918.

The Carpenters' Company adopted a very different attitude during the Gulf War in 1991 when they hastened to offer the Ministry of Defence the use of half the beds at Rustington for convalescent soldiers who had been wounded in the Gulf. Fortunately these beds were not needed.

Of all the Company's properties, the Trades Training School in Great Titchfield Street suffered worst during the First World War; but here the trouble was not the threat of requisition by the War Office, but damage by the enemy. In May 1918 German aircraft dropped a bomb on the Bolsover Hotel in Great Titchfield Street, and damage was done to the nearby Trades Training School, for which the Company made a claim on their insurance company.

When General Sir Douglas Haig was appointed to replace Sir John French as Commander-in-Chief of the British Army on the Western Front, the Carpenters' Company asked him to become an Honorary Freeman. They approached him through General Mackinnon, who was himself an Honorary Freeman, and heard from Mackinnon that Haig would be willing to accept. They therefore sent him the official invitation in November 1916, and received a reply from Haig from General Headquarters, British Army in the Field, telling them of "my deep appreciation of the honour they have done me and my great pleasure in accepting it".

The Court decided to write to Haig suggesting that he might find time to come to Carpenters' Hall to receive the Freedom on one of his visits to London to consult with the Prime Minister, Lloyd George, and the War Cabinet; but the Master did not send the letter after Mackinnon had told him that he was sure that Haig could not possibly find time to come to Carpenters' Hall until the war was over.

When Haig was promoted to Field Marshal in February 1917, the Court sent him a letter of congratulation, telling him that they were sure "that his great services to the Empire will be crowned with complete success". Haig replied from General Headquarters in the Field, telling them of "his very deep appreciation of their inspiring message".

As the war neared its end and victory was at last in sight, the Court wrote to Haig on 5 November 1918 congratulating him "on the continuous series of brilliant victories which he in conjunction with our allies has won". Haig's reply, unlike the earlier correspondence, was not recorded in the Court Minute Book; but it so impressed the Court that they ordered "that the letter be suitably framed and hung in the Clerk's office". The Company no longer has the letter, which was probably destroyed when Carpenters' Hall was bombed during the Second World War.

Even now that the war was over, it was not easy to arrange a date when Haig could come to Carpenters' Hall to receive his Honorary Freedom; but the ceremony finally took place on 17 July 1919. The Freedom certificate was presented to Haig in a silver casket. The presentation was followed by a lunch for Haig which was attended by the members of the Court and their guests.

Five days later the General Court of the Livery was held. The liverymen had read in the press about the presentation and the lunch for Haig, to which none of them had been invited;

59. Memorial roll: members killed in the First and Second World Wars.

no dinner, lunch or any other entertainment for the Livery had been held since the outbreak of war in 1914, although the war had ended eight months before. Some liverymen suggested that one or two liverymen, selected by ballot, might in future be invited to join the Court at lunch on similar occasions. The Master explained that hardly any of the Livery Companies had so far resumed their pre-war entertainments, but that it was hoped to hold a Livery dinner in November, to which the newly-elected Lord Mayor and Haig would be invited. The dinner was duly held in Carpenters' Hall on 13 November 1919. Haig could not come, but the Lord Mayor attended, resuming the practice for the new Lord Mayor to come to the Carpenters before he attended any other Livery dinner.

Very few members of the Court attended the monthly meeting on Tuesday 4 May 1926. The General Strike had begun the day before, halting all trains and public transport; it had been called by the Trades Union Congress to support the miners' strike against a reduction in their wages. Stanley Baldwin's Conservative government declared that the country and the constitution were threatened by this revolutionary action of the TUC; and the Chancellor of the Exchequer, Winston Churchill, called on all loyal subjects to work to maintain the public services and defeat the strike.

As there were not enough members of the Court to constitute a quorum, they discussed what to do. They decided that at the next meeting of the Court at which there was a quorum, the Court would be asked to ratify all the decisions of this meeting of the Court. The Senior Warden, Westbury Preston, "In view of the Existence of the First General Strike" then moved a resolution which was carried unanimously: "that the Court of the Worshipful Company of Carpenters at their meeting this day hereby tender to His Majesty's Government their desire to assist in any way within their power in maintaining order and the essential services for carrying on the business of the country. That the above resolution be communicated to the Prime Minister, the official leaders of the opposition and to each member of the Livery". After some discussion, it was unanimously agreed to add the words: "That the Prime Minister be informed that the Company will be prepared to publish this resolution in the Press if and when the Government think it desirable to do so".

The General Strike collapsed after ten days, and in due course the miners admitted defeat and returned to work at lower wages. At the next meeting of the Court on 1 June 1926 the Court endorsed the decision taken at the meeting on 4 May and decided that that meeting should be considered for all purposes to have been a meeting of the Court. Letters were read to the Court from the Prime Minister, the Home Secretary and the leader of the Liberal Party (Lloyd George), thanking the Court for their resolution of 4 May about the General Strike. Not surprisingly, no reply was received from the Leader of the Opposition, Ramsay Macdonald, for he and the Labour Party had supported the General Strike.

The Carpenters' Company continued to grant the Honorary Freedom to distinguished personages. In 1922 it was given to the Reverend Sir Montagu Fowler, Bart., the Rector of All Hallows-on-the-Wall, who had for so many years conducted the service at his church on the Company's election day. Fowler was invited, and agreed, to become Honorary Chaplain to the Company. The Freedom certificate was given to him, without any special ceremony, at the next Court meeting. Fowler remained Rector of All Hallows and Chaplain to the Company until his death in 1933. The Company did not appoint another Honorary Chaplain to replace him.

60. Honorary Freedom, 1926: Westbury Preston, Master, presents a carved oak casket containing the Freedom of the Company to the Marquess of Reading, 20 October 1926.

In 1926 the Honorary Freedom was granted to the Marquess of Reading. Rufus Isaacs, although he was the son of a Jewish fruit merchant in Aldgate in the City, went to sea as a ship's boy, jumped ship in Rio de Janeiro, was caught and returned to his ship, and sailed around the world scrubbing the decks before returning to London and becoming one of the most famous and highly-paid barristers in England, and Attorney-General in the Liberal Government in 1910. His career was almost ruined when the Government granted concessions in what was then called "wireless telegraphy" to the Marconi Company; for it was found that Sir Rufus Isaacs's brother was a director in the Company, and that Sir Rufus himself, like Lloyd George and other members of the Liberal government, held shares in other Marconi companies and had concealed the fact from the House of Commons. But despite the outcry from the Conservative opposition in Parliament, and a vicious anti-Semitic campaign in certain sections of the press, Sir Rufus was created Lord Reading and appointed Lord Chief Justice of England. This prompted a poem from Rudyard Kipling, who

61. Henry Carl Osborne, 1966: Osborne was Clerk to the Company, 1935–1960. Artist: Jean Clark (b.1902).

denounced the corrupt Judge, "Gehazi, Judge in Israel", and called for "the leprosy of Nathan" to fall "on thee and all thy seed".

Reading survived the storm. After four years as Lord Chief Justice he was sent as ambassador to Washington in 1917, soon after the United States had entered the First World War on the side of the Allies. In 1921 he was appointed Viceroy of India to deal with Gandhi and the Civil Disobedience Campaign and to rule for five years the country that he had first seen forty-four years before as a ship's boy scrubbing the deck of a sailing ship. Soon after his return from India the Carpenters' Company granted the Honorary Freedom to the Most Honourable the Marquess of Reading, GCB, GCIE, etc., "in recognition of the distinguished services which he had rendered to the Empire". He afterwards filled his fifth great office of State, becoming Foreign Secretary for a few months in the National Government in 1931.

By the summer of 1931, the full effects of the economic crisis – "the Slump" – was being felt in Britain. In August Ramsay MacDonald's Labour government, which had held office in a hung Parliament for the last two years, resigned; for most of MacDonald's ministers refused to agree with his decision, in compliance with the wishes of the Treasury officials, to "cut the dole" by reducing unemployment benefit for a single man from 17 shillings to 15s.3d. a week. MacDonald became Prime Minister in a coalition National Government which relied on Conservative support. He asked the King to dissolve Parliament and prepared to fight a general election on a policy of national unity and "equality of sacrifice"; in this hour of crisis, all classes were urged to accept reductions in their income and their standard of living, from the lowest wage-earners on £2 or 30 shillings a week to the top business executives with an income of £10,000 a year.

When the Court of the Carpenters' Company resumed their meetings after the summer recess, the Master, F.O. Keysell, opened the proceedings on 6 October 1931 by reminding the Court of the "crisis", and "the serious times through which the Country was passing". He urged on them the necessity of avoiding taking on any new commitments or extravagances at such a time. The Labour Party, now in opposition, claimed that the talk about a crisis and the need for national unity was a Conservative election ploy, and they violently denounced MacDonald as a traitor for forming the National Government; but the voters rallied to the National Government, who won the greatest election landslide in British history. The National Government was returned to power with 556 members in the House of Commons, 517 of them Conservatives, against 46 Labour MPs and 6 other opposition members.

The Slump had reached its depth, but the first signs of recovery had appeared, when the Carpenters' Company held a great celebration in March 1933. It was in 1911 that a researcher working in the Public Record Office discovered the Book of Ordinances of the Carpenters' Company of 1333. The Company's historian, Edward Basil Jupp, and other scholars had always known that the Carpenters' Company had existed for many years before its charter of 1477 and its regulations of 1455; but this newly-discovered document proved that it had been in existence by the beginning of the reign of Edward III. The Company decided to treat 1333 as the year of its birth and to hold a dinner to celebrate the six hundredth anniversary in 1933.

The dinner was held on 22 March. The Prince of Wales (later King Edward VIII and still later Duke of Windsor) was the guest of honour, and presented the Master (J.E. Lancaster) with a new Badge of Office that the Company had bought. Two of the Company's Honorary Freemen – the Marquess of Reading and the Earl of Albemarle – sat with the Prince of Wales, Lord Wakefield and Lord Plowden on the Master's right, while the Bishop of Southwark, Lord Hayter, Lord Macmillan (a Lord of Appeal in Ordinary) Lieutenant Colonel A.C. Preston (now the Senior Past Master) and Lord Justice Lawrence and other distinguished guests were on the Master's left. They had a seven-course dinner: turtle soup; boiled salmon with lobster sauce; foie gras in champagne jelly; saddles of mutton and vegetables; quail pie; Melba peaches; cheese straws; dessert and coffee. The band played fourteen pieces of music, including Bizet's L'Arlesienne and songs from The Merry Widow, the Grace Laudi Spirituali of 1545, and God Save the King.

In the summer of 1935 Joseph Hutton Freeman, who had been Clerk for thirty-three years, resigned, and at the General Court of the Livery on 23 July he was elected Master; but he was prevented by illness from attending a meeting of the Court on 30 July when the new Wardens were installed. The retiring Master, F. Montague-Smith, was still in office when the members of the Court were recalled from their holidays to attend a Meeting of the Committee of the Whole Court on 29 August. Montague-Smith announced that he had called the meeting because of "very serious information" he had received about the Rustington Home; and he invited the Company Solicitor to make a statement.

The Solicitor was a very eminent man, Sir John Stavridi, whose family was Greek by origin. He had lived and practised for many years in London and had at one time held the post of Greek Consul General there. He had fulfilled a very important diplomatic mission during the First World War when he persuaded the Greek government, although Greece was neutral, not to intern the Serbian troops who retreated into Greece when attacked by the Germans and Austrians. The ultimate result was that Greece entered the war on the Allied side. Sir John Stavridi lived at Holmwood, near Dorking in Surrey, and regularly invited the members of the Court to have tea there with him and Lady Stavridi on their way back to London after their annual visit to the Godalming Almshouses in July.

Sir John Stavridi informed the Committee of the Whole Court, on 29 August 1935, that the Assistant Clerk, Alfred Blackborrow, who was ex officio the Secretary of the Rustington Home Committee, had been defrauding the Home for the last ten years. Cheques had been drawn on the Rustington Home account in favour of a firm that did not exist; Blackborrow had endorsed these cheques in the name of the fictitious payee and had paid them into his own private account at the British Mutual Bank. When Stavridi asked Blackborrow for an explanation, Blackborrow admitted his frauds and wrote him a letter: "Dear Sir John, I beg the Court, through you, not to prosecute me – imprisonment will not clear up the deficit. If the members want to punish me my dismissal, the loss of home, the broken hearts of my dependents and my own marital agony and shame are surely sufficient, and it will give me a chance to make good". He asked the Court to be generous enough to pay his salary for August and return to his wife the money he had paid when becoming a freeman of the Company, for this "will ease my exile – beyond a few pounds it is all she will have . . . In any case, I leave everyone and everything on Friday morning . . . I implore the Court not to kick me now that I am down".

The Court decided to dismiss Blackborrow from his post as Assistant Clerk and to expel him from the Company, but not to prosecute him. They repaid to the Matron at Rustington the £5 which Blackborrow had borrowed from her and had never repaid, and they paid to Mrs Blackborrow £1 a week for the time being; but after two years they stopped the payment and told her to apply for National Assistance. They refused to pay back the money that Mrs Blackborrow's brother had paid to enable Blackborrow to become a freeman of the Company.

The Company asked the British Mutual Bank to compensate it for the money that Blackborrow had misappropriated. As the bank refused, the Carpenters began proceedings in the High Court. The Company approached the British Mutual Bank and suggested a meeting at which some compromise might be reached; but the Bank refused to meet the Company. The case came before Mr Justice Branson in December 1936, and he gave judgment for the Bank, believing that he was bound by a judicial precedent in an earlier case.

At the meeting of the Court of the Carpenters' Company on 12 January 1937, the Solicitor informed them that the Company's counsel, Mr Schiller, KC, had strongly advised the Company to appeal to the Court of Appeal and if necessary to the House of Lords. But Schiller fell ill, and had not yet given his opinion in writing when the Court met again on 2 February. The Court's first reaction was to defer a decision; but Sir John Stavridi pointed out that 8 February was the last date on which they could serve notice of appeal, and that

62. Master's Badge: commissioned by the Company to mark its Sixth Centenary, the badge was made by Omar Ramsden and is still worn by Masters of the Company today.

there were only six days left. The Court agreed to appeal, the notice was served in time, and in July 1937 the Court of Appeal allowed the appeal and gave judgment for the Company with costs. The Bank did not appeal to the House of Lords, and paid up without contesting the Company's claim for costs. The decision of the Court of Appeal was reported in the Law Reports and became a judicial precedent on the point of law involved.

The Company had meanwhile appointed a new Clerk. For the first time in the history of the Company, it was decided to advertise the post. Applicants were to be between the ages of 35 and 45 and to be solicitors by profession. There was argument on the Court as to what salary should be offered; but after £600 per annum had been proposed by the Clerkship Ad Hoc Committee, an amendment was carried to increase this to £750 per annum.

The committee shortlisted five of the applicants for interview. Three of them, including Alan W. Preston, were liverymen of the Company. One of the other two who were not liverymen, was Henry Carl Osborne, who was the Assistant Clerk to the Salters' Company. The committee decided that only the three liverymen should attend the next meeting of the Court, and they were interviewed on 14 October 1935. But as soon as the meeting began, the Reverend G.F. Bartlett intervened. He had joined the Livery in 1875, and had been Master in 1909; when he died in 1949, at the age of 97, he had been a liveryman for 74 years, longer than anyone in the history of the Company. Bartlett proposed that Osborne should also be interviewed and the Court agreed. At another meeting of the Court a week later, a resolution that Osborne be appointed Clerk was carried by 9 votes to 5. He served as Clerk for 25 years until he resigned at the onset of his fatal illness in 1960. His two sons, John and Peter Osborne, had joined the Livery. John became Master in 1986 and Peter in 1989.

63. War damage claims: official photograph taken to record bomb damage to the Hall, viewed from London Wall, May 1941.

13
The Second World War

Preparations for war in the summer of 1939 – the Carpenters' Company in the Second World War – the Carpenters' Company offer the use of their Hall to the Lord Mayor and other Companies after the destruction of the Guildhall and the Livery Company Halls in air raids in October to December 1940 – Carpenters' Hall destroyed in air raid on the night of 10 May 1941 – the Drapers' Company grant the Carpenters the use of their Hall after the destruction of Carpenters' Hall.

In March 1938 Hitler annexed Austria; in September the British Prime Minister, Neville Chamberlain, signed the Munich Agreement which forced Czechoslovakia to cede the Sudetenland to Germany. The Carpenters' Company continued its normal life unaffected by these events in Europe; but when Hitler sent his army into Prague on 15 March 1939 the Carpenters soon felt the repercussions of his latest act of aggression; for Chamberlain realised that the policy of appeasing Hitler could no longer continue, and Britain prepared for war with Germany.

On 4 April 1939 the Court appointed an Air Raid Precautions Committee to consult with the City Corporation's A.R.P. officer on what steps should be taken to prepare for the outbreak of war. On 19 April, on the order of the Committee, 57 volumes of the early records of the Company, the four sixteenth-century "crowns" of the Master and Wardens, the silver-gilt cups, and other valuables were moved from Carpenters' Hall to the storeroom of a bank in the country. At the meeting of the Court on 2 May a discussion took place as to what further air raid precautions should be taken. The Surveyor recommended that £1,381 should be spent on air-raid defences at the Hall. Westbury Preston said that he did not believe that there would be a war, and thought that any expenditure on air raid precautions was unjustified; but Sir Banister Fletcher, who had been Master in 1936, deplored any discussion as to whether or not war would break out, and said that it was the Company's duty to prepare for the possibility of war. Westbury Preston's proposal that the matter should be deferred to the next meeting was carried, with 12 members voting in favour and 5 abstaining.

On 25 May the Court paid their annual visit to the Twickenham almshouses. They asked the almsfolk if they would prefer to be moved from Twickenham to some place in the country in case war broke out and there were air raids on the London area; but all the almsfolk said that they would prefer to stay in Twickenham. On 4 July the Court accepted the recommendation of the A.R.P. Committee that they should spend £60 on building an air raid shelter at Carpenters Hall.

On 1 September 1939 the Germans invaded Poland, and on 3 September Britain declared war. On 5 September the Court of the Carpenters' Company held an emergency meeting at which they unanimously approved the action of the Master in calling the meeting. They decided to spend a further £20 on air raid shelters at Carpenters' Hall and they appointed an Emergency Committee, consisting of the Master, the Wardens, and the Chairmen of the General Purposes, Education and Rustington Committees, with full power to act on behalf of the Court during the national emergency. It was decided that all the Court's employees who were called up for war service should be reinstated in their jobs after the war.

The Livery dinner for the Lord Mayor in November was cancelled and the Clerk reported that the Convalescent Home at Rustington had been taken over by the Ministry of Health under the Emergency Hospital Scheme, and that admission to the Home would have to be stopped.

The Company's most valuable piece of plate – the Master's silver gilt steeple cup of James I's reign – had been sent to the United States for an exhibition, and it was decided to keep it there for the time being. At the October meeting, the Court agreed that the cup should stay in the United States till the end of the war.

The Court continued to meet as usual on the first Tuesday of every month, but all dinners and social events for the Livery were cancelled. The Trades Training School was closed but reopened after a few weeks, having been adapted to fit in with a War Office scheme for training army personnel in carpentry and stonemasonry. Only the almshouses at Twickenham and Godalming continued to function as in peace time and although the almsfolk were subjected to wartime rationing, the Senior Warden succeeded in obtaining an allowance of petrol for the motor mower at Godalming.

The General Court of the Livery and the elections of the new Master and Wardens were held as usual in July 1940; but by now the country faced the danger of invasion after the evacuation from Dunkirk and the fall of France. On 15 July the military authorities informed the Carpenters' Company that they were withdrawing Rustington Convalescent Home from the Emergency Hospital Scheme, and advised the Company that the Home should be evacuated at once, for Rustington, on the coast, was in the zone threatened by German invasion and all entry into the area was banned without a special pass. A pass was issued to the Chairman of the Rustington Home Committee, who regularly visited the Home every month to observe the condition of the property, which sometimes was empty and sometimes occupied by convalescent soldiers. The farm continued to operate with "land girls" from the wartime Land Army working side by side with men who were not called up for the armed forces.

The air raids on London began in September 1940. On the night of 16 October a land mine hit the Dutch church in Austin Friars, totally destroying it. The windows of Carpenters' Hall were shattered and though no serious damage was done to the structure, the stained glass windows were damaged beyond repair. On 29 November there was an air raid on Twickenham in which the Carpenters' Company's almshouses were damaged; but none of the almsfolk were injured, and when the Senior Warden and the Clerk visited them next day they found the morale of the almsfolk was excellent.

On the night of 29 December there was a heavy air raid on the City. Carpenters' Hall suffered no damage, but other Livery Companies lost their Halls, and the Guildhall was destroyed. The Carpenters offered the Lord Mayor the use of Carpenters' Hall, and the Court of Aldermen held their meetings there for several months at the beginning of 1941. The Carpenters also offered the use of their Hall to the Coopers' Company, whose Hall

144

64. War damage claims: view taken from parapet at eastern end of London Wall looking down through the Drawing Room into the Court Luncheon Room, May 1941.

had been destroyed and they used the Hall for nearly three months until finding other accommodation on 20 March.

There was another air raid on the City on the night of 10 May 1941 and at 1.43 a.m. a land mine fell in London Wall shattering a gas main; the time of the explosion is known because it stopped the clocks in Carpenters' Hall. The fire services were unable to deal with the many fires because water pressure was too weak, and Carpenters' Hall was almost totally destroyed by fire. Although some records and valuables were destroyed, many were saved, and so was most of the Company's stock of port. The Drapers' Company, remembering how the Carpenters had offered them hospitality after the Great Fire in 1666, offered the Carpenters the use of their Hall for meetings and lunches. The Carpenters held their Court meetings at their premises at 8 Throgmorton Avenue, going afterwards to Drapers' Hall for the lunch. Guests at lunch were often the members and officers of the refugee Allied governments and armies in London, and American as well as Soviet and Chinese diplomats and officers.

In the Annual Report to the Livery for 1941, which was presented to the General Court of the Livery held at Drapers' Hall on 23 July 1941, the Clerk described the destruction of Carpenters' Hall and the treasures that had been saved. "Carpenters' Hall, with the Halls of many other Guilds, has been destroyed by the fury of the forces of Anti-Christ and it seems almost a challenge to the forces of evil that the first line of the first written record of

145

the Company (the Wardens Account Book of 1438) reads: 'Ihsu and his mother dear Have mercy on Crofften the Carpenter'. The Carpenters indeed, of all Guilds, have received peculiar honour in their craft from Him who was known on earth as 'The Carpenter's Son'. Their Hall has been destroyed but the spirit of the craft is indestructible and in good time and in better days a new Hall will rise from the ruins of the old where the ancient craft will flourish with renewed strength".

At the meeting of the Court on Tuesday, 6 June 1944, when it was recorded that "this day 6th June 1944 the invasion of the Continent of Europe by the Allies had been announced", the Clerk read a letter from the Senior Warden, Captain H.W. Fletcher, R.N., apologising for his inability to attend the meeting because of his service with the Royal Navy; but he was elected Master at the General Court of the Livery in July. The London area still faced the danger from the enemy V.1 flying bombs and V.2 rockets and in July 1944 the almshouses at Twickenham were damaged again, this time by a flying bomb; but no one was injured.

By the time that the General Court of the Livery was held in July 1945 the war in Europe had ended. The Company lost no time in resuming their dinners and other entertainments, and the November Livery dinner, attended as always by the new Lord Mayor, was held in Drapers' Hall in 1945. It took longer before the Carpenters again had their own Hall, and for fourteen years all dinners were held in Drapers' Hall, except for one at Grocers' Hall and one at the Mansion House.

14
Contested Elections

*The system of choosing the Masters of the Carpenters' Company before 1721 –
the present system of appointment by seniority begins in 1721 – contested
elections of Masters and Wardens between 1741 and 1947 – a troublesome
liveryman – Sir Leslie Boyce, Sir Cuthbert Ackroyd and Sir Edmund Stockdale
of the Carpenters' Company become Lord Mayor – The Carpenters' Company's
Clerks since 1960.*

The method of selecting the Master and the Wardens of the Carpenters' Company is laid down
in the Ordinances promulgated by the Lord Chancellor, the Lord Treasurer, and the Chief
Justices of the King's Bench and Common Pleas in 1607, which almost certainly followed the
practice which had been adopted by the Company for the previous two or three hundred years.
The Court nominates a number of candidates to be elected by the Livery at the General Court
of the Livery on election day. Liverymen are entitled to vote only for one of the candidates
nominated by the Court and may not nominate or vote for any other candidate.

There is no limit to the number of candidates who may be nominated by the Court; but
obviously they must nominate at least two for every office so as to give liverymen the
opportunity for choice, and it has been the practice, at least since 1710 and probably much
earlier, for the Court to nominate three candidates for each of the four offices of Master and
the three Wardens. The first name on the list is the candidate whom the Court wish to see
elected and who is almost always elected. In practice, the Master and Wardens are therefore
chosen by the Court.

In earlier times there was no particular rule or pattern by which the Master and Wardens
were chosen. The Court no doubt selected the man whom they thought to be the most
suitable in the particular circumstances. It was common for a liveryman to be selected to be
Master more than once, though often a considerable time, sometimes more than twenty
years, elapsed between the first and the last occasion on which he served as Master. Lawrence
Bradshaw was Master eight times between 1551 and 1580; Thomas Peacock seven times
between 1563 and 1581; Thomas Warham six times between 1456 and 1467 and Thomas
Bynkes six times between 1495 and 1514; William Carter five times between 1474 and 1489,
and Thomas Kydd five times between 1485 and 1499. Two men were Master four times,
and five three times, in the fifteenth and sixteenth centuries. Richard Wyatt, who was Master
in 1604, 1605 and 1616, was the last man to hold the office more than twice.

Since 1721 a pattern is discernible in the selection of Master and Wardens. A liveryman
first comes on to the Court as Junior Warden, serving in that office for a year and progressing
annually through the offices of Middle and Senior Warden before in turn being Master and
then Deputy Master. The office of Deputy Master, whose duty is to represent the Master in
his absence, was first created in 1929. Originally he was elected every year by the Court,
and the Senior Past Master was often, though not always, chosen. Since the Second World
War however, the office has automatically been held by the Immediate Past Master. After

147

ELECTION OF COMMITTEES. JANUARY, 1914.

BALLOT PAPER.

Estates Committee.

4 Members to be elected.

Put a X against the names of those for whom you desire to vote.

If more, or if less, than *4* votes are recorded, the Ballot Paper will be null and void.

Only one vote can be recorded for any one member, and any member may vote for himself.

Mr. B. J. JACOB	✓	8 —
„ NIEMANN SMITH		4
„ EDWARD SMITH		4
„ ~~C. L. SMITH~~		
„ JOHN WILLSON	✓	12 —
„ ~~WALTER SMITH~~		
„ PERCY PRESTON		6
„ F. A. CRISP	✓	8 —
Captain DRUMMOND		
Mr. A. B. HAMMOND		
„ W. ROBERTSON		
Lt.-Col. A. C. PRESTON		
Mr. M. H. POCOCK	✓	5
Rev. C. B. BARTLETT		
Mr. ROBERT COBAY	✓	6
„ WILLIAM R. COBAY		3
„ SPENCER W. MORRIS	✓	4

66. *Tally of votes cast for the election of the Company's Estates Committee, 1914.*

being Master, the liveryman remains on the Court as a Past Master for the rest of his life, or until he chooses to retire.

A liveryman comes forward to election as Junior Warden by virtue of his seniority in the Livery but in practice only about 30 or 40 of the 150 liverymen come on to the Court; the others die before it is their turn, emigrate, ask not to be considered, or very occasionally are passed over because they are considered to be unsuitable. A liveryman therefore ordinarily comes on to the Court as Junior Warden about thirty or thirty-five years after joining the Livery. This system tends to make the average age of the Court rather older than in many Livery Companies, but it has the advantage that there is no canvassing or influence used in order to gain office.

Although the seniority rule is generally observed, there are exceptions. Sometimes the man next in line dies before the time for the election arrives and the usual practice then is for the promotion of the survivors to be accelerated. If the Senior Warden dies before he can be elected Master, or if he refuses to serve, the Middle Warden is promoted directly to Master without having been Senior Warden, and the same rule is followed lower down the line. But occasionally, for some reason, the Court does not wish to do this, and some other arrangement is made; perhaps a Past Master will be nominated to serve for a second time. In the last three hundred years only seven men have been Master twice for a full year – one in the eighteenth, four in the nineteenth, and two in the twentieth centuries. Three more –

148

two in the eighteenth and one in the twentieth century – after serving their full term as Master, have been Master a second time for a few months or weeks after another Master died in office.

On two occasions a retiring Clerk of the Company was nominated to the Court ahead of his turn, one going straight to be Master and the other first serving as Warden. From time to time the Court decided to promote a liveryman to be Master ahead of his turn; this is usually because the man in question is about to be elected Lord Mayor, and the Court wish him to have been Master, or at least a Warden, before he becomes Lord Mayor. Although premature promotions have the effect of postponing for a year the date when the other members of the Livery might take office, usually, but with some notable exceptions, there has been no objection to the Court's decision.

Until 1741 the number of votes obtained at the General Court of the Livery by each of the three candidates in the election was not revealed; the Court minute books merely record the names of the three candidates and which of them had been elected. From 1741 to 1823 the voting figures were recorded in the minutes, and from 1824 to 1880 they were recorded in a rough notebook kept by the Clerk which has survived. From 1903 to 1914 they were recorded in the Court minutes but since then there has been no record, except once after a strongly contested election in 1947. Apart from this, the only guide to the voting figures since 1914 has been that sometimes the Master informed the successful candidate at the

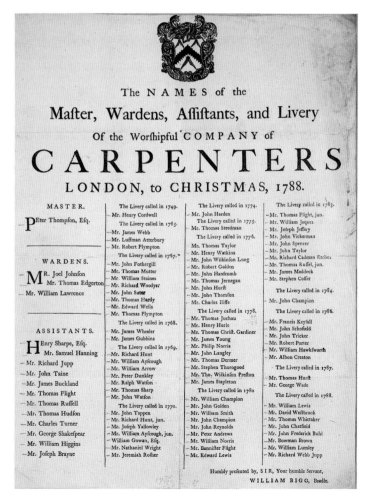

67. Livery List, 1788.

68. Sir Cuthbert Ackroyd: Lord Mayor in 1955 and Master of the Company in 1952. Artist: Allan Gwynne Jones (1892–1982).

General Court that he had been "unanimously elected", and sometimes that he had been "elected", leaving out the word "unanimously". But since 1968 the members of the Livery are not given even this glimpse of the way the voting has gone. At the meeting of the Court on 6 August 1968 Sir Edmund Stockdale (a Past Warden and future Master and a former Lord Mayor) suggested that it was wrong to humiliate a successful candidate by announcing that he had been elected and omitting the word "unanimously", thus making it known that at least one vote had been cast for another candidate. The Court agreed with Sir Edmund, and decided that in future the Master should in every case merely inform the successful candidate that he had been "elected" and never utter the word "unanimously".

Voting figures have therefore been recorded for more than 600 elections and they show that in most cases the Court's nominee was elected unanimously; but it has been very common for a few votes to be cast for other candidates though very unusual for another candidate to obtain more than ten votes. This frequently happened in the eighteenth century, perhaps because the new principle of selecting the Master and Wardens by seniority had not yet been clearly accepted by the liverymen. Sometimes the contest was close; in 1798 the Renter Warden was elected with 17 votes against 16 for the second candidate and two for the third. The Court's nominee was defeated in 16 elections between 1770 and 1812. Since 1812 this has occurred only twice – in the election for Master in 1853 and for Junior Warden in 1903.

In 1853 all the candidates for Master were Past Masters; the Senior and Middle Wardens in 1852 (Hurst and Allen), who would normally have been Master and Senior Warden in 1853, had both died and the Court decided to nominate Flight to serve as Master for a second term. In accordance with the usual practice, two other candidates, both Past Masters (Churchill and R.W. Kennard), were also nominated with no intention that they should be elected. But, at the General Court of the Livery, Flight received 5 votes, Churchill 21 and Kennard 3. So it was Churchill, not Flight, who served a second term as Master.

The next trouble with the elections occurred in 1901. It was known that Alderman H.C. Morris was due to become Lord Mayor in a few years' time, and the Court therefore decided to promote him to be Junior Warden ahead of his turn so that he could be Master before he was Lord Mayor. There had been no objection from the Livery in 1883 when Nottage was elected as Senior Warden two months after he became a liveryman so that he could be Master when he was Lord Mayor; but for some reason many liverymen in 1901 felt differently about Morris.

Morris was named third on the list for Junior Warden in 1901 with a view to his becoming Junior Warden in 1903. At the General Court of the Livery on 23 July 1901 the Court's chosen nominee for the year, Field, was duly elected as Junior Warden; but at the end of the meeting a liveryman moved a resolution in any other business: "That the Livery respectfully ask the Court to withdraw the name of Mr Alderman H.C. Morris from the nomination for Junior Warden until he has served in that position by rotation or until he is elected Lord Mayor when the matter will be further considered by the Court". The Master announced that the members of the Court who were present at the meeting would not vote on the resolution, and, with only the other liverymen voting, it was carried by 17 votes against 7.

The Court considered the effect of the resolution at their meeting on 3 December 1901.

151

They decided to disregard it, and nominated Morris again as second on the list of candidates for Junior Warden in 1902, and in 1903 he was put forward as the Court's nominee for Junior Warden. The other candidates, Captain Drummond and A.B. Hammond, were as usual the next two liverymen on the list. The voting was 10 for Morris, 57 for Drummond and 0 for Hammond. Morris's opponents on the Livery had obviously decided that they would all vote for Drummond to avoid splitting the anti-Morris vote between Drummond and Hammond. Morris was not nominated again. He was never a Warden or Master, and he was never Lord Mayor, but he was Master of the Fanmakers Company in 1905. Drummond and Hammond in due course became Master of the Carpenters' Company, Drummond in 1905 and Hammond in 1906.

There were difficulties about the choice of Masters and Wardens during the Second World War when many of the liverymen who were due to be elected to these offices were unable to accept because of the war and in 1942 the Court found that the next six liverymen on the list who were due to become Junior Warden declined because of war service. At the General Court in July 1942, the Master, Bernays, was nominated to be Master for a second year, and he was duly elected. It was the first time since 1868 that a Master had served a second term.

There were more difficulties in 1943. The Senior Warden, H.W. Morris, was duly nominated for Master, but the Middle Warden, Smith, was unable to accept office as Senior Warden because of ill health; the Master and Wardens Committee therefore recommended that Fletcher move up from Junior Warden to Senior Warden. The next two liverymen in line were John Godwin King and A.B. Rosher; but the Master and Wardens Committee decided to cut out Godwin King, perhaps because of his age – he was 79 – and to nominate H.D. Harben, the grandson of the Company's benefactor Sir Henry Harben, though there were many liverymen ahead of him in the Livery list. They duly nominated Rosher as Junior Warden.

When the report of the Master and Wardens Committee was discussed at the May Court, an amendment to nominate King, not Harben, as Middle Warden was carried. The usual procedure was then adopted of asking King and Rosher, who would be coming on to the Court for the first time, to provide references; and when this formality had been completed, their nominations came up for ratification at the meeting of the Court in June. Harben's supporters then made a final attempt on his behalf. An amendment was moved that Harben, not King, should be nominated as Middle Warden, though it was an unprecedented step to deny the nomination to King after he had been asked to provide references. The amendment was defeated, and King was nominated as Middle Warden.

When the election took place at the General Court of the Livery at Drapers' Hall on 20 July 1943, there was an unexpected development. After Morris, Fletcher and King had been elected as Master, Senior Warden and Middle Warden, an elderly portly liveryman with a white goatee beard rose to address the Master. He was G.P. Pocock, a well-known figure in the Company, who had joined the Livery in 1904. His grandfather, W.W. Pocock (Master in 1883), had been the architect of the new Hall in 1876, and his great-grandfather, W.F. Pocock (Master in 1840) had been architect of the Twickenham almshouses in 1841. He demanded to know why he had not been nominated as Junior Warden, because he was senior in the Livery to the candidates who had been nominated by the Court for election as Master and Wardens. Why had he been passed over?

152

Most of the liverymen present could guess the reason: it was because Mr Pocock had a habit of being too boisterous and vociferous after he had drunk too much at Livery dinners. He often interrupted both the speeches and the musical entertainments by expressing, at the top of his voice, his contempt for the speakers and the singers. On one occasion *The Times* correspondent, who had been invited to a dinner to report the speeches, and had been placed to sit near Pocock, complained to the Clerk that he had not been able to hear what the speaker was saying because Pocock was shouting throughout the speech. When the guests rose from the table, Pocock went downstairs and had an angry altercation with the Beadle, demanding that the Beadle give him more information about the frauds committed by the Assistant Clerk at Rustington. The Clerk, Henry Osborne, arrived on the scene and put an end to an unpleasant incident, which was being noticed by the other guests. The Clerk felt it necessary to write to *The Times* apologising for Pocock's rudeness to their correspondent at the dinner. Pocock sometimes turned up uninvited at the Clerk's office and complained of the way in which he was being treated by the Clerk and the Court.

The fiery Mr Pocock was confronted at the General Court of the Livery in 1943 by Bernays, who was nearing the end of his second term as Master. He was a charming elderly gentleman, with a quiet voice and gentle manner and a soft hand that shook from Parkinson's disease. He was more than a match for Pocock and told him that the Court had complete discretion as to whom they nominated for election to office and were not obliged to give the reasons for their decision. Pocock then called on the liverymen present not to vote for any of the three candidates nominated by the Court but instead to elect him as Junior Warden. The Master told him that such a proposal was out of order, as the only choice before the Livery, under the Ordinances of 1607, was to vote for one of the candidates nominated by the Court. The voting then took place, and the Court's chosen nominee, Rosher, was duly elected as Junior Warden.

Pocock did not accept defeat. He wrote a number of letters to the Clerk in which he threatened to bring an action in the High Court against the Company for breach of contract, because when he joined the Livery by patrimony and paid his admission money, there was an implied term in the contract that he would be nominated by the Court for the office of Junior Warden when it was his turn by seniority. He did not appear at the General Court of the Livery at the elections in July 1944, but in August he had several meetings with the Clerk and Past Master Morris at the Company's offices at 8 Throgmorton Avenue, at which he repeated his threat to sue the Company.

The Court passed the matter to Sir John Stavridi, who was acting as the Company Solicitor in the absence of the regular solicitor, Commander Alan Preston, on war service in the Navy. In November Sir John wrote to Pocock emphasizing that the Court was under no obligation to give their reasons for refusing to nominate him as Junior Warden; but he added that, writing "no longer as Solicitor but as one Carpenter to another", he would give his personal explanation. "I have attended numerous dinners, balls and receptions of the Company at which you were present and I have heard you on various occasions speak in a very loud and perhaps somewhat coarse manner interjecting remarks both during speeches and whilst the music was being played. I have heard guests close to me suggest that the interrupter ought to be asked to 'shut up' and some other less polite remarks. This may seem perhaps a

153

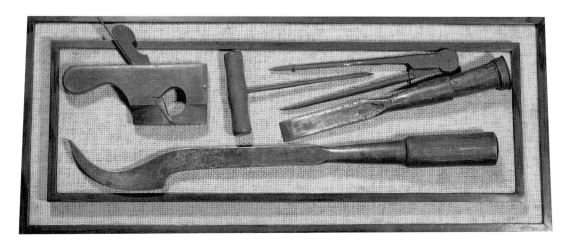

69. Carpentry tools, c.1920: this set of old carpentry tools was collected together and presented to the Company by Mr A.E. Bierton in 1992. The tools comprise (clockwise from top left) *hand rail plane, shell gimlet, plain compasses, firmer chisel and lock mortice chisel.*

somewhat trivial offence, but when one thinks of the position occupied by a Master of one of the great City Guilds, it is easy to realise that a lack of poise, tact and good manners may be a bar to the election of liveryman to that position".

Mr Pocock denied these allegations. He thought that even if they were true he should have been given the opportunity to apologise. He wrote letters in which he referred to the frauds committed in connection with the Rustington Home accounts by the Assistant Clerk, and hinted that other officers of the Company might have been involved in them. He said that he would appeal to the Home Secretary and the Prime Minister. But he took no action until the General Court of the Livery on election day in July 1946. He moved a resolution that the method of election to the Court was out-of-date and that a committee should be set up, consisting of four members of the Court and four from the Livery, to consider "whether the time has arrived for membership of the Court to be thrown open to all Members of the Company by ballot on a system of universal suffrage".

The Clerk replied by reading a carefully prepared statement which pointed out that the Company was forbidden by the Ordinances of 1607 from changing the method of elections to the Court. The Livery supported the Court in their disagreements with a dissatisfied liveryman, as it had done in the Court's dispute with Simmons in 1826. Pocock's resolution was defeated by 36 votes to 2, with 2 abstentions.

Pocock made no more trouble. When he died in 1954 the Clerk wrote a particularly kind letter of condolence to his widow, who acknowledged it most appropriately.

There was more argument at the General Court of the Livery in July 1947. A member of the Livery, Alderman Sir Leslie Boyce, was due to be Lord Mayor in 1949. He was an Australian by birth who came to England in 1920 and established a very successful railway carriage construction business in Gloucester, being elected Conservative MP for Gloucester in 1929, although he lost the seat in the Labour landslide victory at the general election in 1945. At the meeting of the Court on 6 May 1947 it was proposed that he should be

154

70. Sir Edmund Stockdale: Lord Mayor in 1959–1960 and Master of the Company in 1970. Artist: Alfred Kingsley Lawrence (1893–1975).

promoted ahead of more senior liverymen as the Court's nominee for Junior Warden at the election in July, so that he would become Master during his year of office as Lord Mayor in 1950.

But there was opposition on the Court. An amendment was moved that the question of nominating Boyce should be referred to the Livery for discussion at the General Court. After the amendment had been lost by 12 votes against 4, Boyce's nomination as Junior Warden was approved by 15 votes against 2. Every member of the Court agreed "not to initiate or cause to be initiated" at the General Court any opposition to Boyce's nomination, but that if any opposition first arose from the Livery, then any member of the Court was free to express his personal views.

The Court decided to send a letter to every liveryman explaining why they were nominating Boyce as Junior Warden. "The Court considers it proper to nominate a liveryman who in the ordinary course, might be in a position to hold the offices of Lord Mayor and Master of the Company at the same time. It is for this reason that the Court nominated the Senior Sheriff, Sir Leslie Boyce, K.B.E., for election to the Court. Should he be Master of the Company in the year of his Mayoralty, both the Company and he would be naturally honoured. The Court therefore believes that the Livery will approve his nomination".

At the General Court on 22 July 1947 the Master, Senior Warden and Middle Warden were elected in the usual way; but when the Master announced that they would now proceed to the election of the Junior Warden, Pocock protested against Boyce's nomination, and Boyce was asked to withdraw from the room while the discussion took place. Several members of the Livery expressed their views. The Company's Solicitor, Alan Preston, spoke in his personal capacity as a liveryman, saying that although he would vote for Boyce, he thought that the principle of choosing a liveryman to come on to the Court ahead of his turn so that he could be Master and Lord Mayor in the same year, was undesirable; it had been done in Nottage's case in 1883, but this was not a precedent which should be followed. After a long discussion, the election of the Junior Warden took place. Boyce received 30 votes, and 11 were cast for the other two candidates.

The Solicitor's intervention was discussed at the next meeting of the Court. A letter had been received from Alderman Cuthbert Ackroyd, who was a liveryman, protesting strongly against it; Ackroyd thought that no paid officer of the Company should speak at the General Court in his capacity as a liveryman unless he had first resigned his office in the Company. The Master said that the Solicitor had asked his permission in advance to participate in the debate, and that he had granted it; but Past Master Morris gave the required notice that he would move a resolution at the next meeting of the Court: "That, except with the special consent of the Court, a liveryman who was at the same time a paid officer of the Company should neither address the Livery as a liveryman nor vote on matters relating to the internal affairs of the Carpenters' Company". Morris did not, in fact, move this resolution at the next Court, and the matter was dropped. Alan Preston became Master in 1957, and remained an active and highly respected member of the Court until his death in 1987.

In 1948 Boyce moved up and was elected Middle Warden without controversy; but then the Court's calculations went awry. He fell ill, and it became clear that he would not be able to take office as Lord Mayor in 1950; nor was he willing to stand in 1949 for election as

Senior Warden. He held no further office in the Company, but was elected Lord Mayor in 1951. He had also joined the Loriners' Company, and when he was chosen as Lord Mayor he gave the Loriners as his first, or "mother", Company; perhaps he was a little put out at the opposition to his election as Junior Warden in the Carpenters' Company.

Boyce caused some public controversy by his speech at the Lord Mayor's banquet in November 1951. Churchill had become Prime Minister again after the Conservative victory in the general election in October, and Boyce proposed his health at the banquet in what some people regarded as a party political speech. In his usual robust manner, and speaking with his strong Australian accent, he recalled the Lord Mayor's banquet in November 1945, after Churchill's defeat in the general election, saying how shocked they had all been that when the health of the Prime Minister was then proposed, "it was not to you that we raised our glass".

Boyce fell ill during his year as Lord Mayor, and was forced to undergo an operation which prevented him from fulfilling his mayoral duties for several months during his term of office. It also prevented him from accepting the invitation from the Court of the Carpenters' Company to stand for Senior Warden. In November 1954 he resigned from the Court on grounds of ill-health, and died in June 1955.

The Carpenters had two more liverymen who were in line to become Lord Mayor, but made no attempt to arrange for them to be Master and Lord Mayor at the same time. Cuthbert Ackroyd was elected ahead of his turn, without any opposition from the Livery, to be Junior Warden in 1949, progressing in the usual way to be Master in 1952. In 1955 he was elected Lord Mayor. At the meeting of the Court of the Carpenters' Company on 6 December 1955 the Lord Mayor arrived half-way through the meeting, and after apologising for his late arrival took his place as a member of the Court. As he entered the court room the Court rose to their feet to receive him, and the Master thanked him for attending the meeting when he was so busy with his duties as Lord Mayor. Ackroyd attended ten of the twelve meetings of the Court which were held during his year as Lord Mayor, and also came to the General Court of the Livery in July 1956.

Sir Edmund Stockdale was Lord Mayor in 1959. A few months before his election as Lord Mayor he was elected Junior Warden of the Carpenters' Company without any opposition, and during his year as Lord Mayor he became Middle Warden. It was not until 1969 that he was prepared to stand as Senior Warden, and he duly became Master in 1970.

In 1960 Henry Osborne resigned as Clerk, after twenty-five years of outstanding service to the Company; he was already suffering from the fatal illness from which he was to die five years later. He was succeeded by Captain George Baillie Barstow, R.N., who was Clerk from 1960 to 1977. When Barstow resigned, another naval captain, Kenneth Hamon, was appointed Clerk, and served for fourteen years. He was Clerk for a shorter period than any of the Company's Clerks since Robert Prater, who was Clerk from 1750 to 1757; but Hamon's short term was as distinguished as any of his predecessors', none of whom had been more highly regarded than Hamon in the City. When he retired as Clerk in 1991 he was elected Junior Warden, having become a liveryman a few years earlier; and in 1994, like Hutton Freeman 59 years before, he became Master.

The post of Clerk was advertised in 1991, as it had been in 1935, 1960 and 1977. Seven hundred and eighteen men and two women applied for details of the post. Sixteen men were interviewed and four of them were shortlisted and invited to lunch with the Court, accompanied by their wives. Many people in the City believed that the appointment was certain to go, for the third time in succession, to a retired naval officer, and that it was a waste of time for anyone else to apply; but this was not true. Many other applicants, including former ambassadors, high-ranking army officers, and solicitors, were impartially considered.

The four remaining candidates were interviewed again by the Court on 19 February 1991, and the Court then voted, on the exhaustive vote system which had been used in 1960 and 1977. Each member of the Court voted for the candidate that he preferred; the candidate receiving the least number of votes being eliminated, and the others going forward to a second ballot, until the final choice was made between the last two candidates. It was pure coincidence that the successful applicant was again a naval man – Major General Paul Stevenson of the Royal Marines. He had served in the Falklands War in 1982, and from 1988 to 1989 had held the appointment of Commander British Forces in the Falkland Islands. He is only the eighth Clerk that the Carpenters' Company has had since the eighteenth century.

15
The Post-War Years

General Smuts becomes an Honorary Freeman in 1941 – the Honorary Freedom is not offered to Ernest Bevin – the attempt to ban Communists from benefitting from education under the Read's Trust – Field Marshal Montgomery granted the Honorary Freedom in 1951 – Queen Juliana of the Netherlands an Honorary Freeman and Liveryman – the new Hall opened in 1960 – Queen Juliana uses Carpenters' Hall for a dinner given to Queen Elizabeth II in 1972 – The Prime Minister of Malaysia made an Honorary Freeman in 1989 – relations with the Carpenters' Company of Philadelphia – The Rustington Convalescent Home – sale of the Twickenham Almshouses – the Godalming Almshouses – less lengthy Company dinners.

The Carpenters' Company continued to grant the Honorary Freedom to eminent public figures. In 1933 they gave it to Sir Eric Drummond, who had become the first Secretary-General of the League of Nations. He afterwards became British ambassador to Italy and, after succeeding to his family's title of Earl of Perth, was Deputy-Leader of the Liberal Party in the House of Lords. There was disagreement on the Court as to who should be invited to the presentation ceremony on 11 October and to the lunch that followed. The Master and Wardens Committee recommended that the members of the Court and their ladies, and the senior half of the Livery, should attend, and an amendment moved by Westbury Preston and seconded by the Reverend C.B. Bartlett, that all the Livery should be invited, was lost.

Westbury Preston took the lead with regard to Honorary Freemen. Having proposed that it be granted to Sir Eric Drummond, he followed this three years later by moving a resolution, at the Court meeting on 3 June 1936, that "In view of his conspicuous services to the Empire the Honorary Freedom of the Company be offered to General The Right Honourable J.C. Smuts, P.C., C.B., F.R.S., K.C., M.P." Westbury Preston had made private approaches to the South African High Commissioner and had been informed that Smuts was willing to accept the Honorary Freedom. But Smuts was Deputy Prime Minister in the coalition government that he had formed with his political opponent, General Hertzog. On 20 November 1936 Smuts wrote to the Clerk of the Carpenters' Company that as Hertzog would be coming to London for the coronation of King George VI in May 1937, he himself would have to stay in South Africa to carry on the duties of Deputy Prime Minister, and could therefore not attend to receive the Freedom at Carpenters' Hall.

When the Second World War broke out in September 1939, the Afrikaner political organisations, who sympathised with Hitler and the Nazis, wished South Africa to remain neutral; but after a few days' political crisis, Hertzog resigned and Smuts became Prime Minister. Smuts brought South Africa into the war on Britain's side. It was now more difficult than ever for him to leave South Africa. In June 1940 the Court of the Carpenters' Company sent him a message regretting that his duties prevented him from leaving South Africa to receive the Freedom. "They desire to express their continued appreciation of the services he has rendered and is now rendering not only to South Africa but also to the Empire and the cause of world freedom. They sincerely hope that he may be spared to visit England when the present war with Germany has been won".

On several occasions Smuts wrote to the Clerk; in September 1941, after the Company had congratulated him on becoming a Field Marshal, he expressed his sympathy at the destruction of Carpenters' Hall by the German bombers. But he still could not come to England. In view of this, the Court decided on 2 December 1941 to take the unusual step of conferring the Freedom on him in his absence, asking him to make the Freeman's declaration on admission before the Chief Justice of South Africa at a time convenient to him. Smuts agreed to do this, and his Honorary Freedom was dated as from 2 December 1941. The Court told him that they hoped he would come to the Carpenters to sign the Roll of Freemen when he next came to England.

When Smuts came to London in October 1942, he was invited to lunch with the Company, and said that he would come if he could; but in fact he could not find time to do so during his five-week stay or any of the fourteen occasions on which he came to England before his death in 1950, though he three times attended a function in the City. Smuts is the only one of the Company's Honorary Freemen who never visited Carpenters' Hall nor attended a ceremony to receive the Freedom from the Master.

At the end of the Second World War Churchill and the Conservatives were defeated in the general election of July 1945, and a Labour government was elected. There was much controversy between the parties about the Labour programme of nationalisation, and a great deal of opposition from the doctors to the introduction of the National Health Service; but the Labour government's foreign policy of alliance with the United States against the Soviet Union in the Cold War was supported by the Conservative opposition. The Foreign Secretary was the former trade union leader, Ernest Bevin. He won the respect of everyone, except for the left wing in his own party, by his robust exchanges at a series of international conferences with the Soviet Foreign Ministers, Molotov and Vyshinsky. At the meeting of the Court of the Carpenters' Company on 8 January 1946, Past Master Hugh Smith proposed that Bevin should be invited to become an Honorary Freeman; but this was too much for the Court. Past Master Louis Jacob moved an amendment, which was carried, that the motion be postponed sine die. Perhaps Westbury Preston, who seconded the amendment, remembered the General Strike of 1926, when he and Bevin had been on opposite sides.

As the Cold War developed, the fear of Communists and their sympathisers and "fellow-travellers" was played up in the national press. Past Master Montague Smith became alarmed that some student who was a Communist might be sent by the Company to Oxford or Cambridge with the money provided under the terms of the Reads' Trust. At the meeting of the Court on 2 March 1948 he moved a resolution "That Students who hold or may hold Communistic views are debarred from holding scholarships granted by the Carpenters' Company". The mood of the country had changed since 4 January 1944, when, at the height of the wartime alliance with the Soviet Union, the Soviet Military and Naval Attaches, Lieutenant Colonel Kozlov and Captain Morozovski, had been guests at a Carpenters' Court lunch; but Montague Smith withdrew his motion after a full discussion, and it was agreed "that in future the seeded candidates for the University Scholarships be personally inter-

71. Honorary Freedom, 1951: Field Marshal The Right Honourable the Viscount Montgomery of Alamein receives the Freedom of the Carpenters' Company in Drapers' Hall.

viewed before awards are made".

John Read would probably have approved of this attempt to prevent his money from being used to educate Communists. When he was Master in 1650 he had actively supported a revolutionary regicide government, but not the Levellers or Winstanley's Diggers.

In 1951 the Honorary Freedom was conferred on Field Marshal the Viscount Montgomery of Alamein, the victorious commander in North Africa, and later in Western Europe, during the Second World War. In his letter of acceptance, Montgomery wrote how honoured he was to follow his old friend Smuts as an Honorary Freeman of the Company. He came to Drapers' Hall, which was still being used by the Carpenters for their functions, to accept the Freedom on 5 June 1951. On this occasion all the Livery were invited to attend the ceremony and to the lunch that followed. Many of them, seeing Montgomery for the first time, were surprised that he was so small, for this had not been revealed in the photographs of him which had so often been published in the press.

The Freedom was presented to Montgomery in a beautifully-made box in which various types of wood were used. The description of the box, which was printed in the programme of the ceremony, described the wood and compartments of the box in some detail. It mentioned that "the interior is lined with cedar to contain cigarettes in a removable tray of three dimensions. The lower recess beneath the tray will, in the first instance, contain the Freedom Scroll and may later be used for cigars". The Company had slipped up here, for it was well known that Montgomery, rather unusually in 1951, did not smoke. The story had often been told that when Churchill first appointed him to a high command in the Second World War, Montgomery said: "I don't drink and I don't smoke and I am a hundred per

cent fit", and that Churchill had replied: "I do drink and I do smoke and I am two hundred per cent fit". When Montgomery was handed the box, he commented on the beauty of the design, and said that as he did not smoke he would not be able to use it for cigarettes, but had no doubt that he would find some other use for it.

The word had gone round that Montgomery had come to Drapers' Hall, and a crowd of several hundred people gathered in the street to see him leave. He barked at them: "Why are you all waiting here? Haven't you any useful work to do?"

The next distinguished personage to receive the Honorary Freedom, Queen Juliana of the Netherlands, was, unlike Montgomery, a smoker. She was awarded the Freedom at a ceremony at Drapers' Hall on 7 May 1954. As in the case of the granting of the Honorary Freedom to Montgomery, the Livery were invited to attend; but through an unfortunate slip-up some of the younger liverymen were unable to get in to the lunch. They were shunted into a small room which was lined with books, where they remained for a long time until they eventually left, having been given nothing to eat or drink.

The Master, K.M. Roberts, in his speech, told Queen Juliana that "the Guilds of the City of London in general, and the Carpenters in particular, hold in grateful memory the House of Orange Nassau" because of the part played by William III in reversing the quo warranto proceedings. "Thus at the hands of William III the City Guilds regained the rights and privileges they had cherished for centuries past of which they were deprived by King James

72. The Dining Hall, 1992.
◀

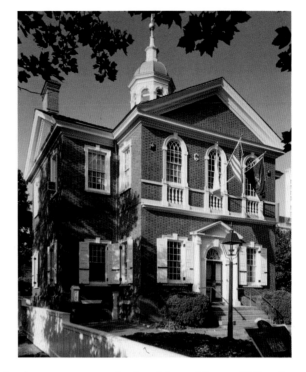

73. Carpenters' Hall, Philadelphia,
1992: north elevation of the Hall.
▶

II". The Master was by no means the first commentator who has blamed James II for the actions which were in fact initiated by Charles II.

It had been decided that when coffee was served after the lunch, gentlemen guests should be offered a cigar and two cigarettes, and the ladies two cigarettes. When the cigarette box was offered to Queen Juliana, she took one cigarette which she immediately lit. The Assistant Beadle then offered her another cigarette. "What shall I do with it?" she asked, "shall I put it behind my ear?" It is not surprising that the members of the Carpenters' Company have always regarded their royal Freewoman with affection as well as with respect.

When Queen Juliana came to London in 1966, the Company were able to entertain her to lunch in their own Hall. Plans for building a new Hall were first made in 1950, when a Committee for the Building of Carpenters' Hall was set up; Geoffrey Ridley, who was an architect and Master in 1955, was active on the committee during his year of office, and afterwards served as chairman of the committee until his death in 1957. It was decided to make no attempt to produce an imitation of an old building, but to erect a Hall in the modern contemporary style within the Victorian walls which had survived more or less intact. It would have been difficult to recreate the first Hall of 1429, of which there were only a few drawings; and the 1880 Hall, which had been destroyed in 1941, was not to the taste of everyone in the 1950s. The decision to build a modern Hall, in which wood was an important feature, seemed to be the most satisfactory solution.

74. Honorary Livery, 1966: Queen Juliana of the Netherlands was the first person to be made an honorary member of the Livery, by the Master, K.B. Jacob.

Some aspects of the building seem strange to the members of the Company forty years later. It is surprising that the lifts go up only to the fourth floor, leaving a flight of 38 stairs leading up to the top storey. It was impossible to do anything about the lift when improvements were made in the 1980s and 1990s to bring the Hall up to date; but an impressive Master's flat, and a flat for the Clerk, were installed, and rooms which had been let as offices were taken back by the Company in order to convert them into bedrooms and bunks for members of the Court who have to stay overnight when they are attending meetings or functions at the Hall.

After enjoying the hospitality of the Drapers' Company for eighteen years, the Carpenters were able to open their offices in their new Hall, and to hold their first Court meeting and Court lunch there, in the very hot summer of 1959. The Hall was officially opened by the Lord Mayor, Sir Edmund Stockdale, who was Junior Warden of the Carpenters' Company, on 4 May 1960, and the first Livery dinner was held there in November 1960.

The dining hall, which was built on a bridge spanning Throgmorton Avenue, is lined with cedar and other woods; behind the high table is a wooden carving of the Tree of Life, by Sir Charles Wheeler of the Royal Academy. At first the Hall was not to everyone's liking. Some of the liverymen thought it was too modern, and would have preferred a Hall more in the style of the 1880 building, but posterity did not agree with the objectors, and today nearly

164

all liverymen and their guests, and other Companies and organisations who hire the Hall for their functions, warmly praise the building, the dining hall, and Sir Charles Wheeler's Tree.

In April 1972 a great State occasion was held in Carpenters' Hall. Queen Juliana came on a State visit to London, and after being entertained to a banquet by Queen Elizabeth II at Windsor Castle, wished to be hostess to the Queen at a reciprocal dinner. As there was not enough room at the Dutch Embassy, the Dutch ambassador asked if they could use Carpenters' Hall and the Court eagerly agreed to this. Queen Juliana awarded the Order of Orange Nassau to the Master (V.J.G. Stavridi), and a lesser order to members of the staff at the Hall, and invited the Master and Wardens to the banquet.

The other guests included, as well as Queen Elizabeth II, the Duke of Edinburgh, the Queen Mother, Princess Margaret, and other members of the royal family; the Prime Minister (Edward Heath), the Foreign Secretary (Lord Home) and several Cabinet and junior ministers; the Lord Mayor; and many other dignitaries. The guests sat at a number of small tables and at the beginning of the banquet Queen Juliana sat at a table with Queen Elizabeth II and other members of the royal family. For the next course she moved to another table where she sat with Heath and some cabinet ministers, and then to a third table occupied by other guests. An official of the embassy explained to the Master of the Carpenters' Company that, in accordance with tradition, Queen Juliana dined first with royalty, then with the Government, and last with the common people.

The architect of the new Carpenters' Hall, Mr. Herbert Austen Hall, was made an Honorary Freeman in November 1960 and in January 1967 the Honorary Freedom was granted to Sir Charles Wheeler. Neither in Hall's case nor in Wheeler's were liverymen invited to be present at the ceremony nor to attend a lunch.

In 1989 the Honorary Freedom was granted to Dr. Mahathir Bin Mohamad, the Prime Minister of Malaysia. Relations between Malaysia and Britain had not always been cordial since Dr. Mahathir came to power in Kuala Lumpur; but after 1985 there was a great improvement, and the British Prime Minister, Mrs. Margaret Thatcher, established a relationship with Dr. Mahathir based on mutual respect, with an agreement to disagree on certain matters and to co-operate on others. Dr. Mahathir's favourite hobby was carpentry; on one occasion, in 1987, he attended a wood-turning course in Buxton, Derbyshire. In 1988 the Lord Mayor, who was about to visit Malaysia, suggested to the Carpenters' Company that it would be particularly appropriate if Dr. Mahathir could, in some way, be associated with the Company.

The Court decided that it would be pleased to confer the Honorary Freedom of the Company on Dr. Mahithir which he was pleased to accept. For various reasons it was impossible to perform the ceremony until he came to London on a very hurried visit to Margaret Thatcher in May 1989. It was not practicable to organise the ceremony and a lunch at Carpenters' Hall on a Friday – the only day when Dr. Mahathir was free – so the Honorary Freedom was granted to him by me, as Master, accompanied by the Wardens and the Clerk, at the Malaysian High Commissioner's office in Belgrave Square before Dr. Mahathir had to go to meet Mrs. Thatcher in Downing Street. The ceremony was broadcast on Malaysian television.

In 1966 the Carpenters' Company created and conferred a new honour when they

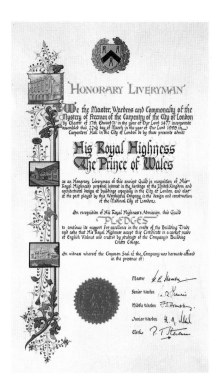

promoted their honorary member of the Freedom, Queen Juliana, to be an honorary member of the Livery. This was the first time in 700 years that honorary membership of the Livery had been awarded. On 22 March 1995 His Royal Highness Charles, Prince of Wales, came to Carpenters' Hall and was made an Honorary Liveryman. On this occasion both freemen and liverymen, some 120, were invited to witness the ceremony.

This was only the second occasion in the Company's history that the heir to the throne had attended a Company function at the Hall, which by a coincidence took place on the anniversary of the visit of Edward Prince of Wales to the sexcentenary dinner on 22 March 1933. In 1995 no formal banquet was held but the members of the Court and their wives, and as many liverymen and freemen as wished, attended a buffet lunch. Students from the Building Crafts College exhibited their work to the Prince who spoke to many of them during the lunch.

The Company grants the Honorary Livery to the Presidents for the time being of the Carpenters' Company of the City and County of Philadelphia. The origin of the Company, like the Carpenters' Company of London, is a little uncertain; but probably it had been founded by 1724, no doubt by English emigrants to Pennsylvania. It has been impossible to prove that there is any direct connection with the London Carpenters; although it has a similar coat-of-arms.

Carpenters' Hall in Philadelphia played an important part in the history of the American

75. Honorary Livery, 1995: The Master, Captain K. G. Hamon RN, presents HRH the Prince of Wales with an illuminated address to mark the Prince's admission to the Carpenters' Company.
◀

76. The Carpenters' and Dockland Centre, Stratford, 1993. Facilities at the Centre include a sports hall, judo training room, pool room, multi-gym, meeting rooms, recreation area and bar.
▶

77. Building Crafts Training School, 1970: initially teaching all building crafts, the College now concentrates on woodworking and stonemasonry.
◄

Revolution. As events moved to a final break between the American colonists and the British Government, the first Continental Congress met in Philadelphia in Carpenters' Hall on 5 September 1774; the forty-four delegates included "George Washington, Esquire" from Virginia and John Adams from Massachusetts. Before they dispersed on 25 October they had issued a "Declaration of Rights" and had formed the "Association" to boycott British goods; but they disappointed their extremist followers by not declaring independence from Britain. When the second Continental Congress met in Philadelphia on 10 May 1775 the first armed clashes with British troops had taken place, and the delegates began the discussions which led to the issuing of the Declaration of Independence on 4 July 1776; but the second Continental Congress met in the State Hall (today Independence Hall), not in Carpenters' Hall. While these discussions were taking place, representatives of the colonists had a secret meeting in Carpenters' Hall with an agent of King Louis XVI of France, and began the negotiations which ended with France declaring war on Britain and intervening on the American side. When the British army captured Philadelphia, Carpenters' Hall was occupied by British troops.

For the next 175 years there was very little association between the Carpenters of London and Philadelphia. They were kept apart by wars and strained relations between Britain and the United States, and by the width of the Atlantic Ocean in the days of sailing ships; but there was an occasional exchange of greetings towards the end of the nineteenth century.

It was not until after the Second World War that any real links were established between the two Companies. The first initiative came from Philadelphia in 1950 and by 1951 close relations had been established. The President of the Philadelphia Company and his wife have frequently attended the London Company's Court Ladies Dinner and other functions; and in 1977 a number of members of the Philadelphia Company visited England and were entertained by the London Carpenters, both at Carpenters' Hall and elsewhere, on the five hundredth anniversary of the grant of the English Company's charter in 1477. The London Company's visits to Philadelphia have been less frequent, chiefly because of the difficulties, at various periods, of obtaining the necessary foreign currency; but the Master and other members of the Court of the London Company have visited Philadelphia, and have been very hospitably entertained there at Carpenters' Hall on several occasions, including the celebrations of the bicentenary of American independence in 1976, and more recently in 1990.

One particularly happy development has been a scheme for the exchange of scholars, under which an American student of one aspect of the construction industry comes to London, and a British student goes to Philadelphia, for a year's work experience training. This idea was proposed by the Philadelphia Company in 1964. It continued very successfully till 1991, when it had to be temporarily suspended because of the trade recession and the unemployment in the building industry both in Britain and in the United States. The Exchange Scholarship was resumed in 1995.

The Carpenters' Company still owns much of the land at Stratford in East London that it bought in 1767. In the nineteenth century the farmland was converted into factory sites by the Company's tenants. The value of the land fell in the years immediately after the Second World War, and the Court – unwisely, as it seems today – let the property on long leases at rents which are barely one per cent of today's market rent. The Company has bought in some of these long leases although it has consistently refused to sell any of the freeholds. It is still too early to say whether the development of the Channel Tunnel Rail Link to London, and a possible international railway station at Stratford, will greatly increase the value of these lands.

Every year in May the Master has the delightful duty of visiting the Carpenters Road Junior and Mixed Infants School, where he presents the annual school prizes, which are funded by the Company.

The social centre in the Church Hall at Stratford became the Carpenters' Institute and was organised in turn by Cecil Barnes and Commander Alan Preston. Afterwards Hugh Barnes-Yallowley was appointed secretary, and he formed a small committee with representatives of Yardleys and other industries on the Carpenters' Estate. Cecil Barnes, Alan Preston and Hugh Barnes-Yallowley all became Masters of the Carpenters' Company, Barnes in 1950, Preston in 1957, and Barnes-Yallowley in 1991.

In the first years after the Second World War the youth club was situated in a disused domestic science building alongside Carpenters' School, and was entirely staffed by volunteers; but the policy of successive governments after 1945 made it possible to obtain financial help from the local council in Newham and the State under the auspices of the

169

78. Sitting Room, Rustington, 1992: the portrait over the fireplace is of Sir Henry Harben, founder of the Home.

Albemarle Trust. In March 1973 a new centre, which had been designed by Kenneth Lindy and cost nearly £100,000, was opened by Princess Margaret and the Master, Brigadier George Evelegh. At that time Hugh Barnes-Yallowley was President of the London Junior Chamber of Commerce. He persuaded an old-established charity, the Dockland Settlements, to take on the trusteeship of the club, which was then renamed The Carpenters' and Dockland Youth Centre; and the local youth centre, known as the Tom Alan Club, moved their staff and members to the new buildings. There is now an average attendance of some 90 members a night. The Carpenters' Company made a substantial grant to the refurbishment fund in 1993.

The Trades Training School has continued to flourish since it was opened in 1893. Its name was changed in 1948 to the Building Crafts Training School and in 1993 to the Building Crafts College. The original building, which had been a drill hall, was rebuilt in 1968 and re-opened as a full-time craft training centre. Students from the School contributed to the restoration of York Minster after it was struck by lightning in 1984, and because of this the Master of the Carpenters' Company was invited to the Dedication Service in the presence of the Queen in November 1988.

The War Office took longer than the Company hoped to derequisition the Rustington

79. Godalming visitation, 1994: the Master, Wardens and Beadle of the Company together with the Mayor and Town Clerk of Godalming at Puttenham Church.

Convalescent Home after the Second World War, but finally handed over possession of the Home and it reopened for patients on 2 July 1948. The Company claimed £4,000 compensation for the use of the Home and any damage done to it, but were quite happy to accept the War Office's offer of £3,821. The Company continued to run the farm adjacent to the Convalescent Home on a profitable basis; on one occasion in 1943 they sold three pigs for £32.5s.0d. and bought six for £21.

The Home and the farm were placed under the control of a Warden, Brigadier Napier, under whom a staff of three sisters provided convalescent care, but a disagreement arose as to the extent of the Warden's authority over the nursing staff and when Brigadier Napier resigned in 1950 he was not replaced as Warden. The Home was placed under the control of a Matron, whilst the farm was managed by a bailiff until it was sold by auction for £170,000, in 1968, to a developer who converted it into a housing estate. In 1971 this money was used to fund a major conversion programme to modernise the Home.

Although the Home at Rustington had originally been called "The Rustington Convalescent Home for Working Men", Sir Henry Harben's Deed of Gift to the Company provided that it should be open to "persons of the working class and others". This was sufficiently wide to allow for the admission of persons of all classes and both sexes. Women were first admitted in 1980 and today about 70% of the patients are women.

The Rustington Convalescent Home has been an outstandingly successful institution.

171

Almost without exception the patients enthusiastically praise the treatment they receive, and some of them have made substantial gifts of money to the Home, in gratitude. The only serious complaint has been that in recent years some patients have objected to sharing a bedroom. The sharing of rooms, though perfectly acceptable to people of an earlier generation, fails to conform to the standards expected today; and in 1994 it was decided to offer a single room to every patient who requires one, although this has reduced the number of patients who can be accommodated. It marks the final transition from the large open-plan dormitories of the original Home to the single bedrooms of today.

The Home, with its potting-sheds, outhouses and former laundry building, was regarded as a typical modern house in the 1890s. It was considered ugly by many people in the 1930s but today, it is scheduled as a Grade 2 building of historic interest. Although this status has drawbacks with regard to maintenance, the Company are proud to be the Trustees of this splendid example of 1896 architecture. They are even more proud of the commitment shown by the Matron, Mrs Patricia Neild, and the nursing staff, and of the facilities offered to the patients in this convalescent home. These include a high degree of skilled nursing, which has become more essential than ever since changes in the National Health Service have meant that patients are often discharged from hospitals to convalesce only a few days after undergoing major surgery.

The almshouses at Twickenham were taken over by the Twickenham Borough Council in 1947. The Borough Council offered the Company the choice of negotiating a sale by agreement or of acquiring them under compulsory powers, and offered to adopt whichever course was to the greater advantage of the Company. The Company chose to sell them by agreement. The almshouses at Godalming however, remain under the trusteeship of the Company, as they have been since 1622. They were modernised in 1957, when electric light, bathrooms and similar facilities were installed without spoiling the outside appearance of this fine Jacobean building.

The choice of the almsmen to fill the eight places in the almshouses rests with the Carpenters' Company, who are required by the terms of Richard Wyatt's will to choose residents from the parishes of Godalming (now including Farncombe), Puttenham, Hambledon, Compton and Dunsfold. In the nineteenth century the Company took great care in selecting suitable almsmen. It was the practice, whenever a vacancy occurred, for the Master, the Senior Warden, the Clerk, and the "Father of the Company" (the most Senior Past Master) to go to Godalming to interview applicants – normally at least four or five. The Master and his colleagues wrote a full report on the merits and drawbacks of each applicant, which often ran to several pages, and presented it to the next meeting of the Court, where it was fully discussed. The Court then decided whom to choose, relying largely on references from the local vicars and others, and on the personal impression which the committee had formed of the applicants. A favourable reference from Lord Middleton for one of his old servants certainly helped an applicant in 1875, but it was not enough to obtain the vacancy for him.

Some of the almsmen were married, and their wives lived with them in the almshouse though sometimes wives were required to leave after the death of their husbands. In 1863 a widowed almsman who was crippled, and in need of help in walking, was allowed to have his sister living with him, after the Court had verified that she was a respectable woman and was over fifty years of age.

One of the almsmen was always appointed to be supervisor of the almshouses and placed in a position of authority over his fellow-almsmen. It was his duty to see that the almsmen attended divine service in the tiny chapel, and periodically to read aloud to them the terms of Richard Wyatt's will, which contained the regulations that the almsmen were obliged to observe. For this reason the Court in choosing which applicants to accept for the almshouses, preferred those who could read and write. Today there are fewer applicants than in earlier times, and the procedure for choosing them is simpler. Only the Senior Warden and the Clerk go to Godalming to interview the applicants, and they make recommendations, through the Master and Wardens Committee, to the Court for approval.

The clause in Wyatt's will which has always caused the greatest difficulty is the stipulation that the almsmen must not be drunkards. On one occasion in 1962 an almsman was threatened with expulsion because he insisted on keeping a dog which frightened the other almsmen; but it is the provision about drunkenness which in every century has caused the trouble. On several occasions over the years an almsman has been warned by the Court that he would be expelled if he continued to get drunk; and on at least one occasion, in 1866, the offending almsman was in fact expelled.

The Court has continued to visit Godalming once a year, as they have done ever since 1623 whenever they have not been prevented by war, civil war or plague. The visit originally took place in August, but in 1880 was changed to July. Since 1961 it has been in late May or early June. The proceedings begin with a meeting in the chapel at the almshouses, at which part of Wyatt's will is read aloud by the Clerk, and the almsmen are given the opportunity to raise any matter or make any complaint. The Court, and any liverymen present, then attend a service in one of the six parish churches before lunching in a local hotel.

Until 1971 the religious service was always held in the parish church in Godalming; but in 1972, when repairs were being carried out at the church, it was suggested that the service should be held at Compton parish church. After the Clerk had made sure that this would not contravene the terms of Wyatt's will, the service in 1972 was held at Compton; and now it is held each year in one of the six parish churches – Godalming, Farncombe, Compton, Puttenham, Hambledon or Dunsfold.

The Mayor of Godalming, who is just beginning his mayoral year, is always invited to the church service and lunch, at which he replies to the toast proposed by the Master; and he, in return, invites the Master to the Mayor's dinner in the following March or April.

In reflecting on the Company's responsibilities for endowments and charitable giving and on entertainment, it is worth noting that the Carpenters today spend about 3 per cent of their income on entertainment – a smaller percentage than at any time in their history. Until the Second World War, they had seven or more courses at dinners; on 31 March 1914 thirteen courses were served. Today four or five courses are normal but these figures are deceptive. Dishes were served as separate courses in the 1930s which today would be served together as one, and chocolates are now passed around with the coffee without being noted as a separate course. Older liverymen and guests who remember the former dinners say that

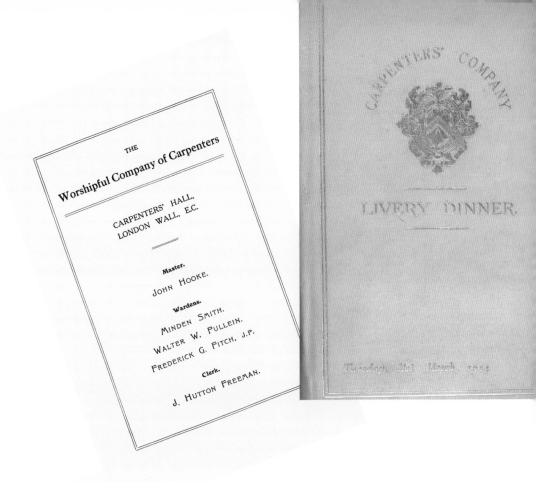

THE

Worshipful Company of Carpenters

CARPENTERS' HALL,
LONDON WALL, E.C.

Master.
JOHN HOOKE.

Wardens.
MINDEN SMITH.
WALTER W. PULLEIN.
FREDERICK G. FITCH, J.P.

Clerk.
J. HUTTON FREEMAN.

CARPENTERS' COMPANY

LIVERY DINNER.

Tuesday, 31st March, 1914

GRACE.   *John Reading, 1675*

CANTOR.
Benedictus sit Deus in donis suis,

RESPONSUM.
Et Sanctus in omnibus operibus ejus.

CANTOR.
Adjutorium nostrum est in nomine Domini.

RESPONSUM.
Qui fecit cœlum et terram.

CANTOR.
Sit nomen Domini benedictum.

RESPONSUM.
Et hoc nunc usque in secula seculorum.   Amen.

Fac Regem salvum Domine,
Da pacem in diebus nostris,
Et exaudi nos in die
Quocunque invocamus Te.—Amen.

80. Menu, 1914: various pages from the menu of a Livery Dinner, March 1914. Dinner menus of this period also included seating plans and song sheets. Surprisingly, given that the Company had an Entertainments Committee and tremendous enthusiasm for its drink, no list of wines was included. Prior to the First World War, the Company spent around £2000 a year on

174

Programme of Music

(Under the Direction of Mr. CHARLES CAPPER).

Artists:

Miss ANNIE BARTLE.
Miss VIOLET OPPENSHAW.
Mr. IVOR WALTERS.
Mr. CLIFTON YATES.

| Violincello | - | - | - | Mr. J. EDWIN PARR. |
| Accompanist | - | - | - | Mr. P. MAVON-IBBS. |

GRACE... ..."Benedictus sit Deus" (*Old Winchester Grace*)

NATIONAL ANTHEM. "God save the King"

"God save the Queen" and "God bless the Prince of Wales"

QUARTETTE "In England, Merrie England" (*Merrie England*)
E. German

Miss ANNIE BARTLE. **Mr. IVOR WALTERS.**
Miss VIOLET OPPENSHAW. **Mr. CLIFTON YATES.**

SONG ... ... "Christina's Lament" *Antonin Dvôrak*
Miss ANNIE BARTLE.

SONG ... "Lorraine, Lorraine, Lorrée" ... *Jno Capel*
Mr. CLIFTON YATES.

SONG ... ... "A Summer Night" ... *Goring Thomas*
('Cello Obligato: Mr. J. EDWIN PARR.)
Miss VIOLET OPPENSHAW.

RECIT. AND ARIA "O Vision Entrancing" *Goring Thomas*
Mr. IVOR WALTERS.

VIOLINCELLO SOLO ... "Berceuse" ... ... *Godard*
Mr. J. EDWIN PARR.

SONG ... ... "Wake-up" ... *Montague Phillips*
Miss ANNIE BARTLE.

SONG ... ..."The Lute Player" *Frances Allitsen*
Mr. CLIFTON YATES.

QUARTETTE ... "The Lass of Richmond Hill" *Old English*
Miss ANNIE BARTLE. **Mr. IVOR WALTERS.**
Miss VIOLET OPPENSHAW. **Mr. CLIFTON YATES.**

The Master will feel obliged if gentlemen will refrain from asking for encores as they cannot be allowed.

TOAST LIST.

H.M. THE KING.

H.M. THE QUEEN, QUEEN ALEXANDRA.
H.R.H. THE PRINCE OF WALES,
and
THE OTHER MEMBERS OF THE ROYAL FAMILY.

THE VISITORS.

THE WORSHIPFUL COMPANY OF CARPENTERS.

hospitality with wine consumption accounting for about a quarter of this bill. During the war, expenditure was drastically cut. For example, in 1913, the Company spent £574 on wine consumption whereas between 1915–1918 expenditure was around £150 a year. Company hospitality did not regain its former style until 1925.

MENU.

Hors d'Œuvres.

Tortue, Tortue Claire
Saumon, Sauce Mousseline.
Blanchaille.
Filets de Ris de Veau aux Truffes,
Bonnes Bouches Moderne.

Selle de Mouton.
Canetons, Petits Pois.
Jambon, Salade.
Asperges,
Gelée à l'Imperiale, Meringues.
Bombe Creole.
Crèmes d'Anchois,
Glaces,
Dessert.

the amount of food consumed was no more than is eaten today as the helpings were much smaller; but serving the many courses meant that the dinners then took much longer, and though they started earlier they ended later than now. This did not matter when most of the Livery had a house in the London area and a coachman who could drive them home in their carriages at any hour; but thirteen course dinners are unacceptable to the liverymen today who are conscious of the drink-drive law or have to catch the last train home.

Unlike most Livery Companies, the Carpenters do not have a wine committee. Before the Second World War dinners were organised by the Entertainments Committee, which later merged with the Master and Wardens Committee; and the committee's recommendations would be solemnly debated at meetings of the Court, where a Past Master would move an amendment, which was put to the vote, that a different wine should be served and that the band should play selections from a different Gilbert and Sullivan operetta than had been recommended by the Entertainments Committee. Now the arrangements for the food and wine at the dinner are left in the capable hands of the Master, the Clerk and the Assistant Clerk.

After tobacco reached England in 1595 the Carpenters smoked pipes at their dinners until smoking became socially unacceptable in the 1770s and was replaced by snuff; but cigars were served at dinners after the Crimean War, and cigarettes by the 1880s. In the first half of the twentieth century one cigar and two cigarettes were offered to each guest although now only cigars are offered, and only a minority of the liverymen and guests accept them. Few of the Livery and guests take the snuff which is offered in one or other of the Company's silver snuffboxes. Only one man within living memory has smoked a pipe at a Carpenters' Livery dinner – a former Bishop of London.

Since the middle of the nineteenth century white tie has been worn at Carpenters' dinners, although, following some discussion, black tie is now optional. When the Livery were asked to express their opinion some amusement was caused by my observation that full evening dress, which had been designed to be worn by gentlemen who had valets, was now 100 years out of date; "at no other period in the last 650 years had the Livery dressed for dinner in clothes that were 100 years out of date. The Livery in Charles II's reign did not dress for dinner in the costume of Elizabeth I's time". Though some senior members of the Livery were in favour of abandoning full evening dress this was not the view expressed by a majority of the junior members. The Court decided that the Livery should be given the option of wearing black tie instead of white.

16
The Carpenters' Company Today

Participation of junior liverymen in the running of the Carpenters' Company – arguments as to the power to co-opt liverymen who have not been Master or Warden to serve on the Court, 1665 to 1993 – opposition to the proposal to co-opt liverymen to Court Committees in 1962 – the principle accepted in 1992 – the attendance of ladies at dinners and social events, 1477 to 1985 – the admission of women to the Livery rejected in 1977 – there is no justification for the criticism of Livery Companies today – the Carpenters' Company's future.

During the last seventy years there has been a great deal of discussion and controversy in the Carpenters' Company as to the extent to which liverymen who are not on the Court should be invited to take part in running the Company's affairs. The idea has taken root that all liverymen should take an interest in the management of the Company and not merely think of it as an institution that provides them with excellent dinners free of charge, for there is no doubt that for many years this was all that the Company meant to most. A liveryman who joined as a young man at the age of 23 or 24 greatly enjoyed the Livery dinner every year in November, to which he was entitled to bring a male guest every other year, and the Livery Ladies Dinner in April or May, to which he could bring his wife or girl friend every year. He was also invited once a year to attend the monthly Court lunches after the Court meetings, as well as the General Court of the Livery every July, with the procession to the church and another excellent lunch before the election of the Master and Wardens. Many members of the Court will admit that the Company meant nothing more than this to them until, after thirty-five or forty years, they came on to the Court as Junior Warden and discovered for the first time about the Company's property and charitable endowments and the day-to-day administration of their Company.

There is one practical difficulty in involving the younger members of the Livery in the Company's affairs. Many liverymen, until they reach retirement age, may be too busy pursuing their careers to find time to do more than attend the occasional social function. The wish to generate the greater involvement of the Livery is so universally accepted today that it is surprising to discover how strongly the idea was opposed by many members of the Court in the 1930s and even as late as the 1960s. The strongest argument of the opponents has been the provision in the Ordinances of 1607 that the affairs of the Company shall be administered by the Master and Wardens and by those who have been Master or Wardens. This seems to exclude any other members of the Livery, and to prevent the Court from bringing liverymen on to the Court in any other way than by nominating them for election as Junior Warden at the General Court of the Livery.

It is strange that so much importance has been attached to this provision in the Ordinances of 1607, because most of the other 47 provisions of these Ordinances are regarded as obsolete and have long since been ignored by the Company. No one suggests that the Master and Wardens still have the power to enter the premises of any carpenter in the City of London

81. Dining Hall, 1995: HRH The Duke of Edinburgh (Patron) and H.M. Neal (President) preside over a dinner of the City and Guilds College Association.

and within four miles from its boundaries in order to inspect his work and materials to ensure that he is complying with the Company's regulations; that the Master may order a carpenter to inflict corporal chastisement on any of his apprentices who has not attended church on Sundays or who has been "haunting taverns"; that no carpenter's apprentice may get married without the Master's consent; that if any member of the Court fails to attend a meeting to which he is summoned, the Master may imprison him for three days in Carpenters' Hall as a punishment for his misconduct. The provision in the Ordinances that a General Court of the Livery shall be held at least four times every year has not been complied with for several centuries, and was ignored even in the seventeenth century. It is only the provision about the Court consisting of "the Master and Wardens and such others as had been Master or Warden" which is still considered to be sacred.

In 1665, after many members of the Court had died of the Great Plague, the Court co-opted liverymen who had never been either Master or Warden, and this was done again on several occasions during the next twenty years. It was not until 1846 that the power of the Court to co-opt members of the Livery was challenged. The Court then proposed to bring on to the Court a liveryman who had not been Master or Warden but had just been elected as a Sheriff of London; but it was said that this would be illegal under the Ordinances of

178

82. *Dining Hall windows: Mr Alfred Fisher's original designs for stained glass windows in the Hall.*
a. City window, 1991
◀

b. Company window, 1988 ▼

1607. It was decided to take counsel's opinion, and the papers were sent to Serjeant Manning, Q.C. He expressed the view that under the Ordinances of 1607, the Court had no power to co-opt members of the Livery on to the Court; he thought that the General Court of the Livery might be entitled to change the regulations to enable this to be done, but believed that it might also be necessary to obtain the consent of the Crown.

In February 1923 the Court considered the desirability of altering the method of election to the offices of Master and Wardens and the matter was discussed at the General Court of the Livery in July. They decided to take no action, but in October 1929 they appointed a committee to consider the problem. The committee reported that the Ordinances of 1607 prevented the Company from altering the method of election or from bringing anyone on to the Court except by nominating him to be Master or Warden. The question was further considered in 1938, when the Clerk, Henry Osborne, prepared a memorandum on the subject. He referred to Serjeant Manning's opinion in 1846 and was sure that the Ordinances of 1607 prevented not only the Court, but probably also the Livery at a General Court, from altering the method of election or from granting the Court the power to co-opt. He thought that any change would require the consent of the Crown.

In 1993 the Court wished to appoint to the Court a most distinguished liveryman, Sir Desmond Heap. He had formerly been Master of the Solicitors' Company, and Comptroller and Solicitor to the City Corporation. He had pointed out to the Company, when they were planning to build their new Hall, that by constructing an arcade in London Wall they would prevent the acquisition by compulsory purchase of their land for the widening of London Wall. He also pointed out that they would not require special permission to build their banqueting hall on a bridge across Throgmorton Avenue because it was not a public highway. Sir Desmond felt unable, because of his age, to accept office as Junior Warden and in due course to become Master; so the Court decided to appoint him as an honorary member of the Court. It was argued that this could not be done because of the Ordinances of 1607; but the majority of the Court took the view that the Standing Orders could be changed to create the status of "honorary members" of the Court, and that the Court could appoint these honorary members. Sir Desmond Heap was appointed to the Court in April 1993.

There has been less resistance to the plan to prepare senior members of the Livery for their work on the Court by co-opting them to the standing committees; but when it was proposed at a meeting of the Court on 6 March 1962 that a certain number of liverymen should be co-opted to the General Purposes Committee, there was strong opposition.

Past Master J.B. Rosher spoke particularly strongly against the proposal. "A similar Scheme had been proposed many years before because it was thought that the Court had become so moribund that nothing got done. The Scheme did not go through then, and he saw no reason for it now. The present Court was certainly not moribund ... The members of the Court had all joined it as Junior Wardens and had sat and listened during their first years. He could not see a young liveryman presuming to argue with the experienced members of the Court; they would therefore contribute nothing. Every effort that had been made in the past 35 years to bring the Livery in touch with the Court had failed". Past Masters B.J. Nicholson, K.M. Roberts and Alan Preston strongly supported the proposal, and denied that it was inspired by the feeling that the present members of the Court were "moribund".

When the proposal was put to the vote, there were 8 in favour and 8 against. The Master, Lewis Grece, gave his casting vote in favour of the motion. But at the next meeting of the Court he apologised for his action, and regretted that he had ignored the tradition that if an equal number of votes were cast for and against a proposal, the Master should always give his casting vote against it. He said that "he had been surprised by the extent, quality and vehemence of the opposition". He had "considered only the merits of the recommendation itself, and not the larger issue that so revolutionary a change in practice and procedure should be carried by a single vote".

A compromise was reached which was in effect a victory for the opponents of the involvement of the Livery. Under Standing Orders a three-fourths majority is necessary to rescind a resolution of the Court which has been passed within the previous five years; but at the meeting of the Court on 1 May 1962 it was agreed unanimously to rescind the decision to co-opt liverymen to the General Purposes Committee. In November it was decided instead to introduce a scheme by which members of the Livery should be invited in turn to accompany the Wardens when they paid their regular visits to Godalming, Rustington and the Building Crafts Training School. This failed to work in practice, because the liverymen were too busy to accept the invitation.

In 1992 the Court agreed, without opposition, that two members of the Livery should be co-opted to serve on all executive committees of the Company, except the Master and Wardens and the Admissions Committees. These liverymen may not serve for more than two years at a time though they may be co-opted again after a break of a year.

Another matter of controversy has been the admission of women to the Freedom and Livery, and their participation in social events. There are references to the "brothers and sisters" of the Freedom in the Company's first charter of 1477, but no freewoman was admitted to the Livery. The wives of the Master and Wardens were regularly invited to dinner with the Lord Mayor, to the Election Day dinner, and to other Company functions in the Middle Ages and the sixteenth and seventeenth centuries, and in the eighteenth century a Court Ladies Dinner was regularly held. But Edward Jupp, in his History in 1848, writes as if this was a thing of the past. "Up to quite a recent date the ladies partook of the hospitalities of Carpenters' Hall. In this respect the gallantry of the Company has sadly evaporated".

Balls have occasionally been held, as well as ladies dinners. There was a ball in 1749 and also in 1752 and 1753; but they did not become a regular feature of the Company's social engagements in either the eighteenth, nineteenth or twentieth centuries, though dances have been held irregularly from time to time; the last one was in 1983. The pattern is always the same; dances are proposed and eagerly supported by some members of the Court, but when the dance takes place very few members of the Livery attend.

At the November Livery Dinner for the Lord Mayor in 1882 the members of the Court were entitled to introduce two ladies to watch from the gallery. Since 1985 the ladies of members of the Court dine separately and enter the gallery to listen to the speeches at the Livery Dinner in November. A Livery Ladies Dinner, to which every liveryman may bring a lady as a guest, was first held in 1897, and is now held every year. There is also an annual Court Ladies Dinner, to which every member of the Court is entitled to bring two ladies and one gentleman as guests – for example, his wife and a married couple. For many years

181

83. Building Crafts College, 1994: students in the woodwork workshop.

the Court Ladies Dinner was held in April or May, and the Livery Ladies Dinner in June; but since 1958 the Livery Ladies Dinner has been held in April or May, and the Court Ladies Dinner in June. In 1956 the wives of the members of the Court were invited for the first time to accompany their husbands on the annual visit to Rustington and to attend the lunch there in the summer.

In 1918 J. Godwin King (who became Master in 1945) asked the Clerk to inform him as to the position about freewomen in the Company. He had no son, but his daughter had been born in 1897; he himself had become a freeman of the Company in 1907 and a liveryman in 1908. The Clerk prepared a memorandum on the subject. A woman who was born after her father became a freeman was eligible to become a freewoman by patrimony; but she ceased to be a freewoman when she married, presumably because she then passed from her father's into her husband's control. When her husband died and she became a widow, her position as a freewoman revived; but her Freedom gave no patrimonial rights to her children because when they were born during her marriage she herself was not Free. No woman could join the Livery either by patrimony or by redemption. In view of this memorandum, King arranged for his daughter's husband, Major G.W. Ridley, to join the Livery by redemption in 1919. He became Master in 1955.

Not for the first or last time in the history of the Carpenters' Company, a legal opinion or a memorandum by counsel or the Clerk has been completely forgotten or ignored by the

182

Company. The daughters of liverymen and freemen who become Free by patrimony do not now cease to be Free when they marry, and married women have often been admitted to the Freedom by patrimony.

The question of the admission of women to the Livery was raised after the enactment of the Sex Discrimination Act of 1975. The Solicitor gave his opinion that the Act did not apply to the admission of women to Livery Companies; but the question was discussed with some vehemence at several meetings of the Court. It was decided to consult the Livery, who were invited to write to the Clerk giving their opinions. Some of those who objected to the admission of women believed that there would one day be a reaction against the present concept of a "single sex society", and that the Court should not now take a decision which would prevent the Company from taking advantage of this reaction when it occurred.

The Court was considerably influenced by the opinion of liveryman R.L. Woolley, who next year was elected Junior Warden and was Master in 1980. "Admission to the Livery implies a willingness to serve on the Court at the appropriate time. With no intention of disrespect to the ladies, I nevertheless suspect that the proportion of women experienced and able to serve on the Court satisfactorily is smaller than the proportion of men able to do so". He also pointed out that if women were to be admitted to the Livery there were about 100 daughters of liverymen who could be admitted by patrimony, which would cause great complications.

The Middle Warden, Douglas Eggleton, spoke particularly strongly against the admission of women. Others advocated caution before adopting so far-reaching a change in the composition of the Company, believing that "Marry in haste and repent at leisure", and that "Fools rush in where angels fear to tread".

The decision was finally taken at a special meeting of the Court on 16 March 1977. A resolution "That as a matter of principle women be not admitted to the Livery at this time" was moved by Eggleton and carried by 10 votes against 4. The issue has not been raised since, though several other Livery Companies have admitted women. Some women – one of them, Her Royal Highness The Princess Royal – have been Masters of Livery Companies; and some Livery Companies have very efficient women Clerks, who are regularly invited as guests to the Carpenters' Court lunches and Livery dinners. The greatest argument against admitting women is the practical problem which it would cause at a time when there was a waiting list of men wishing to be admitted and when for several reasons – above all the size of the dining hall – the Company does not wish to increase the numbers of liverymen above 150.

What then is the Carpenters' Company today? Like many other English institutions, it is something which has evolved through the centuries as a result of a number of historical accidents, and has not been planned or designed to fulfil its present function; and like other English institutions which have arisen in the same way, it works surprisingly well in practice. Anyone who attends a Carpenters' Company Livery dinner will soon discover that very few of the people present are carpenters, but as the master carpenters in the fourteenth century combined the function of builder and architect, any builder or architect can justly be called a carpenter for the purposes of membership of the Company. Some 38% of the Livery today are connected with the building industry.

The Carpenters' Company today attaches great importance to its links with the craft. In

May 1977 the Court decided that "in considering applications to the Livery, the importance of a strong representation of the building trades and allied professions shall be borne in mind". In recent years the Company has allowed this principle of links with the building trade to prevail over that other historical tradition of the Company – the hereditary family ties of the liverymen, though a balance has always been kept. The Company has also ruled that a liveryman of another Company may not become a member of the Carpenters' Company, except in very special circumstances, in order to strengthen the links with the craft, and to limit the number of the Livery to 150.

There is no opposition to Livery Companies today from any substantial section of the public; indeed their popularity is shown by the fact that new Livery Companies are always being formed. The Chartered Architects, the Constructors, and the Information Technologists have been created only recently. The only people who oppose Livery Companies are small minorities who do so from some theoretical objection to what they see as privileged and "elitist" bodies. It is possible that at some future date the press and the media might whip up hostility to Livery Companies on these grounds. The lavish dinners given by the Companies may again be denounced, as they were 120 years ago, but there is no justifiable reason to criticise Livery Companies on these grounds, or for some liverymen to be as apologetic as they are about the dinners. The Carpenters now help many deserving causes. In 1994 they made grants to 46 different charities, to 36 individuals to assist with their training for a career in the craft, and to four students to help with university or school studies.

The Carpenters' Company today is a property-owning company whose members are freemen and liverymen, not shareholders; who have acquired their membership not by buying shares but by paying their admission fees; who have inherited from their fathers not their shareholdings but the right to join the Company by patrimony. Its governing body consists of men from differing backgrounds who collectively have wide experience of the world and are worthy trustees of their heritage.

Let us suppose for a moment that the Livery Companies did not exist, and that their assets were confiscated and their property sold to other bodies. Who would replace the Livery Companies as the owners and landlords of their property? Unless it was the State or the local authorities – not always the most popular of landlords – it would be some property-owning company. Like the Carpenters' Company they would spend a large part of their income on maintaining and improving their property, and would then consider how to spend the rest of their rents. They would spend far more in paying dividends to their shareholders (who would spend some of these dividends on expensive dinners) than the Livery Companies spend on dinners and entertainments for their liverymen. The fees and perks paid to their directors would be perhaps a hundred times higher than the Court fees and other benefits paid by the Livery Companies to the members of the Court for attending the meetings of the Court and committees. Most of the shareholders would know less about the working and management of the company than the liverymen know about the Carpenters' Company; and the proportion of shareholders attending the company's annual general meeting would be much lower than the 20 per cent of liverymen who usually attend the General Court of the Livery on election day. Many property-holding companies give donations to charity and good causes; but what commercial company follows the example of the Carpenters' Company

84. HMS Norfolk: in 1989 the Company became affiliated to HMS Norfolk, a Type 23 frigate. The ship was commissioned for service in June 1990 at Plymouth. The Company entertains members of the ship's company annually and contributes to the ship's welfare fund.

185

85. Reception area, 1995: the first picture of the refurbished Reception area. This light and spacious L-shaped room adjoins the Dining Hall.

in giving more than three times more to charity than it pays in directors' fees and in dividends to its shareholders?

The Carpenters' Company is flourishing in 1995 after having been in existence for about seven hundred years. Liverymen and freemen die; on the Court, where most of the members are over seventy, a death occurs on average once a year. But the Carpenters' Company shows no sign of dying. It survived Judge Jeffreys; it survived the French Revolution; it survived the criticisms of Firth. At the Company's Livery dinners the last toast of the evening has been proposed since 1937 by the junior liveryman present, in words almost identical with those used by the Master, Alfred Preston, at the Livery dinner to the Lord Mayor in November 1881: "The Carpenters' Company root and branch, and may it continue and flourish for ever". There is no reason to think that in the foreseeable future the Carpenters' Company will cease to flourish.

186

APPENDIX I
LIST OF DATES

1271   First mention of a Master Carpenter in the City of London building regulations.

1333   Book of Ordinances.

1389   Richard II is presented with the 1333 Ordinances.

1429   First Hall built on land rented from the Hospital of St. Mary without Bishopsgate.

1438   Wardens' Accounts, the earliest written records.

1455   Ordinances institute the Court of Assistants of the Company.

1466   Grant of Arms.

1477   First Charter from Edward IV.

1477   Lime Street property given to the Company by Thomas Wareham.

1487   Ordinances.

1558   1st Charter confirmed by Philip and Mary I.

1560   1st Charter confirmed by Elizabeth I.

1561   Master's Crown presented.

1607   Ordinances.

1607   2nd Charter from James I.

1611   Master's cup given by John Reeve.

1620   Richard Wyatt died leaving land and money for almshouses at Godalming.

1630   Norton Folgate estate purchased.

1640   3rd Charter from Charles I.

1664   New wing built to Carpenters' Hall.

1666   Great fire of London. Carpenters' Hall survived.

1673   4th Charter from Charles II.

1686   5th Charter from James II.

1767   Company decided to purchase marsh land at Stratford.

1841   Almshouses built at Twickenham, Middlesex.

1876   Old Hall demolished and new Hall built.

1880   New Hall opened.

1891   Stratford Institute school started.

1893   Building Crafts College founded.

1897   Sir Henry Harben built and endowed the Rustington Convalescent Home.

1905   Stratford Institute school closed.

1941   Hall destroyed when a bomb ignited a gas main in London Wall.

1944   Supplemental Charter from George VI.

1947   Twickenham almshouses acquired by local council and demolished.

1956   Foundation stone of present Hall laid by Sir Cuthbert Ackroyd, the Lord Mayor of London.

1960   New Hall opened by Sir Edmund Stockdale, Junior Warden and Lord Mayor of London.
1971   Building Crafts College reopened in new building.
1971   Rustington Convalescent Home modernised.
1973   Carpenters & Dockland Centre opened at Stratford.

86. Honorary Livery, 1995: HRH The Prince of Wales meets students from Building Crafts College in the course of his admission to the Livery.

APPENDIX II
LIST OF HONORARY MEMBERS

Sir John Lubbock, Bt, MP	12 April, 1988
Sir Albert K. Rollit, MP	30 July, 1894
The Very Revd. Henry Wace, DD	30 July, 1894
Professor William Robert Smith, MD	30 July, 1894
Sir Joseph Fayrer, Bt, KCSI, MD	4 December, 1894
General The Rt. Hon. Sir Redvers H. Buller, VC, GCB, GCMG, PC	26 March, 1901
Major General W.H. Mackinnon, CB	26 March, 1901
Colonel H.C. Cholmondeley, CB	26 March, 1901
Rt. Hon. The Earl of Albemarle, CB	23 April, 1901
Rt. Hon. Sir George Houston Reid, KCMG, PC, KC	22 June, 1910
Thomas Wharrie, JP	1 June, 1915
Mrs. Mary Woodgate Wharrie	3 July, 1917
Field Marshal The Rt. Hon. The Earl Haig of Bemerside, OM, KT, GCB, KCIE, GCVO	17 July, 1919
The Revd. Sir Montague Fowler, Bt, MA	7 November, 1922
Most Hon. The Marquess of Reading, GCB, GCSI, GCIE, GCVO	20 October, 1926
Rt. Hon. Sir Eric Drummond, PC, KCMG, CB, subsequently Earl of Perth	11 October, 1933
Field Marshal The Rt. Hon. J.C. Smuts, PC, CH, FRS, KC	2 December, 1941
Field Marshal The Rt. Hon. The Viscount Montgomery of Alamein, KG, GCB, DSO	5 June, 1951
Her Majesty Queen Juliana of the Netherlands	7 May, 1954
Herbert Austen Hall, FRIBA	1 November, 1960
Sir Charles Wheeler, KCVO, CBE, PPRA, FRBS	10 January 1967
Mahathir bin Mohamad, Dato Seri Dr.	24 May 1989
His Royal Highness The Prince of Wales, KG, KT, GCB	22 March, 1995
The President for the time being of the Carpenters' Company of the City and County of Philadelphia	

APPENDIX III
LIST OF MASTERS AND WARDENS

Names in italic type are of Masters or Wardens who succeeded those who either died in office or did not serve a full term.

Until 1456 the Company was governed by Wardens.

Year of Election	Masters	Wardens
1437		Richard Punchon
		William Crofton
		Thomas Coventry
1438		John Blomvile
		John Tanner
		Richard Aas
1439		William Sefowl
		Thomas Sexteyn
		Thomas Iseleon
1440		John Salisbury
		William Goldington
		Richard Bird
1441		Thomas Smyth
		Thomas Warham
		Hugh Blyton
1442		John Wyse
		William Waleys
		John Silkwith
1443		John Stock
		Thomas Finch
		William Chacombe
1444		Robert Cowper
		Thomas Coventry
		William Bentham
1445		William Seryll
		Piers Sexteyn
		William Bowle
1446		Richard Punchon
		Thomas Ungyll
		Thomas Winchcombe
		William Carter
		Simon Chacombe
1447		William Sefowl
		Robert Knight
1448–1450		Not known

Year	Masters	Wardens
1451		John Silkwith
		John Punchon
		John Bentley
1452		John Wyse
		William Waleys
		John King
1453		Thomas Smyth
		Robert Churchman
		John Glover
1454		Thomas Coventry
		Thomas Ungyll
		Simon Chacombe
1455		John Wyse
		Thomas Ungyll
		Edward Stone
		Simon Chacombe
		Symon Clenchwarton
1456	Thomas Warham	Edward Stone
		Robert Knight
		William Brown
1457	Thomas Warham	Robert Knight
		William Brown
		Thomas Fenne
		William Robert
1458	Thomas Warham	John Punchon
		William Robert
		Thomas Fenne
		Walter Orchard
1459	Thomas Warham	John Punchon
		John King
		Walter Orchard
		John Brook
1460	Thomas Sexteyn	John King
		John Brook
		John Hankyn
		Harry Shadd
1461	Thomas Ungyll	Symon Chacombe
		William Ray

1462	Edmond Gravely	Thomas Wright		1479	John White	Andrew Essex
		John Punchon				Thomas Kydd
		William Warham				Robert Crosby
1463	Walter Orchard	Thomas Pert		1480	William Ray	Walter Constantine
		John Forster				William Chacombe
		William Carter				Robert Tyrell
1464	Walter Orchard	Robert Knight		1481	William Carter	Thomas Payne
		Thomas Pert				William Chacombe
		John Shornall				John Ruddock
1465	Robert Knight	John Shornall		1482	John White	Thomas Kydd
		John Scalton				Robert Crosby
		Christopher Baker				Walter Wilson
1466	Thomas Warham	John Haynes		1483	Christopher Baker	Stephen Scales
		Roger Lee				Christopher Kechyn
		John Sampson				John Davy
1467	Thomas Warham	Thomas Ungyll		1484	Christopher Baker	Stephen Scales
		John King				Christopher Kechyn
		William Carter				John Davy
1468	William Ray	Christopher Baker		1485	Thomas Kydd	Robert Crosby
		Thomas Payne				William Chacombe
		John Davy				Walter Wilson
1469	William Ray	Christopher Baker		1486	Thomas Kydd	Thomas Bynckes
		Thomas Pert				Symon Birlingham
		John White				John Pope
1470	Walter Orchard	Thomas Pert		1487	William Carter	Thomas Bynckes
		John Scalton				John Pope
		John White				Roger Ovenell
1471	Walter Orchard	John Scalton		1488	Robert Crosby	Christopher Kechyn
		Thomas Wilcox				Roger Ovenell
		Walter Constantine				William Barfoot
1472	Thomas Ungyll	John Sampson		1489	William Carter	Christopher Kechyn
		Thomas Wilcox				Thomas Bynckes
		Walter Constantine				William Barfoot
1473	Thomas Ungyll	John Sampson		1490	Thomas Kydd	Thomas Bynckes
		John Shornall				Walter Wilson
		Andrew Essex				Symon Birlingham
1474	William Carter	Christopher Baker		1491	Thomas Kydd	Walter Wilson
		Andrew Essex				John Pope
		Edmund Denys				John Manecke
1475	Thomas Pert	Christopher Baker		1492	Robert Crosby	John Manecke
		Thomas Kydd				Thomas Mauncy
		Robert Crosby				John Bird
1476	Thomas Pert	John White		1493	Robert Crosby	Thomas Mauncy
		Robert Crosby				Roger Ovenell
		Piers Baily				John Bird
1477	William Carter	John White		1494	William Chacombe	Roger Ovenell
		Piers Baily				John Davy
		John Berns				Thomas Smart
1478	Christopher Baker	Andrew Essex		1495	Thomas Bynckes	Thomas Smart
		Thomas Kydd				Richard Smyth
		John Berns				Thomas Clement

192

Year	Name	Officers
1496	Thomas Bynckes	Symon Birlingham
		Thomas Clement
		Thomas Wood
1497	John Pope	Roger Ovenell
		John Bird
		Thomas Wood
1498	John Pope	Roger Ovenell
		John Bird
		Richard Smyth
1499	Thomas Kydd	Thomas Mauncy
		Thomas Smart
		John Wyneates
1500	Thomas Bynckes	Thomas Smart
		John Wyneates
		Philip Cosyn
1501	Thomas Bynckes	Thomas Wood
		Philip Cosyn
		William Reynold
1502	John Pope	Thomas Wood
		John Bird
		William Reynold
1503	John Pope	John Davy
		John Bird
		Richard Smyth
1504	John Davy	Richard Smyth
		John Wyneates
		John Jackson
1505	John Bird	John Wyneates
		John Jackson
		William Cony
1506	Roger Ovenell	Thomas Wood
		William Cony
		Humphrey Cooke
1507	Richard Smyth	Philip Cosyn
		Humphrey Cooke
		William Prest
1508	Thomas Smart	John Wyneates
		John Jackson
		William Prest
1509	Thomas Wood	William Reynold
		William Cony
		John Dryver
1510	Thomas Bynckes	Humphrey Cooke
		(Not known)
		Robert Isodson
1511	John Wyneates	Philip Cosyn
		John Jackson
		Robert Isodson
1512	Philip Cosyn	John Jackson
		William Cony
		Thomas Hall
1513	Thomas Smart	William Cony
		Thomas Hall
		Christopher Brown
1514	Thomas Bynckes	John Jackson
		Christopher Brown
		Robert Short
1515–1518	Not known	
1519	Philip Cosyn	Humphrey Cooke
		Christopher Brown
		Richard Madock
1520–1532		Not known
1533	Stephen Punchon	
1534	James Nedam	
1535	James Nedam	
1536–1537		Not known
1538	Philip Cosyn	William Walker
		John Russell
		William Collins
1539	? William Walker	
1540	John King	John Russell
		John Arnold
		Thomas Gyttons
1541	John Russell	
1542	James Nedam	
1543	Richard Madock	Thomas Ellis
		Wolston Wynde
		William Collins
1544	William Walker	John Arnold, d.,
		Thomas Ellis
		John Tryll
		Richard Tylton
1545	Thomas Sheres	John Abbot
		William Lugg
		Francis Stelecrag
1546	Richard Amrys	Wolston Wynde
		Richard Tylton
		George King
1547	Thomas Ellis	John Tryll
		Francis Stelecrag
		Lawrence Bradshaw
1548	John Abbot	Richard Tylton
		Lawrence Bradshaw
		George Stalker
1549	John Russell	Lawrence Bradshaw
		George King
		Thomas Shereman
1550	Wolston Wynde	Richard Tylton
		George King
		William Mortimer

1551	Lawrence Bradshaw	John Tryll	
		Francis Stelecrag	
		Edward Whytwell	
1552	Richard Amrys	Francis Stelecrag	
		Thomas Shereman	
		Thomas Peacock	
1553	Thomas Ellis	George King,	
		William Mortimer	
		John Revell	
1554	John Tryll	William Mortimer	
		Thomas Peacock	
		William Wetherby	
1555	Lawrence Bradshaw	Thomas Peacock	
		John Revell	
		William Hamond	
1556	Wolston Wynde	John Revell	
		William Wetherby, d.,	
		Thomas Shereman	
		John Owtyng	
1557	John Russell	Thomas Peacock	
		William Hamond	
		Christopher	
		Riddlesden	
1558	John Abbot	William Mortimer	
		John Owtyng	
		William Ruddock	
1559	John Revell	John Owtyng	
		William Ruddock	
		William Buttermore	
1560	William Mortimer, d.,	Thomas Peacock	
	John Tryll	Christopher	
		Riddlesden	
		Richard More	
1561	John Tryll	William Ruddock	
		William Buttermore	
		Robert Quoyney	
1562	Lawrence Bradshaw	John Owtyng	
		Christopher	
		Riddlesden	
		Richard Bradshaw	
1563	Thomas Peacock	William Ruddock	
		Richard More	
		Henry Wreste	
1564	Thomas Peacock	Christopher	
		Riddlesden	
		Robert Quoyney	
		John Hawthorne	

1565	John Russell, d.,	Christopher	
	Thomas Peacock	Riddlesden	
		William Buttermore	
		John Wolmer	
1566	William Ruddock	Richard More	
		Henry Wreste	
		Richard Smart	
1567	Lawrence Bradshaw	Robert Quoyney	
		Henry Wreste	
		William Fisher	
1568	Christopher	William Buttermore	
	Riddlesden	John Hawthorne	
		Roger Reynolds	
1569	John Owtyng	Richard More	
		Richard Smart	
		John Dorrant	
1570	Thomas Peacock	Henry Wreste	
		William Fisher	
		William Royse	
1571	Lawrence Bradshaw	William Buttermore	
		John Hawthorne	
		John Lyffe	
1572	William Buttermore	Henry Wreste	
		Roger Reynolds	
		Anthony Bear	
1573	Thomas Peacock	John Hawthorn	
		John Lyffe	
		Lawrence Puddle	
1574	Lawrence Bradshaw	Henry Wreste	
		Thomas Harper	
		Christopher	
		Mortimer	
1575	Henry Wreste	Roger Reynolds	
		John Lyffe	
		Roger Shers	
1576	William Buttermore	John Lyffe	
		Thomas Townson	
		William Sylvester	
1577	Thomas Peacock	Thomas Harper	
		Anthony Bear	
		Thomas Watts	
1578	Thomas Harper	Anthony Bear	
		Lawrence Puddle	
		Robert Cawsey	
1579	Lawrence Bradshaw	Thomas Townson	
		Christopher	
		Mortimer	
		Thomas Hubie, d.,	
		John Bond	
1580	Lawrence Bradshaw	Thomas Townson	
	Thomas Peacock	Thomas Watts	
		Gregory Newland	

1581	Thomas Townson	Roger Reynolds	1595	William Allen	T. Haslowe

Year	Name	Officers	Year	Name	Officers
1581	Thomas Townson	Roger Reynolds	1595	William Allen	T. Haslowe
		Roger Shers			J. Worrall
		Gilbert Thomplinson			T. Payne
1582	Roger Reynolds	John Lyffe	1596	John Bland	J. Worrall
		William Sylvester			J. Toulson
		Robert Cawsey			J. Abbott
		William Taylor	1597	John Saxbye	R. Kinge
1583	John Lyffe	Roger Shers			J. Abbott,
		John Bond			P. Cobb
		John Bland	1598	Richard Smith	J. Ansell
1584	John Lyffe	Robert Cawsey			P. Streete
		Gregory Newland			T. Armatroyding
		Thomas Gittins	1599	Richard Kinge	G. Abbott
1585	Anthony Bear	John Bond			R. Wyatt
		Gilbert Thomplinson			R. Fysher
		Richard Smith	1600	John Worrall	P. Cobb
1586	Thomas Townson	Thomas Watts			R. Kerbye, d.,
		William Taylor			*R. Bushe*
		John Bland			J. Sharpe
		John Saxby	1601	John Ansell	R. Wyatt
1587	Roger Shers	Thomas Gittins			G. Isack
		John Bland			J. Petley
		Thomas Eaton	1602	Geoffrey Abbott	R. Bushe
		George Bowes			J. Hedlund
1588	John Bond	Gilbert Thomplinson			J. Reeve
		Richard Smith	1603	Peter Cobbe	R. Fysher
		Robert Maskall			J. Sharpe
1589	Thomas Watts	Richard Smith			R. Bentley
		John Saxby	1604	Richard Wyatt	J. Sharpe
		Thomas Hasilloe			J. Petley
1590	John Bland	Thomas Eaton			E. Harwyn
		John Evans	1605	Richard Wyatt	G. Isack
		William Allen			J. Reeve
1591	Richard Smith	John Saxby			W. Wilson
		George Bowes	1606	John Ansell	J. Petley
		Robert Maskall			R. Bentley
		Richard King			T. Fawcon
1592	Roger Shers	Robert Maskall	1607	John Sharpe	J. Hedlund
		John Evans			H. Harwyn
		William Allen			J. Joyse
		John Abbott			*J. Cockshutt*
1593	John Saxby	Willian Allen	1608	George Isack	J. Reeve
		Robert Ledyman, d.,			W. Wilson
		R. Kinge			E. Moore
		John Ansell	1609	John Petley	H. Harmyn
1594	William Allen	R. Kinge			T. Fawcon
		J. Ansell			W. Wheatley
		J. Fymby	1610	John Reeve	W. Wilson
					J. Brock
					P. Thornton

1611	John Reeve	T. Fawcon	
		E. Moore	
		W. Bonner	
1612	John Worrall	J. Cockfield	
		P. Thornton	
		T. Edmond	
1613	Thomas Fawcon	E. Moore	
		W. Bonner	
		T. Haydon	
1614	John Cockfield	J. Brock	
		T. Edmond	
		J. Daye	
1615	Edward Moore	P. Thornton	
		J. Daye	
		A. Messenger	
1616	Richard Wyatt	W. Bonner	
		W. Burnham	
		W. Kinge	
1617	Peter Cobb	T. Edmond	
		A. Messenger	
		T. Rushall	
1618	George Isack	J. Daye	
		W. King	
		J. Blinckhorne	
1619	John Petley	W. Wheatley	
		T. Rushall	
		E. Baker	
1620	William Bonner	A. Messenger	
		J. Bird, d.	
		J. Blinckhorne	
		T. Blemell	
1621	John Daye	William King, d.,	
		Thomas Rushall	
		E. Baker	
		J. Merryman	
1622	A. Messenger	E. Baker	
		J. Blemell	
		T. Fenor	
1623	Thomas Rushall	J. Blinkhorne	
		G. Arnold	
		W. Guye	
1624	Edward Baker	T. Blenell	
		J. Merryman	
		R. Norman	
1625	John Blinckhorne	J. Merryman	
		T. Fenor	
		T. Potham	
1626	Thomas Blenell	T. Fenor	
		W. Grey	
		R. Standish	
1627	John Merryman	G. Arnold	
		R. Smyth	
		A. Forman	
1628	Thomas Fenor	T. Potham	
		R. Standish	
		J. Prestwood	
1629	George Arnold	R. Smyth	
		A. Jarman	
		M. Bancks	
1630	Thomas Potham	R. Standish	
		J. Prestwood	
		H. Cordwyn	
1631	Ralph Smyth	A. Jarman	
		W. Freeman	
		J. Brewer	
1632	Richard Standish	J. Prestwood	
		M. Bancks	
		T. Birckhead	
1633	Anthony Jarman	W. Freeman	
		H. Cordwyn	
		J. Hilliard	
1634	John Prestwood	M. Bancks	
		J. Brewer	
		T. Brewer	
1635	William Freeman	H. Cordwyn	
		T. Birkett	
		J. Copland	
1636	Mathew Bancks	J. Brewer	
		J. Hilliard	
		T. Kinge	
1637	Henry Cordwyn	T. Birkett	
		J. Copland	
		R. Sanderson	
1638	John Brewer	J. Hilliard	
		T. Kinge	
		J. Hone	
1639	Thomas Birkett	J. Copland	
		R. Sanderson	
		P. Petley	
1640	John Hilliard	T. Kinge	
		J. Hone	
		R. Wade	
1641	John Copland	R. Sanderson	
		P. Petley	
		G. Andrews	
1642	Thomas Kinge	J. Hone	
		R. Wade	
		T. Hunt	
1643	Richard Sanderson	P. Petley	
		G. Andrews	
		S. Lynn	

1644	Peter Petley	R. Wade
		T. Hunt
		H. Standish
1645	Richard Wade	G. Andrews
		J. Berrey
		N. Guy
1646	George Andrews	J. Berrey, d.,
		S. Lynn
		H. Standish
		J. Read, sen.
1647	Samuel Lynn	H. Standish
		N. Guy
		T. Dorebarre
1648	Hugh Standish	N. Guy
		J. Read, sen.
		J. Joyse
1649	Nicholas Guy, d.,	J. Read, sen.,
	Thomas Birkett	T. Dorebarre
		T. Atkinson
1650	John Read, sen., d.,	T. Dorebarre
	John Brewer	W. Blunden
		R. Frith
1651	Thomas Dorebarre	W. Blunden
		J. Joyse
		W. Taylor
1652	William Blunden	J. Joyse
		T. Atkinson
		J. Wildgoose
1653	John Joyse	T. Atkinson
		R. Smith
		G. Gilpin
1654	Thomas Atkinson	N. Woodgate
		W. Taylor
		H. White
1655	Richard Sanderson	R. Frith
		T. Edmonds
		W. Pilling
1656	Nicholas Woodgate	W. Taylor
		J. Wildgoose
		J. Darvoll
1657	Richard Frith	T. Edmonds
		H. White
		J. Hawkins
1658	William Taylor	J. Wildgoose
		W. Pilling
		J. Pitt
1659	Thomas Edmonds	H. White
		J. Darvoll
		S. Berry
1660	John Wildgoose	W. Pilling
		J. Hawkins
		W. Ligborne

1661	Henry White	J. Darvoll
		J. Pitt
		T. Audley
1662	William Pilling	J. Hawkins
		S. Berry
		J. Seagood
1663	Joseph Darvoll	S. Berry
		W. Ligborne
		J. Figgins
1664	John Hawkins	W. Ligborne
		T. Audley
		L. Blanford
1665	Samuel Berry	T. Audley
		J. Seagood
		W. Wildgoose
1666	Thomas Audley	J. Seagood
		J. Figgins
		N. Fox
1667	John Seagood	J. Figgins
		J. Read
		J. King
1668	John Figgins	J. Read
		T. Wildgoose
		T. Charman
1669	John Read	T. Wildgoose
		N. Fox
		J. Marshall
1670	John Seagood	N. Fox
		J. King
		W. Pope
1671	Nathaniel Fox	J. King
		T. Charman
		E. Buckley
1672	John King	T. Charman
		J. Marshall
		S. Linn
1673	Thomas Charman	J. Marshall
		W. Pope
		W. Willis
1674	Joseph Marshall	W. Pope
		E. Buckley
		T. Brockwell
1675	William Pope	E. Buckley
		T. Brockwell
		A. Attwell
1676	Edward Buckley	T. Brockwell
		T. Attwell
		R. Jarman
1677	Edward Buckley	T. Attwell
		I. Knowles
		O. Lyde

1678	Thomas Attwell	I. Knowles B. Spencer B. Lipscombe	1695	John Warren	E. Withers W. Miller W. Biggs

Year	Name	Wardens	Year	Name	Wardens
1678	Thomas Attwell	I. Knowles B. Spencer B. Lipscombe	1695	John Warren	E. Withers W. Miller W. Biggs
1679	Israell Knowles	B. Spencer H. Wilkins P. Barber	1696	Edward Withers	T. Scott H. Joyce S. Knapp
1680	Thomas Brockwell	O. Lydd B. Lipscombe W. Young	1697	Thomas Scott	H. Joyce T. Buttamore T. Donning
1681	Ben. Spencer	H. Wilkins N. Kilby T. Cass	1698	Mathew Banckes	W. Champion J. Rawlins W. Attwell
1682	Henry Wilkins	N. Kilby H. Peirson R. Horton	1699	Henry Joyce	W. Mills S. Knapp R. Norman
1683	William Young	H. Peirson J. Deane C. Stanton	1700	William Champion	T. Buttamore J. Collyer J. Freeman
1684	Phillip Barber	J. Deane R. Horton J. Chitty	1701	Thomas Buttamore	J. Rawlins E. Rainsford W. Lawe
1685	Phillip Barber	J. Deane R. Horton J. Chitty	1702	Jasper Rawlins	Captain Knapp R. Norman E. Calcutt
1686	John Deane	T. Cass W. Gray W. Peacock	1703	Samuel Knapp	E. Rainsford J. Greene A. Arlidge
1687	Henry Peirson	R. Horton C. Stanton T. Buttamore	1704	John Foltrop	R. Norman J. Freeman A. Jordan
1688	Thomas Cass	W. Gray E. Clarke J. Warren	1705	Edward Rainsford	J. Greene T. Lockwood T. Dennett
1689	William Gray	T. Kentish J. Haynes S. Tovey	1706	Richard Norman	J. Freeman R. Calcutt G. Faulkner
1690	Robert Horton	E. Clarke J. Chitty W. Champion	1707	John Greene	T. Lockwood A. Arlidge J. Abbott
1691	Thomas Kentish	C. Stanton J. Warren T. Haynes	1708	John Freeman	R. Calcutt R. Andrews S. Rickward
1692	Edmond Clarke	J. Chitty S. Tovey T. Scott	1709	Thomas Lockwood	A. Arlidge T. Howes T. Bowcher
1693	Charly Stanton	J. Warren W. Champion H. Joyce	1710	Robert Calcutt	R. Andrews G. Faulkner R. Hedges
1694	Joseph Chitty	H. Pottinger E. Withers J. Rawlins	1711	Sir John Cass	A. Jordan S. Rickward T. Arnold

198

1712	Abraham Arlidge	T. Dennett		1729	Thomas Willmore	J. Spencer
		J Brydon				E. Bowcher
		P. Rogerson				Capt. B. Osgood
1713	Robert Andrews	G. Faulkner		1730	Joseph Spencer	E. Bowcher
		J. Chamberlen				M. Deane
		H. Stevenson				B. Barlow
1714	Thomas Dennett	S. Rickward		1731	Edward Bowcher	M. Deane
		J. Moore				J. Meard
		J. Walker				J. Williams
1715	George Faulkner	J. Chamberlen		1732	Matthew Deane	R. Norman
		J. Brittaine				J. Prater
		J. Headland				J. Russell
1716	Samuel Rickward	J. Moore		1733	Richard Norman	J. James
		T. Bowcher				J. Chitty
		T. Dawson				T. Haddon
1717	John Chamberlen	J. Brittaine d.,		1734	John James	J. Meard
		T. Bowcher				B. Osgood
		T. Arnold				N. Ward
		T. Arlidge		1735	John Meard	S. Burgin
1718	James Grove	T. Arnold				B. Barlow
		P. Rogers				N. Benbridge
		E. Cordwell		1736	Samuel Burgin	J. Prater
1719	John Moore	P. Rogerson				Col. J. Williams
		W. Abby				S. Horton
		S. Boughton		1737	John Prater	J. Chitty, d.,
1720	Thomas Bowcher	W. Abby				*Maj. B. Osgood*
		J. Headland				T. Haddon
		T. Boddell				R. Plimpton
1721	William Abby	J. Headland		1738	Maj B. Osgood	Col. J. Williams
		T. Dawson				N. Ward
		E. Oliver				S. Hawkins
1722	John Headland	T. Dawson		1739	Col J. Williams	T. Haddon
		W. Ogborne				N. Benbridge
		W. Hazard				J. Brookes
1723	Thomas Dawson	W. Ogborne		1740	Thomas Haddon	N. Ward
		J. Edden				T. Ripley
		R. Grasswell				T. Keene
1724	William Ogborne	J. Edden		1741	Nat. Ward, d.,	T. Ripley
		T. Arlidge			*Nat. Benbridge*	G. Newland
		J. Buckland				J. Bush
1725	John Edden	T. Arlidge		1742	Thos. Ripley	G. Newland
		S. Boughton				R. Plimpton
		W. Smith				J. Cordwell
1726	Sir William Ogborne	S. Boughton		1743	George Newland	R. Plimpton
		T. Boddell				S. Hawkins
		E. Littlefoild				W. Champion
1727	Samual Boughton	T. Boddell		1744	Robert Plimpton	S. Hawkins
		T. Willmore				J. Bush
		T. Davis				J. Stedman
1728	Thomas Boddell	T. Willmore		1745	Samuel Hawkins	J. Cordwell
		J. Spencer				W. Champion
		J. Brittan				B. Sparruck

1746	John Cordwell	W. Champion	
		J. Stedman	
		A. Mason	
1747	W. Champion, d.,	James Stedman	
	J. Stedman	B. Sparruck	
		R. Boulton	
		A. Natt	
1748	Barth. Sparruck	R. Boulton	
		T. Moore	
		Col. J. Steere	
1749	Richard Boulton	T. Moore	
		R. Langton	
		H. Denning	
1750	Thomas Moore	R. Langton	
		J. Lamborne	
		J. Dutton	
1751	Richard Langton	J. Lamborne	
		J. Price	
		W. Robinson	
1752	James Lamborne	J. Price	
		A. Russell	
		J. Lawrence	
1753	John Price	A. Russell	
		R. Sparkes	
		T. Bates	
1754	Augustus Russell	R. Sparkes	
		T. Funge	
		E. Johnson	
1755	Richard Sparkes	T. Funge	
		T. Radcliffe	
		A. Pullen	
1756	Thomas Funge	T. Radcliffe	
		A. Mason	
		R. Plimpton	
1757	Thomas Radcliffe	A. Mason	
		W. Reynolds	
		W. Alingham	
1758	Anthony Mason	W. Reynolds	
		S. Chitty	
		R. Jupp	
1759	William Reynolds	S. Chitty	
		W. Robinson	
		J. Holden	
1760	Samuel Chitty	W. Robinson	
		R. Mount	
		S. Oliver	
1761	William Robinson	R. Mount	
		E. Johnson, d.,	
		I. Ware	
		J. Spencer	
1762	Richard Mount	I. Ware	
		A. Pullen	
		R. Day	
1763	Isaac Ware	A. Pullen	
		W. Bigg	
		J. Read	
1764	Abraham Pullen	W. Bigg	
		R. Plimpton	
		W. Witcher	
1765	William Bigg	R. Plimpton	
		W. Allingham, d.,	
		W. Dermer	
		A. Atterbury	
1766	Robert Plimpton	W. Dermer	
		R. Jupp	
		G. Bellas	
1767	William Dermer	R. Jupp	
		J. Biddlecom	
		W. Jones	
1768	Richard Jupp	J. Biddlecom	
		S. Oliver	
		J. B. Turner	
1769	Joseph Biddlecom	S. Oliver	
		J. Spencer	
		T. Whittaker	
1770	Sanders Oliver	J. Read	
		W. Witcher	
		T. Steedman	
1771	John Read	W. Witcher, d.,	
		A. Atterbury	
		A. Atterbury	
		G. Ballas	
		R. Withers	
1772	Abraham Atterbury	G. Ballas	
		W. Jones	
		R. Fawson	
1773	William Jones	J. B. Turner	
		T. Whittaker	
		M. Fairless, d.,	
		T. Jernegan	
1774	John B. Turner	T. Whittaker	
		T. Steedman	
		J. Payne	
1775	Thomas Whittaker, d.,	T. Steedman	
	J. Biddlecom	R. Withers	
		J. Buckland	
1776	Thomas Steedman	T. Withers	
		T. Jernegan, d.,	
		S. Hanning	
		C. Mills	

Year	Name	Assistants
1777	Robert Withers	S. Hanning
		R. Jupp, jnr.
		E. Gibbs
1778	Samuel Hanning	R. Jupp, jnr.
		J. Taine
		T. Russell
1779	Richard Jupp	J. Taine
		J. Buckland
		T. Hudson
1780	John Taine	J. Buckland
		T. Flight
		J. Johnson
1781	James Buckland	W. Dermer
		John Jordan
		W. Jupp
1782	Thomas Flight	J. Jordan
		C. Mills
		W. Palmer
1783	John Jordan	C. Mills
		E. Gibbs
		T. Edgerton
1784	Charles Mills	E. Gibbs
		T. Russell
		W. Higgins
1785	Edward Gibbs	T. Russell
		T. Hudson
		S. Parker
1786	Thomas Russell	T. Hudson
		P. Thompson
		J. Webb
1787	Thomas Hudson	P. Thompson
		J. Johnson
		J. Brayne
1788	Peter Thompson	J. Johnson
		T. Edgerton
		W. Lawrence
1789	Joel Johnson	T. Edgerton
		W. Higgins
		T. Mutter
1790	Thomas Edgerton	W. Higgins
		G. Shakespear
		J. Suter
1791	William Higgins	W. Lawrence
		W. Staines
		E. Wells
1792	William Lawrence	Ald. W. Staines
		R. Woodyer
		W. Arrow
1793	Ald. William Staines	R. Woodyer
		J. Suter
		J. Tappen
1794	Richard Woodyer	J. Suter
		T. Hardy
		J. Yallowley
1795	John Suter	T. Russell
		R. Hunt
		W. Ayscough
1796	James Wheeler	W. Arrow
		P. Dunkley
		J. Rosher
1797	William Arrow	P. Dunkley
		J. Yallowley
		N. Wright
1798	Peter Dunkley, d.,	J. Yallowley
	Richard Jupp, d.,	W. Ayscough
	Sir William Staines	T. Taylor
1799	Joseph Yallowley	J. Sutter
		N. Wright
		C. Iliffe
1800	Nathaniel Wright	T. Taylor
		R. Golden
		J. Golden
1801	Thomas Taylor	R. Golden
		C. Iliffe
		T. Flight
1802	Robert Golden	C. Iliffe, d.,
		Sir W. Staines
		J. Golden
		J. Vickerman
1803	John Golden	P. Norris
		T. W. Preston
		J. Taylor
1804	Thomas W. Preston	W. Smith
		J. Champion
		T. Russell
1805	William Smith	J. Champion
		W. Norris
		S. Cosser
1806	William Norris	B. Flight
		T. Flight
		J. Champion
1807	Banister Flight	T. Flight
		J. Vickerman
		R. Porter
1808	Thomas Flight	J. Vickerman
		J. Spencer
		W. Hawksworth
1809	John Vickerman	J. Spencer
		J. Taylor
		A. Creaton

1810	John Spencer	J. Taylor
		T. Russell
		D. Westbrook
1811	John Taylor	T. Russell
		D. Schofield
		J. F. Buhl
1812	Thomas Russell	J. Schofield
		R. Porter
		W. Lumley
1813	John Schofield	R. Porter
		A. Creaton
		R. Field
1814	Robert Porter	A. Creaton
		D. Westbrook
		J. Wilkinson
1815	Albon Creaton	D. Westbrook
		J. F. Buhl
		J. Flight
1816	David Westbrook	J. F. Buhl
		W. Lumley
		E. Trimmer
1817	John F. Buhl	W. Lumley
		R. Field
		J. Rosher
1818	William Lumley	R. Field
		J. Wilkinson
		R. Ashton
1819	Richard Field	J. Wilkinson
		J. Flight
		T. Lett
1820	John Wilkinson	J. Flight
		E. Trimmer
		J. Bury
1821	Joseph Flight	E. Trimmer
		J. Rosher
		H. Hurle
1822	Edward Trimmer	J. Rosher
		R. Ashton
		T. Reid
1823	Jeremiah Rosher	R. Ashton
		T. Lett
		J. Simmons
1824	Robert Ashton	T. Lett
		J. Bury, d.,
		J. Yallowley, jnr.
1825	Thomas Lett	J. E. Cook
		T. Long, d.,
		W. Woodyer
1826	John E. Cook	H. Hurle
		J. Yallowley, jnr.
		J. Richardson d.,
		P. J. Harrison

1827	Henry Hurle	J. Yallowley, jnr.
		W. Woodyer
		W. Jupp
1828	Joseph Yallowley, d.,	W. Woodyer
	Banister Flight	P. J. Harrison
		C. Maxey
1829	William Woodyer	P. J. Harrison
		W. Jupp
		R. Hillcock
1830	Parker J. Harrison	W. Jupp
		C. Maxey
		W. Payne
1831	William Jupp	C. Maxey
		R. Hillcock
		M. Warton
1832	Charles Maxey	R. Hillcock
		W. Payne
		W. P. Ulgate
1833	Mat. Warton	W. P. Ulgate
		J. Taylor
		J. Kershaw
1834	W. Phil. Ulgate	J. Taylor
		J. Kershaw
		T. W. Snelson
1835	John Kershaw	T. W. Snelson
		T. Wright
		J. Watts
1836	Thomas W. Snelson	T. Wright
		J. Watts
		T. Long
1837	Thomas Flight	J. Watts
		T. Long
		W. F. Pocock
1838	John Wilkinson	T. Long
		W. F. Pocock
		E. Staple
1839	Thomas Long	W. F. Pocock
		E. Staple
		T. Ayscough
1840	William F. Pocock	E. Staple
		T. Ayscough
		T. Flight, jnr.
1841	Edward Staple	T. Ayscough
		T. Flight, jnr.
		W. Churchill
1842	Thomas Ayscough	J. Flight, jnr.
		W. Churchill
		J. Harvey
1843	Thomas Flight, jnr.	W. Churchill
		J. Harvey
		J. Fleetwood

1844	William Churchill	J. Harvey	1861	George Faith	T. A. Brew

Year	Name	Officers	Year	Name	Officers
1844	William Churchill	J. Harvey	1861	George Faith	T. A. Brew
		J. Fleetwood			J. Archer, d.,
		T. W. Browne			R. Warton
1845	Thomas Long	J. Fleetwood			J. C. Smith
		T. W. Browne	1862	Thomas A. Brew	J. C. Smith, d.,
		M. Savory			*W. Biggerstaff*
1846	John Fleetwood	T. W. Browne			R. Warton
		M. Savory			R. J. Stuckey
		J. Foot	1863	Robert Warton	R. J. Stuckey
1847	R. W. Kennard	J. Foot			W. Biggerstaff
		J. Taylor			J. Blyth
		J. Browne	1864	Robert J. Stuckey	W. Biggerstaff
1848	Ald William Lawrence, Snr.	J. Taylor			J. Blyth
		J. Browne			G. Rosher
		R. S. Jupp	1865	William Biggerstaff	John Blyth
1849	John Foot	J. Browne			W. Rosher
		R. S. Jupp			E. Rosher
		T. Martyr	1866	John Blyth	W. Rosher
1850	James Browne	R. S. Jupp			E. Rosher
		T. Martyr			J. M. Morris
		C. Rosher	1867	Edward Rosher	J. M. Morris
1851	Richard Samuel Jupp	T. Martyr			G. Hensman
		C. Rosher			W. H. Warton
		J. Hurst	1868	Edward Ward	G. Hensman
1852	Charles Rosher	J. Hurst			W. H. Warton
		J. Allen			W. Robertson
		H. Rosher	1869	George Hensman	W. H. Warton
1853	William Churchill	J. B. Rosher			W. Robertson
		H. Rosher			B. Jacob
		R. Waylat	1870	William H. Warton	W. Robertson
1854	Henry Rosher	J. Allen			B. Jacob
		R. Waylat			J. T. Preston
		J. F. Bury	1871	William Robertson	B. Jacob
1855	James F. Bury	T. Lett			J. T. Preston
		J. Atkinson			R. S. Faulconer
		E. Ward	1872	Benjamin Jacob	J. T. Preston
1856	Ald William Lawrence, Jnr.	E. Ward			R. S. Faulconer
		F. W. E. Jowers			S. W. Preston
		T. G. Smith	1873	Joseph T. Preston	R. S. Faulconer
1857	Thomas Lett	F. W. E. Jowers			S. W. Preston
		T. G. Smith			J. Foot
		T. Finden	1874	Robert S. Faulconer	S. W. Preston
1858	Edward Ward	T. G. Smith			J. Foot
		T. Finden			G. H. Ellis, d.,
		G. Faith			*T. D. D. Robertson*
1859	Francis W. E. Jowers	T. Finden	1875	Stanton W. Preston	J. Foot
		G. Faith			T. D. D. Robertson
		T. A. Brew			R. Grace
1860	Thomas G. Smith, d.,	G. Faith	1876	John Foot	T. D. D. Robertson
	Thomas Finden, d.,	T. A. Brew			R. Grace
	James C. Lawrence	J. Archer			J. P. Long

Year	Master	Wardens
1877	Thomas D. D. Robertson	R. Grace / J. P. Long / S. Gibbins
1878	Richard Grace	J. P. Long / S. Gibbins / J. W. Browne
1879	J. Pollock Long	S. Gibbins / J. E. Cook / A. Preston
1880	Samuel Gibbins	J. E. Cook / A. Preston / T. W. Long
1881	Alfred Preston	T. W. Long / W. W. Pocock / F. P. Keysell
1882	Thomas W. Long	W. W. Pocock / F. P. Keysell / F. Rosher
1883	William W. Pocock	G. S. Nottage / F. Rosher / H. J. Kennard
1884	George S. Nottage, d., *John E. Cook*	F. Rosher / H. J. Kennard / H. C. Smith
1885	Francis P. Keysell	H. J. Kennard / H. C. Smith / A. Rosher
1886	Howard J. Kennard	H. C. Smith / A. Rosher / B. Fletcher
1887	H. Clifford Smith	A. Rosher / B. Fletcher / W. Robertson
1888	Alfred Rosher	B. Fletcher / W. Robertson / T. Robertson
1889	Banister Fletcher	W. Robertson / T. Robertson / B. J. Jacob
1890	Jasper W. Browne	T. Robertson / B. J. Jacob / W. Faith
1891	Thomas Robertson	B. J. Jacob / W. Faith / N. Smith
1892	Benjamin J. Jacob	W. Faith / N. Smith / Edward Smith
1893	Henry Harben	N. Smith / E. Smith / J. Jacob
1894	Nieman Smith	E. Smith / J. Jacob / J. H. Gibbins
1895	Edward Smith	J. Jacob / J. H. Gibbins / J. C. Preston
1896	Jesse Jacob	J. H. Gibbins / J. C. Preston / A. Jacob
1897	Joseph H. Gibbins	J. C. Preston / A. Jacob / T. R. Smith
1898	J. Classon Preston	A. Jacob / T. R. Smith / J. Willson
1899	Arthur Jacob	T. R. Smith / J. Willson / W. Smith
1900	Prof T. Roger Smith	J. Willson / W. Smith / P. Preston
1901	John Willson	W. Smith / P. Preston / E. Field
1902	Walter Smith	P. Preston / E. Field / F. A. Crisp
1903	Percy Preston	E. Field / F. A. Crisp / G. R. B. Drummond / *A. B. Hammond*
1904	Frederick A. Crisp	G. R. B. Drummond / A. B. Hammond / W. Robertson
1905	Capt George R. B. Drummond, MVO, RN	A. B. Hammond / W. Robertson / A. C. Preston
1906	A. Baily Hammond / *William Robertson*	W. Robertson / A. C. Preston / M. H. Pocock / *C. B. Bartlett*
1907	Lt Col Alfred C. Preston	M. H. Pocock / C. B. Bartlett / R. Cobay
1908	Maurice H. Pocock	C. B. Bartlett / R. Cobay / W. R. Cobay
1909	Revd Charles. B. Bartlett	W. R. Cobay / W. R. Cobay / S. W. Morris

1910	Robert Cobay	W. R. Cobay
		S. W. Morris
		J. Hooke
1911	William R. Cobay	S. W. Morris
		J. Hooke
		F. Preston
1912	Spencer W. Morris	J. Hooke
		F. Preston
		M. Smith
		W. W. Pullein
1913	John Hooke	M. Smith
		W. W. Pullein
		F. G. Fitch
1914	Minden Smith	W. W. Pullein
		F. G. Fitch
		F. Sutton
1915	Walter W. Pullein	F. G. Fitch
		F. Sutton
		E. T. Pullein
1916	Frederic G. Fitch	F. Sutton
		E. T. Pullein
		W. T. Birts
1917	Frederic Sutton	E. T. Pullein
		W. T. Birts
		W. J. Minn
1918	Ernest T. Pullein	W. T. Birts
		W. J. Minn
		E. S. Preston
1919	William T. Birts	W. J. Minn
		E. S. Preston
		C. Denny
1920	William J. Minn	E. S. Preston
		C. Denny
		W. H. Evans
1921	Ernest S. Preston	C. Denny
		W. H. Evans
		J. H. Browne
1922	Charles Denny	W. H. Evans
		J. H. Browne
		F. Barnes
1923	William H. Evans	J. H. Browne
		F. Barnes
		D. W. Stable
1924	J. Harris Browne	F. Barnes
		D. W. Stable
		H. W. Preston
1925	D. Wintringham Stable	H. W. Preston
		F. A. Smith
		W. Jacob
1926	H. Westbury Preston	F. A. Smith
		W. Jacob
		G. D. Minn

1927	F. Adams Smith	W. Jacob
		G. D. Minn
		C. A. Robertson
1928	Walter Jacob	G. D. Minn
		C. A. Robertson
		L. Jacob
1929	Gayford D. Minn	C. A. Robertson
		L. Jacob
		R. E. Smith
1930	Louis Jacob	R. E. Smith
		F. O. Keysell
		F. S. Punnett
		R. H. Smith
1931	Francis O. Keysell	J. R. Lancaster
		H. C. Preston
		F. M. Smith
1932	J. Roy Lancaster	H. C. Preston
		F. M. Smith
		A. Roberts
1933	Herbert C. Preston	F. M. Smith
		A. Roberts
		F. S. Sutton
1934	F. Montague Smith	A. Roberts
		F. S. Sutton
		F. Hugh Smith
1935	J. Hutton Freeman	F. S. Sutton
		F. Hugh Smith
		G. Smith
1936	Sir Banister F. Fletcher	F. Hugh Smith
		G. Smith
		A. E. Robertson
1937	F. Hugh Smith	G. Smith
		A. E. Robertson
		R. Jacob
1938	Gregory Smith	A. E. Robertson
		R. Jacob
		A. E. Bernays
1939	Arthur E. Robertson	R. Jacob
		A. E. Bernays
		W. T. W. Birts
1940	Reginald Jacob	A. E. Bernays
		W. T. W. Birts
		H. W. Morris
1941	Albert E. Bernays	W. T. W. Birts
		H. W. Morris
		R. H. Smith
1942	Albert E. Bernays	H. W. Morris
		R. H. Smith
		H. U. Fletcher
1943	Humphrey W. Morris	H. U. Fletcher
		J. G. King
		A. B. Rosher

1944	Capt Hugh U. Fletcher, RN	J. G. King A. B. Rosher G. M. Hamilton	1960	Bernard J. Nicholson, MBE	G. L. F. Grece Ald Sir Edmund V. M. Stockdale
1945	J. Godwin King CBE	A. B. Rosher G. M. Hamilton A. J. M. Binny	1961	G. Lewis F. Grece	F. Halliburton Smith F. Halliburton Smith
1946	Grahame M. Hamilton	A. J. M. Binny F. R. Freeman A. Faith			D. L. Jacob H. F. Groves
1947	Lt Col Alan J.M. Binny	F. R. Freeman A. Faith Ald Sir Leslie Boyce	1962	Frank Haliburton Smith	D. L. Jacob H. F. Groves H. M. Mace
1948	F. Roy Freeman	A. Faith Ald Sir Leslie Boyce R. C. Barnes	1963	Douglas L. Jacob	H. F. Groves H. M. Mace K. B. Jacob
1949	Aubrey Faith	R. C. Barnes J. B. Rosher Ald C. L. Ackroyd	1964	H. Frank Groves	H. M. Mace K. B. Jacob F. Morton-Smith
1950	R. Cecil Barnes	J. B. Rosher Ald C. L. Ackroyd K. M. Roberts	1965	Herbert M. Mace	K. B. Jacob F. Morton-Smith F. C. Braby
1951	John B. Rosher, DSO, MC	Ald C. L. Ackroyd K. M. Roberts W. W. Dove	1966	Kenneth B. Jacob	F. Morton-Smith F. C. Braby P. B. C. Watson
1952	Ald Cuthbert L. Ackroyd	K. M. Roberts W. W. Dove G. W. Ridley	1967	Frederick Morton-Smith	F. C. Braby P. B. C. Watson V. J. G. Stavridi
1953	Kenneth M. Roberts	W. W. Dove G. W. Ridley A. M. D. Robertson	1968	Frederick C. Braby, CBE, MC	P. B. C. Watson V. J. G. Stavridi G. C. Evelegh
1954	Lt Col William W. Dove	G. W. Ridley A. M. D. Robertson A. W. Preston	1969	Peter B.C. Watson	Sir Edmund V. M. Stockdale V. J. G. Stavridi G. C. Evelegh
1955	Geoffrey W. Ridley, CBE	A. M. D. Robertson A. W. Preston H. M. Merriman	1970	Sir Edmund V.M. Stockdale Bt	V. J. G. Stavridi G. C. Evelegh O. Lancaster
1956	Albert M. D. Robertson, OBE	A. W. Preston H. M. Merriman R. W. Gordon Dill	1971	Valieri J.G. Stavridi	G. C. Evelegh O. Lancaster D. R. Stuckey
1957	Cdr Alan W. Preston RN	H. M. Merriman R. W. Gordon Dill B. J. Nicholson	1972	Brig George C. Evelegh, CBE	O. Lancaster D. R. Stuckey J. A. Moody
1958	Hugh M. Merriman	R. W. Gordon Dill B. J. Nicholson G. L. F. Grece	1973	Osbert Lancaster, CBE	D. R. Stuckey J. A. Moody C. E. Keysell
1959	Maj Richard W. Gordon Dill, MC	B. J. Nicholson G. L. F. Grece Ald Sir Edmund V. M. Stockdale	1974	Derek R. Stuckey	J. A. Moody C. E. Keysell J. G. Jacob
			1975	Dr J. Arthur Moody, OBE	C. E. Keysell J. G. Jacob D. W. M. Eggleton

1976	Christopher E. Keysell, MBE	J. G. Jacob D. W. M. Eggleton H. C. Payne	1992	Douglas V.J. Galbraith	V. F. Browne K. G. Hamon M. R. Francis
1977	John G. Jacob	D. W. M. Eggleton H. C. Payne R. L. Woolley	1993	Victor F. Browne	K. G. Hamon M. R. Francis F. D. Hornsby
1978	Douglas W.M. Eggleton	H. C. Payne R. L. Woolley A. R. Robertson	1994	Capt Kenneth G. Hamon, RN	M. R. Francis F. D. Hornsby H. M. Neal
1979	Henry C. Payne	R. L. Woolley A. R. Robertson P. Braby	1995	Malcolm R. Francis	F. D. Hornsby H. M. Neal C. W. Preston
1980	Dr Robert L. Woolley	A. R. Robertson P. Braby R. B. A. Smith			
1981	Arthur R. Robertson	P. Braby R. B. A. Smith F. E. Newman			
1982	Revd Peter Braby	R. B. A. Smith F. E. Newman R. P. G. Dill			
1983	Ralph B.A. Smith	F. E. Newman, MBE R. P. G. Dill A. T. C. Binny			
1984	Maj Richard P. G. Dill	A. T. C. Binny H. J. Osborne W. F. Felton			
1985	A. Trevor C. Binny	H. J. Osborne W. F. Felton J. G. Ridley			
1986	H. John Osborne	W. F. Felton J. G. Ridley P. C. Osborne			
1987	Dr William F. Felton	J. G. Ridley P. C. Osborne D. H. Marriott			
1988	Jasper G. Ridley	P. C. Osborne D. H. Marriott d., *R. B. A. Smith* H. M. F. Barnes			
1989	Peter C. Osborne	W. F. Felton H. M. F. Barnes D. V. J. Galbraith			
1990	Jasper G. Ridley	H. M. F. Barnes D. V. J. Galbraith V. F. Browne			
1991	Hugh M. F. Barnes-Yallowley	D. V. J. Galbraith V. F. Browne K. G. Hamon			

Seventeenth century Dutch ceramic tile depicting a carpenter at work

APPENDIX IV
LIST OF CLERKS AND BEADLES

(Until 1573 Clerks and Beadles
are not clearly distinguished)

Date of
Appointment

1438–(1448)	William Mendham
1452–(1463)	'Thomas'
1482	'Hugh'
1483	John Braban (Clerk)
1483	Thomas Batman
1487	Banaster
1489	Robert Pert
1490	John Forster (Clerk)
1500	Harry Bagott
1510	Thomas Cutler
1515	'Wayter' (March–June)
1515	George Maxwell
1541	Bartholemew Sampson
1543	Henry Townson
1544	Richard Burdon
1561	Richard Sowthye
1563	Robert Armstrong
1566	John FitzJohn

CLERKS

1573	John FitzJohn
1595	Thomas Bowes
1602	Thomas Tanner
1636	Peter Hodgson
1642	Andrew Baker
1652	Roger Goodday
1674	Thomas Ley
1683	John Smalley
1685	James Stone
1709	Joseph Knapp
1712	Richard Hutton
1723	John Michell
1728	Nathaniel Poole
1750	Robert Prater

1757	Thomas Wall
1778	Hawkins Wall
1798	Richard Webb Jupp
1852	Edward Basil Jupp
1878	Stanton William Preston
1902	Joseph Hutton Freeman
1935	Henry Carl Osborne, MC
1960	Captain George Baillie Barstow, RN
1977	Captain Kenneth George Hamon, RN
1992	Major General Paul Timothy Stevenson, OBE

BEADLES

1608	John Adams
1629	Samuel Taleford
1632	John Walter
1657	Thomas Heake
1665	Joseph Hutchinson
1687	Samuel Hughes
1699	Edmund Clarke
1703	John Manuell
1731	Thomas Barnard
1738	Benjamin Barlow
1739	Richard Danes
1741	Peter Vestille
1767	Richard Young
1771	William Bigg
1810	William Lewis
1843	Thomas Standage
1856	Thomas Carter
1895	Frank Carter
1928	Frederick William Powell
1964	William Henry Hopkins
1976	John Henry Palfery-Smith
1987	Lieutenant Commander Brian Frank Dutton, DSO, QGM, RN

BIBLIOGRAPHY
MANUSCRIPT SOURCES

Carpenters' Company MSS.:

Bernard G. Pocock Correspondence
Book of Ordinances, 1333
Building Crafts Training School Prospectus 1954–55
Card Index of Liverymen and Freemen
"Ceremonial Re-opening of the Carpenters' Hall by
    The Rt. Hon. The Lord Mayor Alderman Sir Edmund Stockdale, Wednesday, 4th
    May 1960."
Charters 1477–1690
Committee Minute Books
Court Minute Books 1533–1994
Dinner Bills 1786–87
Court Minute Book (Rough Draft) 1825–82
Dinner Menus 1913–94
"The Dutch Royal Banquet in Carpenters' Hall, 13 April 1972"
Livery Lists 1746–1876, 1883–1921, 1946–93
Miscellaneous Records
Newspaper Cuttings Book
"Order of Service for the Reconsecration of the Guild Church of All Hallows on the
    Wall by Robert Lord Bishop of London at a Solemn Eucharist on 10th July 1962 at
    11.00 a.m."
"Ordinances: Abstract made by their Solicitor Mr. George Hensman, 25 College Hill,
    London, in 1885."
Photograph Album
"Queen Juliana": Presentation of the Honorary Freedom to Queen Juliana on Friday
    7 May 1954
"Sexcentenary Dinner, Wednesday 22nd March 1933"
Wardens Accounts 1647–70.

Grocers' Company MSS.:

Court Minute Books 1846–1924
Invitation Book 1925–39

PRINTED WORKS

ALFORD, B. W. E. and BARKER, T. C., *A History of the Carpenters' Company* (London, 1968)

BEAVAN, Revd. A. B., *The Aldermen of the City of London* (London, 1908–13)

BLAKESLEY, G. H., *London Companies Commission; A Comment on the Majority Report* (London, 1885)

"The 'Boke' of the Ordinances of the Brotherhood of Carpenters of London, 7 Edward III (1333)", See Preston, *The Worshipful Company of Carpenters*

BRENTANO, L., "On the History and Development of Gilds" (in *English Gilds* (ed. J. Toulmin Smith) (London, 1870)

CARPENTER, W., *The Corporation of London as it is, and as it should be* (London, 1847)

The Citizen (London, 1881)

City Press (London, 1880)

CLODE, C. M., *The Early History of the Guild of Merchant Taylors* (London, 1888)

Country Life (London, 1964)

Debate in the House of Commons, 10th April 1877 (London, 1877)

Dictionary of National Biography (Oxford, 1921–37 edn.)

DONOUGHUE, B. and JONES, G. W., *Herbert Morrison, Portrait of a Politician* (London, 1973)

DOOLITTLE, I. G., *The City of London and its Livery Companies* (Dorchester, Dorset, 1982)

The Dutch Church (London, 1986)

FIRTH, J. F. B., *Municipal London* (London, 1876)

—— *Reform of London Government and of City Guilds* (London, 1888)

FLETCHER, Banister, *The City and Guilds of London: Lecture at Toynbee Hall, 25 November 1889* (London, no date)

GROSS, C., *The Gild Merchant* (Oxford, 1890)

HALL, J., *The Works of Joseph Hall, DD, Successively Bishop of Exeter and Norwich* (Oxford, 1837–9)

HANCOCK, W. K., *Smuts* (Cambridge, 1962–8)

Hansard (*Official Parliamentary Report*) (London, 1876–1977)

HARVEY, J., *English Medieval Architects* (London, 1954)

HERBERT, W., *The History of the Twelve Great Livery Companies of London* (London, 1836; New York, 1968)

The History and Activities of the Worshipful Company of Carpenters (script of video) (London, 1994)

History of a Family: Barnes (no place, 1967–8)

HOPE, Valerie, *My Lord Mayor* (London, 1989)

—— *The Worshipful Company of Weavers of the City of London* (London, 1994)

HUNTING, Penelope, *A History of the Drapers' Company* (London, 1989)

HYDE, H. Montgomery, *Judge Jeffreys* (London, 1940)

INGRAM, T. A., "Livery Companies" (in *Encyclopaedia Britannica*, 11th edn.) (London, 1910)

JEFFERY, Sally, "John James and Carpenters Buildings" (in *Transactions of the London and Middlesex Archaeological Society*, xxxiv. (187–94) (London, 1983)

Journals of Congress: containing their Proceedings from 5 September 1774 to 1 January 1776 (Philadelphia, 1800)

JUPP, Edward Basil, *An Historical Account of the Worshipful Company of Carpenters of the City of London* (2nd edn. with a Supplement by William Willmer Pocock) (London, 1887)

KIPLING, Rudyard, *Rudyard Kipling's Verse* (London, 1943)

KIRBY, J. W., "Building Work at Placentia 1543–1544" (in *Transactions of the Greenwich and Lewisham Antiquarian Society*, iv. 285–307) (London, 1954)

L.B.S., *The City Livery Companies and their Corporate Property* (London, 1885)

A Letter from Mercvrivs Civicvs to Mercurius Rusticus: Or, Londons Confession but not Repentance. Shewing, That the beginning and the obstinate pursuance of the accursed horrid Rebellion is principally to be ascribed to that Rebellious City (Oxford ?, 1643)

Letters and Papers (Foreign and Domestic) of the Reign of King Henry VIII (ed. J. Brewer and J. Gairdner) (London, 1862–1920)

LEVIN, Jennifer, *The Charter Controversy in the City of London 1660–1688, and its Consequences* (London, 1969)

Livery Companies' Exhibition 1994: Official Guide (London, 1994)

MONYPENNY, W. F. and BUCKLE, G. E., *The Life of Benjamin Disraeli, Earl of Beaconsfield* (London, 1910–20)

MOSS, Roger W., Junior, "The Origin of the Carpenters' Company of Philadelphia" (in *Building Early America*, ed. C. E. Paterson) (Radnor, Penn., 1976)

One Hundred Years' History of the Institute of Carpenters 1890–1990 (no place or date)

OSBORNE, H. C., *Carpenters' Hall 1428–1959* (London, 1960)

PEARL, Valerie, *London and the Outbreak of the Puritan Revolution* (Oxford, 1961)

PORTER, R., *London: A Social History* (London, 1994)

PRESTON, H. Westbury, *The Worshipful Company of Carpenters* (no place, 1955 edn.)

READING, Marquess of, *Rufus Isaacs, First Marquess of Reading by his Son* (London, 1942–5)

Records of the Worshipful Company of Carpenters (Ed. B. Marsh and J. Ainsworth) (Oxford and London, 1913–68)

Report and Statement of Accounts of the Rustington Convalescent Home for Working Men for the year ending 31st December 1921 (London, 1922)

The Rustington Convalescent Home Littlehampton for Working Men (no place or date (1908 ?))

SIMMONS, J., *A letter to His Grace the Duke of Northumberland on the very Extraordinary Transactions of the Society for the Encouragement of Arts, Manufactures, and Commerce Relative to His Royal Highness the Duke of Sussex* (London, 1824)

——*A Letter to the Liverymen of the Worshipful Company of Carpenters, 1825* (London, 1825)

TAYLOR, J. R., *Reform your City Guilds: "Behold the Spoiler Cometh"* (London, 1872)

THORNLEY, J. C. and HASTINGS, G. W., *The Guilds of the City of London and their Liverymen* (London, no date)

The Times (London, 1847–1986)

TREVELYAN, G. M., *English Social History* (London, 1944)

213

WALLAS, G., *The Life of Francis Place* (London, 1898)

WELCH, C., *A Lecture on the City Guilds and their Relation to Commerce and Education* (London, 1902)

Who was Who 1897–1990 (London, 1915–92)

Index

Please refer to the specific subject required. Page numbers in bold refer to an illustration or an illustration caption. Appendices have not been indexed.

A

Ackroyd, Sir Cuthbert **150**, 156, 157
Acland, James 107
Act for Rebuilding the City of London (1667) 75–6
admissions 25, 28, 80; and apprenticeship 21, 28, 53, 91; and architects 91; early ban on non-carpenters 85–6; effect of plague (1479) on number 33; occupation of members 86, 89, 91; and patrimony 28, 85, 89, 182, 183, 184; percentage of carpenters 24, 51, 183; and redemption 28, 29, 85, 89, 91, 182; and women 181, 182–3; *see also* Honorary Freedom
Air Raid Precautions Committee 143
air raids 144; damage sustained during First World War 134; damage sustained during Second World War 13, 135, 144–5; precautions taken against 143
Albemarle, 8th Earl of 129, 139
Albemarle Trust 169
Aldermen 65, 79, 94, 144
Alexandra of Denmark, Princess 110
All Hallows-on-the-Wall 13, **14**, 15, 33, 48, 136
Allen, William 54
almshouses: dispute over building at Portsoken Ward 87–8; *see also* Godalming almshouses; Twickenham almshouses
American Revolution 166, 168
Anne, Queen 84–5
Ansell, John **18**, **61**
Apocryphal Book of Ecclesiasticus XLII **22**
apprentices 51; attack on foreigners on Evil May Day 35; opposition to Charles I 59, 61, 63
apprenticeship 21, 28, 53, 91
Aragon, Catherine of 35, 37, 43
architects 91, 183
Architects Club 91
Armada, Spanish 50–1
Arts Society 95–6
Assistant Clerk 13; *see also* Blackborrow
Augustinian Friary *see* Austin Friars
Austin Friars 13, 48, 49, 50, **50**; destroyed by air raid **50**, 144
Avebury, Lord *see* Lubbock, Sir John

B

badge, Master's 139, **141**
Baldwin, Stanley 136

ballot box 15, **146**
balls *see* entertainments
banquets, state: for Charles I (1641) 64; for Cromwell (1654) 68; for Charles II (1660) 69; for Queen Juliana (1972) 164–5; *see also* Dinners
Barbers' Company 55
Barnes, Cecil 169
Barnes-Yallowley, Hugh 169
Barstow, Captain George 157
Bartlett, Rev. G.F. 141
Beadle 13 *see also* Appendix IV
Bernays, Albert E. 152, 153
Bevin, Ernest 160
Birkett, Thomas 67
Black Death (1348) 28, 71
Blackborrow, Alfred 140, 153
Boer War 130
Boleyn, Anne 43, 44
Bolton, Sir William 74
Book of Ordinances (1333) *see* Ordinances
Boyce, Sir Leslie 154, 156–7
Bradshaw, Lawrence 47, 147
Bramshott 56: plan of **55**
Branson, Sir George (Mr. Justice) 140
Brass, William 119
Brewers' Company 55, 123
British Expeditionary Force (in France): gifts sent to 131
British Mutual Bank 140–1
Buckingham, George Villiers, 1st Duke of 61
Builder, The (newspaper) 119
building: licences **51**; regulations 75- 6, 84
Building Crafts College **129**, **168**, 170, 181, **182**, **190**; *see also* Trades' Training Schools
Buller, Sir Redvers 129–30
Bynkes, Thomas 147

C

Cambridge University 68, 160
Campbell-Bannerman, Henry 120
Cardinal's College, Oxford 40
Caroline, Queen (wife of George IV) 94
carpenters: early resentment of control of Company 61; increase in unemployment 76, 83; number working in London 24, 51; and serfdom 23; wages 13, 21, 24, 28, 30, 76

Carpenters' Buildings 84, **118**

Carpenters' Company: adaptation to religious changes 47–8, 49; justification for 184, 187; close connection with craft 29, 183–4; criticism of 113; early role 24; family affair 100; first history published (Jupp) 100, 106, 181; flourishing of 18,187; formation 23, 24

Carpenters' Company of Philadelphia *see* Philadelphia

Carpenters' and Dockland Centre **167**, 169–70

Carpenters' Hall *see* Hall, Carpenters'

Carpenters' Institute 169

Carpenters' Road Junior and Mixed Infant School (Stratford) 169

Carter, William 147

Cass, Sir John **85**, 85, 87–8, 91

Catholicism 24–5, 49

Cavaliers 65, 67, 68

ceremonies: crowning of Master and Wardens 16, 17; election day 13–17; foundation (new Hall) 119, **126**; presentation of Honorary Freedom 135, **137**, 159, 161–3; presentation of Honorary Livery to Prince Charles (1995) 165–6, **166**

Chamberlain, Joseph 127

Chamberlain, Neville 143

Chapuys, Eustace 43–4

charity 184, 187; change in attitude towards 88–9, 125; expansion of Company's activities 125; influence of religion on 24–5, 88; reduction in Company's grants to 87–8, 89

Charles I, King 79; and charter **62**, 62–3; City of London's opposition to 59, 61, 62; and civil war 64–5, 67; dissolution of Parliament 61, 62; execution 67; return from Scotland (1641) 63–4

Charles II, King 68–9; confiscation of Livery Company charters 77, 79, 162; entering into London 69; and Great Fire 74; war against Dutch 71; Whig opposition to 76–7

Charles V, Emperor 36, 40, 43, 48, 49

Charles, Prince of Wales 165–6, **166**, **188**

charter(s) (of Company): (Edward IV: 1477) 32–3, 169; (Philip and Mary: 1558) 49; (Elizabeth I: 1560) 51; (James I: 1607) **52**, 53; (Charles I: 1640) **62**, 62–3; (Charles II: 1673); surrendering of to Charles II (1684) 77, 79, 162; (James II: 1686) 80

Chitham, Robert **42**

Cholmondeley, Colonel H.C.129

Christ Church, Oxford (previously known as Cardinal's College) 40

Churchill, William 151

Churchill, Winston 136, 157

cigarettes, cigars 161–3, 176

City Corporation *see* Corporation of London

City and Guilds of London Institute 125

City of London *see* London, City of

City of London Municipal Reform Association 107

City of London Rifle Brigade 109

civil war: First (1642–46) 64–5; Second (1648) 67

Clarenceux King of Arms **30**

Clerk 13, 149; advertising for position of 141, 157–8; members in post of 83, 121, 141, 157; voting procedure 158; *see also* Appendix IV

Cleves, Anne of 44–5

clothing *see* uniform

Clothworkers' Company 113

coat-of-arms: granting of **30**, 32

Cobay, William **43**

Cobb, Peter 54

Cobden, Richard 127

Cold War 160

Committee of the Whole Court 131, 139

communism: fear of 160–1

competitions, woodwork 127

Conservatives 115, 116

Cooke, Humphrey 36, 37, 40

Coopers' Company 55, 144–5

Copperplate Map **20**

Corporation of London 23, 28, 31, 69, 106; attack by Radicals 107, 109, 110; contribution to Ulster scheme 54; and Great Plague 71; and Joiners' and Carpenters' dispute 61–2; and Labour government 115–16; and Livery Companies 51; scheme for emigration to Virginia 53–4; support of rebellion against Somerset 48; surrendering of charter to Charles II 77; *see also* London, City of

costume 110

Cotton, Alderman 114

Cotton, Sir Robert Bruce 34

Court of Assistants 17, **19**, 31; annual visit to Godalming 57–8, 62, 65, 71, 96, 100, 131, 140, **171**, 173, 181; contest over nominations 151–6; co-option of liverymen who have not been Master or Warden 73, 76, 77, 83, 178, 180–1; death of members due to Great Plague 73, 76, 178; on designation of 'Esquire' 91; and election of Clerk 157–8; meetings 17, 87; members of 13, 53, 83; nomination of candidates for elections 15, 147–8, 151–2; and regulations laid down by Ordinances 15, 31; selling of plate 67

Court Room 15, **130**

craftsmen: struggle between merchants and 23

Cranmer, Archbishop Thomas 42, 44, 48

Cromwell, Oliver 65, 67, 68

Cromwell, Thomas 41–2; arrest and execution of 45; and Henry VIII wives 43–4, 45; house **42**, 42–3; meeting with Chapuys 43–4

crowns, Master and Wardens' **18**, 143;

cups, Master and Wardens' **60**, 67, 143, 143, 144

customs: bidding prayer 15; General Court meeting day 17; gift at Christmas 68; Lord Mayor's attendance at Livery dinner 102, 105–6, 136

D

Dance, George, the Younger **14**

Declaration of Indulgence (1688) 80

Defence of the Realm Act (DORA) 132

demarcation disputes: Joiners' Company and Carpenters' Company (1621) 61–2; Ordinances (1455) and settlement of 32

Deputy Master 15, 147

Diamond Jubilee (Queen Victoria) 123

dinners 25, 100, 127, 177; attire worn at 176; cancellation of during First and Second World Wars 131, 194; cost 68, 89; courses served 173; economies made on 65, 87, 89; Election Day 15, 53, 89, 109, 181; foundation ceremony and opening of new Hall (1880) 119, 120–1; Ladies: Court 89, 168, 181- 2; Livery 177, 181, 182; menus **134, 174–5**; origin of Lord Mayor's attendance at annual 102, 105–6, 136; resumption of after wars 136, 146; Sexcentenary (1933) **134**, 139, 166; times of 25; toasts 187; venue 89, 120, 146, 161; wine **174–5**, 176; *see also* banquets, state; entertainment

Disraeli, Benjamin, Earl of Beaconsfield 109, 113, 116

Dove, W.W. 15

Drapers' Company 24, 113; acquiring of Thomas Cromwell's house as Hall **42**, 45; charter (1364) 31; contribution to Henry VII war on France 35; destruction of Hall by Great Fire 74, 145; dinners of Carpenters' Company held at Hall 146, 161; and Judge Jeffreys 79; letting of Carpenters' Hall to 74; offer of use of Hall 145; and Throgmorton Avenue 117

Drummond, Sir Eric 159

Drummond, Capt. George 152

Dudley, John *see* Northumberland, Duke of

Dutch Church *see* Austin Friars

Dutchmen: association between Company and 30–1; *see also* Austin Friars

E

Early Closing Act (1904) 129

East India Company 91

Edinburgh, HRH Duke of **178**

Edmones, Thomas **61**

education: Exchange Scholarships 169; support of technical 125–6, 127, 128; university scholarships 68, 160–1; *see also* Building Crafts College

Edward I, King 23, 31

Edward II, King 23

Edward III, King 29

Edward IV, King 32

Edward VI, King 47–8, 49

Edward VII, King 123, 125

Edward VIII, King 139

Eggleton, Douglas 183

Election Day 13–17, **16**; ballot box 15, **146**; change in 16, 17, 53; church ceremony 13–14; dinner 15, 53, 89, 109, 181; crowning of new Master and Wardens 16, 17; voting 15–16

elections 80: Clerk 157–8; contested 151–6: (1853) 151 (1903) 151–2; (1943) 152–4; (1947) 154, 156; difficulties of choice during Second World War 152; exceptions to seniority rule 148–9; method for Master and Wardens selection 147–8, 180; regulations on 31, 53; seniority rule 147–8, 151; voting figures 149, 151

Elizabeth I, Queen 49, 50, 51, 52, 59

Elizabeth II, Queen 164

entertainment: amount spent on 35, 173, **174–5**; balls 181; cancellation due to plague 59, 71, 73; cancellation during First and Second World Wars 131, 135–6, 144; economies on meals 87; on state occasions: Henry VII welcome 35; Anne of Cleves welcome 44; James VI welcome 52; Charles II welcome 64; marriage of Princess Alexandra of Denmark to Prince of Wales 110; Queen Victoria's Jubilees 123; coronation of Edward VII 123, 125; women's participation in 181- 2; *see also* banquets, state; dinners

'Esquire', designation of 91

Estates Committee: tally of votes cast for election of **148**

Evil May Day (1517) 35

Exchange Scholarship 169

F

Fairfax, Sir Thomas 65, 67

Fairholt, Frederick William **26**

Faith, George 101, **106**

Father of the Company 18, 172 ; *see also* Senior Past Master

Fayrer, Sir Joseph 129

Feast: of St. John the Baptist 25; of St. Lawrence 17, 31, 53; of St. Thomas of Canterbury 32

feasting *see* banquets, state; dinners

Feltworkers' Company 74

feudal system 21, 23

Field, E. 151

Field of Cloth-of-Gold 36–7, **38–9**; pavilions built 37, 40; royal tents **34**

Finden, Thomas 101

Finsberg, Geoffrey 116

Fire of London *see* Great Fire

fires 21

First World War 131–5; air raid damage 134; cancellation of entertainment during 131; death of liverymen 131; gifts sent to forces 131; memorial roll **135**; proposed requisitioning of Hall 132–3; Rustington Convalescent Home 133–4

Firth, J.F.B. 110, **111**, 112, **112**, 114, 115, 116, 125

Fisher, Alfred **179**

Fishmongers' Company 24, 29, 114; charter 31; and Radicals 94

Fitzailwin, Henry 24

Fletcher, Sir Banister 125, **129**, 143

Fletcher, Capt. H.W. 146

Flight, Thomas (jr) 18, 151

Fordham, James 84, 117

'foreigns' (foreigners) 49; attacks on Evil May Day (1518) 35; from Netherlands 48, 49; from outside London 23

Fowler, Rev. Sir Montagu 136

Foxe, Richard, Bishop of Winchester 36

Foxe, John: *Book of Martyrs* 50

France: war against 35, 36, 40, 45, 168

Francis I, King of France 36–7, 40, **38–9**

freemen 25, 28, 32, 47, 51, 85; *see also* Honorary Freedom

French Revolution 93

G

Galbraith, Douglas **104**

General Court of the Livery 17, 53, 77, 79, 135–6, 177, 178, 180; and election day 13–15

General Purposes Committee 180–1

General Strike (1926) 136, 160

George IV, King 94–6

Giffard, Sir Hardinge (Lord Halsbury) 114

Gladstone, William 113, 114, 115

gloves: gift of 68

Godalming almshouses (Surrey) **56**, **57**, **58**, 172; annual visit to 57–8, 62, 65, 71, 96, 100, 131, 140, **171**, 173, 181; demands for increase in almsmen pension 88; distinction between Twickenham almsmen and 100, **101**, 110; during Second World War 144; gift to almsmen 110; opening 57; selection of almsmen to fill places at 172–3; Wyatt's bequest **54**, **55**, 56–7, 100

Golden Jubilee: Queen Victoria 123

Goldsmiths' Company 24, 29, 113; charter 31; contribution to Henry VII war in France 35; letting of Carpenters' Hall to 74

Grant of Arms (1466) **30**, 32

Great Eastern Railway 99

Great Fire (1666) 45, **70**, 73–4, 102, 106; rebuilding after 74–6

Great Plague (1665) 71, **72**, 73, 76, 178

Great Reform Bill (1832) 107

Great Twelve Livery Companies 51–2, 123

Greater London Council 115–16; *see also* London County Council

Grece, Lewis 181

Grey, Lady Jane 49

Grey, Lord 107

Grocers' Company 24, 29, 46, 102, 106; contribution to Henry VII war in France 35; Hall of 30; and Judge Jeffreys 79

Guildhall 32, 74, 144

Gulf War 134

H

Haberdashers' Company 74

Haig, Sir Douglas 134–5, 136

Hall, Carpenters' Company

[(1429) 33; additional storey and buildings built (1737) 84; additions to (1779) 89; building of 29–30; demolishment 117, 119; escape from Great Fire 73, 74; insurance of 83; interior **92**; letting of 30–1, 76, 84, 117; letting to Livery Companies and Lord Mayor after Great Fire 74; map showing **20**; new wing built (1664) 71, **82**; ordinance survey map (1874) **118**; plan of **87**; prevention of quartering by Cromwell's soldiers 67, 68; tax paid on 83; Tudor wall paintings **26–7**]

[(1880): air raid shelter built 143; bomb damage during Second World War 135, **142**, 144, **145**, 145–6; building of 117, 119–20, 152; dining hall **111**, 119, **120**; foundation ceremony 119, **126**; offer of use to Lord Mayor and Livery Companies whose Halls were destroyed 144–5; opening 120–1; proposed requisitioning of during First World War 132–3];

[(1960): building of 163–4; dining hall **162**, 178; opening 164; Queen Juliana's state banquet at (1972) 164–5; reception area **186**; reception of Lord Mayor **104**; stained glass windows **179**]

Hall, Carpenters' Company of Philadelphia **163**, 166, 168

Hall, Herbert Austen 165

Hall, Joseph 59

Hammond, A.B. 152

Hamon, Captain Kenneth 157, **166**

Harben, H.D. 152

Harben, Sir Henry 126, 127–8, **132**, 152, **170**, 171

Hawkeslowe, William **30**

Heake, Thomas 73

Heap, Sir Desmond 180

Henry II, King 23, 31

Henry VI, King 29, 32

Henry VII, King 35

Henry VIII, King 35, 41; contributions from Livery Companies to fund war in France 35; declares war on France 40, 45; dissolution of monasteries 45; and Field of Cloth- of-Gold **34**, 36–7, **38–9**, 40; and Nedeham 41; palaces of 42; treatment of rioters on Evil May Day 35; wives 43–5;

Hensman, Ernest 121

Hensman, George 121

Hertzog, General 159

Hervey, Walter 23
History of the Carpenters' Company (Jupp) (1848) 100, 106, 181
Honorary Chaplain 136
Honorary Freedom 128, 129–30, 136, 159, 165; Sir Douglas Haig 134–5, 136; Queen Juliana 133, 162–3; Field Marshal Montgomery **161**, 161–2; Marquess of Reading **137**, 137–8; General Smuts 159-60, 161; *see also* Appendix II; individual names
Honorary Livery: Prince Charles 165–6, **166**; Queen Juliana **164**, 165
houses: built of wood 21, 32; built of brick after Great Fire 75–6
Hundred Years War 29
Hutton Freeman, Joseph 121, 139, 157

I

immigrants *see* Austin Friars; 'foreigns'
income: (1700) 83, 87; (1788) 87; (1800–30) 99; (1880) 123; (1900) 125
Independents 65, 67, 68
Innholders' Company 99, 113
Institute of Carpenters 125–6
insurance: of Carpenters' Hall 83
investments 84, 87; South Sea Bubble 84
Ireland: Ulster scheme 54–5
Irish Land Acts 55
Ironmongers' Company 55
Isaacs, Rufus *see* Reading, Marquess of

J

Jacob, Benjamin **126**
Jacob, Kenneth B. **164**
Jacob family 91, 100
Jacobins 93
James I, King 16, **52**, 52–3, 54, 59
James II, King (formerly James, Duke of York) 73, 76, 77, 79–80, 162
James, W.H. 112–13, 114
Jarman, Anthony **61**
Jeffreys, Sir George ('Judge') 77, **78**, 79, 80, 81, 93
Jesus Christ **27**, 33
Joiners' Company 113; demarcation dispute with Carpenters' Company (1621) 61–2
journeymen 21
Juliana, Queen of the Netherlands: Honorary Freedom 133, 162–3; Honorary Livery **164**, 165; state visit 164–5
Jupp, Edward Basil 100, **105**, 106, 121, 139, 181
Jupp, Richard (jr) 91
Jupp, Richard (sr) 91
Jupp, Richard Webb 96, 100, **102**, 121
Jupp, William (sr) 89, 91

K

Keysell, F.O. 139
King, John Godwin 152, 182
King, Thomas 64
King's Carpenter(s): Cooke 36, 37, 40; Nedeham 40–3, 44–5, 46; Russell 47
Kipling, Rudyard 137–8
Knapp, Joseph 83
Kozlov, Lt. Col. 160
Kydd, Thomas 147

L

Labour party 136, 138, 139, 160; and City of London 115–16
Lamb, Dr. 61
Land Tax (1691) 83
Lasco, John à 48
Lawrence, Sir James Clarke 101–2, **103**, 105–6, 109, 114, 119, 120, 121
Lawrence, Sir William (jr) 100–1, 101–2, **103**, 105, 106, 128
Lawrence, William (sr) 101
Leathersellers' Company 123
Leicester, Robert Dudley, Earl of 117
Liberal Party 102, 115, 128–9
licences, building **51**
life assurance: for working class 126–7
Lime Street 74
Lindy, Kenneth 169
Livery Companies 15; admission of women 183; arguments for 113- 14, 184; attack on by Radicals 25, 93, 107, 110, 112–13, **113**; charters 31, 77, 80; confiscation of charters by Charles II 77, 79, 162; contributions to Henry VII war against France 35; criticism of extravagant dinners 112, **112**, 113, 114; demarcation disputes between 61–2; dinner with Lord Mayor 102, 105; and Firth 110, **111**, 112, **112**, 114, 115, 116, 125; gentlemen as members 29; Great Twelve 51–2, 123; Halls destroyed by air raids 144; increase in wealth 93; Judge Jeffreys control over 79; letting of Carpenters' Hall to 74; and Metropolitan Board of Works Bill 109; occupation of Halls by Cromwell's army 67; origin 24; popularity 184; Royal Commission (1880–84) 114–15, 129; and Second Civil War (1648) 67; *see also* individual companies
Livery list (1788) **149**
Liverymen, Carpenters 47; admission of 25, 28, 80, 85 *see also* admissions; characteristics of 91; and Company regulations 32; co-option on to Court without being Master or Warden 73, 76, 77, 83, 178, 180–1; death of in First World War 131; and election day 13, 15, 17; non-carpenters as 28, 85–6, 89, 91; numbers of 51, 85, 89; participation of

219

Liverymen, Carpenters—*cont*
  junior in running of Company 177–8; progression
  through offices of 147–8; *see also* General Court of
  the Livery
London, City of: air raids during Second World War
  144–5; attack by Radicals 93–4, 107, 109, 110;
  attempt to set up Metropolitan Board of Works 109;
  contribution to Ulster scheme 54; copperplate map
  (1558/9) **20**; early governance 23–4; expansion of
  86, 93, **108**; extent of at 1300, 21; failure of action
  against 115–16; foreigners in 23, 35, 48; Great Fire
  (1666) 45, **70**, 73–4, 102, 106; increase in wealth
  28–9, 93; and Judge Jeffreys 79; opposition to King
  Charles I 59, 61, 62, 64–5, 67; panorama of (1520)
  36–7; Peasants Revolt (1381) 28; and plague 52–3,
  59, 71, **72**, 73; population 21, 28, 51, 93; quo
  warranto proceedings on charter 77; rebuilding after
  Great Fire 74–6; struggle between craftsmen and
  merchants 23; Whig opposition to Charles II 76–7;
  see also Corporation of London; Lord Mayor
London Bridge 21
London County Council 115, 128–9; *see also* Greater
  London Council
London Tavern 89
London Wall 13, **16**, 21, 84, **95**, 117, 145, 180
Lord Mayor 13, 23–4, 54, 68, **104**, 144; banquets:
  (1945) 157; (1951) 157; Carpenters as 91, 100–1,
  121, 149, 156, 157; and Judge Jeffreys 79; lease of
  Carpenters' Hall to after Great Fire 74; origin of
  attendance at Carpenters' annual dinner 102, 105–
  6, 136
Lord Mayor's Show **43**, 107
Loriners' Company 157
Louis XIV, King of France 77, 83, 168
Lubbock, Sir John (Lord Avebury) 128, 129
Luck and Kent (partnership) 117

M

MacDonald, Ramsay 136, 138–9
Mackinnon, General 129, 134, 135
Mahathir, Dr. Bin Mohamad 165
Malaysia 165
Manning, Serjeant 180
maps: copperplate of London **20**; ordinance survey of
  area surrounding Carpenters' Hall **118**
Marconi Company 137
Mary I, Queen 49
Mary II, Queen 80–1
Mary, Princess (King George V's daughter) 133
Masons' Company 32, 35
Master 33; badge 139, **141**; chair **105**; crown **18**;
  cup **60**; election day 13, 15–16, 17–18; [method of
  selection 147–8, 180: contested elections 151–6;
  difficulties over choice of during Second World War
  152; exceptions to seniority rule 148–9]; and Ordi-

nances 31, 32, 53; *see also* Appendix III; individual
  names
Master Carpenter 21, 25, 32
Mayor of London *see* Lord Mayor
McWilliams, Sir Francis **104**
membership *see* admissions
Memorial roll **135**
Mercers' Company 24, 29, 102; charter (1393) 31;
  contribution to Henry VII war effort 35
Merchant Taylors' Company 24, 25, 54, 94; *see also*
  Taylors and Linen Armourers
merchants: struggle between craftsmen and 23; and
  wool trade 28–9
Metropolitan Board of Works 109, 115
monasteries: dissolution of 45; gifts to 25, 88
Monck, General 68
Monmouth, Duke of 79
Montague-Smith, F. 139
Montgomery, Field Marshal **161**, 161–2
Morozovski, Capt. 160
Morris, H.C. 151–2
Morris, Humphrey **111**, 152, 156
Morrison, Herbert 115
motto 15, 32
Mount, Richard 86
Municipal Corporations Act (1835) 107

N

Napier, Brigadier 171
Napoleon III, Emperor of France 109
Navy: gifts sent to in First World War 131
Neal, H.M. **178**
Nedeham, James 40–3, 44, 45–6; background 40–1;
  building of Thomas Cromwell's house **42**, 42-3;
  death 45; employed by Henry VIII as Surveyor of
  King Works 41-2, 45; as Master of Carpenters'
  Company 46; receiver of monastic lands 45
Neild, Patricia 172
Netherlands 83; export of wool to 28, 29; Charles II
  war with 71; Protestants in London 30–1; *see also*
  Austin Friars; Queen Juliana; revolt against tyranny
  of Philip II of Spain 50
Norfolk, HMS **185**
Norris, Sir Henry 41, 44
Northumberland, John Dudley, Duke of 48–9
Nottage, Alderman 121, 151, 156

O

Ordinances: (1333) Book of 23, 24, 25, 31, 32, 139;
  (1455) 17, 25, 31–2, 53; (1607) 15, 53, 76, 147,
  154, 177–8, 180
Osborne, Henry Carl **138**, 141, 153, 157, 180
Osborne, John 141

Osborne, Peter 141
Oxford University 40, 68, 160

P

paintings, Tudor wall **26–7**
Palmerston, Lord 109
patrimony, freedom by 28, 85, 89, 182, 183, 184
patron saint (Virgin Mary) 33
Peacock, Thomas 147
Peake, Sir William 74
Pearson, Charles 107
Peasants' Revolt (1381) 28
pensions 88
Pergami, Bartolommeo 94
Pewterers' Company 55
Philadelphia, The Carpenters' Company of the City and County of **163**, 166, 168–9
Philip II, King of Spain 49, 50
Pilgrimage of Grace 45
Place, Francis 107
plague 13; Black Death (1348) 28, 71; (1479) 33; (1603) 52–3; (1625) 59; (1636) 62; Great (1665) 71, **72**, 73, 76, 178
Plaisterers' Company 32
plate: safety precautions during Second World War 143, 144; selling of 61, 65, 66, 67
Plumbers' Company 32
Pocock, G.P. 152–4, 156
Pocock, William Fuller **98**, 100, 152
Pocock, William Willmer 119, 152
Pocock family 91, 100
poor relief 24; *see also* almshouses; charity
population, London 21, 28, 51, 93
Portsoken Ward: dispute over building of almshouses 87–8
Powell, Frederick William **16**
Prater, Robert 157
prayer, bidding 15
Presbyterians 59, 63, 65, 67, 68–9, 71
Preston, Commander Alan 154, 156, 169
Preston, Stanton W. 119, 121, **122**, 127
Preston, Westbury 136, **137**, 143, 159, 160
Preston family 100, 131
Progressives 129
Protestantism 17, 48, 88
Prudential Mutual Assurance Investment and Loan Association 126, 127, 133
Puritans 59, 62, 64

Q

Quo Warranto 77, 79; reversal of **75**, 80, 162

R

Radicals: attack on City of London 93–4, 107, 109, 110; attack on Livery Companies 25, 93, 107, 110, 112–13, **113**
railways: selling of Company's land to 99, 117
Ramsden, Omar **141**
Read, John 68, 161
Reading, Marquess of (Rufus Isaacs) **137**, 137–8
Read's Trust 68, 160
redemption, freedom by 28, 29, 85, 89, 91, 182
Reeves, John **61**
Reform Bill: (1832) 107; (1867) 110
Reformation 17, 48, 88
Reid, Sir George Houston 130
religion: adaptation to changes in by Carpenters 47–8, 49; importance of in fourteenth century 24–5
Representation of the People Act (1918) 115
Restoration (1660) 68–9, 76, 77–8
Richard II, King 24
Richard, Duke of York 32
Ridley, Major Geoffrey W. 163, 182
Ridley, Jasper G. 165, 176
Ridley, Nicholas, Bishop of London 48
rifle brigades 109
Roberts, Sir Gabriel 76, 83, 84
Roberts, K.M. 162
Rollit, Sir Alfred 129
Roman Catholic Church: influence of 24–5
Rosher, A.B. 152, 153
Rosher, J.B. 180
Rosher family 100, 131
Roundheads 63, 64, 65
Royal Commission: Livery Companies (1880–84) 114–15, 129; reforming electoral system and local government 109
Royal Exchange 74
rules *see* Ordinances
Rupert, Prince 64
Russell, John 47
Russell, Lord John 107
Rustington Convalescent Home **124**, **170**, 170–2; adjacent farm 128, 170, 171; defrauding of by Assistant Clerk 139–41, 154; and First World War 133–4; Grade 2 building status 172; and Gulf War 134; opening 126, 127–8; in Second World War 144; reopening after Second World War 170; success 171, 172; visits to 181, 182

S

Saddlers' Company 123
Schiller, Ferdinand, K.C. 140
scholarships: Exchange 169; university 68, 160–1
Scotland 63

Scriveners' Company 55

Second World War 143–6, 159; air raid damage 13, 135, **142**, 144–5, **145**; air raid precautions taken 143; destruction of Hall 145–6; difficulties about choice of Masters and Wardens during 152; memorial roll **135**

Selborne, Lord 114

Senior Past Master 18, 147, 172; *see also* Father of the Company

serfdom 21, 23, 28

Serles, William 30

servitude *see* apprenticeship

Seymour, Edward *see* Somerset, Duke of

Seymour, Queen Jane 43, 44

Sex Discrimination Act (1975) 183

Shackleford (Surrey) 56, **58**

Shaftesbury, Anthony Ashley Cooper, 1st Earl of 76–7

Sheres, Roger 55

Shipmoney tax 61

silver *see* plate

Simmons, John 94, 95–8; expulsion 97–8

Skinners' Company 85, 112, 113

'Slump', the 138–9

Smalley, John 79, 80–1

Smart, Thomas 30

Smith, Minden 18

Smith, Montague 160

Smith, Thomas 101

Smith, Prof. William 129

smoking 71, 73, 161–3, 176

Smuts, General J.C. 159–60, 161 snuff 176

solicitor: appointment of 121

Somerset, Duke of (Edward Seymour) 47–8, 49

South Africa 159, 160

South Sea Bubble 84

Soviet Union 160

St. John the Baptist, church of 25, 33

St. Paul's Cathedral 123

St. Thomas of Acon, church of 25, 33

Staines, Sir William **90**, 91, 94

Stavridi, Sir John 140, 154

Stavridi, V.J.G. 18, 165

Stevenson, Major General Paul 158

Stockdale, Sir Edmund 151, **155**, 157, 164

stocks and shares *see* investments

Stone, James 79, 80, 81, 83

Strafford, Earl of 63

Stratford estate 169; Carpenters' and Dockland Centre **167**, 169–70; plan of **86**; purchase of 87; social centre (later named Carpenters' Institute) 125, 169; technical school 127

Stuckey, Robert 132

Sumptuary Laws 25

Surveyor of the King's Works 41, 42, 47

Sussex, H.R.H. Prince Augustus Frederick, Duke of 95–6

T

taxation: Land Tax (1691) 83; Shipmoney 61

Taylors and Linen Armourers 24, 29; charter (1327) 31; *see also* Merchant Taylors' Company

technical education 125–6, 127, 128

Tennyson, Alfred 109–10, 119

Thatcher, Margaret 165

Thornton, Peter **18**

Throckmorton, Sir Nicholas 117

Throgmorton Avenue 117, 145, 164, 180

Throgmorton Street 42, 117

timber business 55–6

tobacco 73

Tom Alan Club 169–70

tools, carpentry **154**

Tories 76, 80, 107

Tower of London 41, 42

Trades' Training Schools **129**, 170; air raid damage during First World War 134; during Second World War 144; founding 126; *see also* Building Crafts College

Trades Union Congress (TUC) 136

traditions *see* customs

training 184; *see also* education

Tree of Life 164

Tryll, John **18**

Tudor Crowns **18**

Twickenham almshouses **98**, **101**, 152; air raid damage during Second World War 144, 146; annual visit 100, 143; construction 99–100; distinction between Godalming almsmen and 100, **101**, 110; gift to almsmen 110; sale of to Borough Council 172

Twickenham Borough Council 172

Tyler, Wat 28

Tylers' Company 32

U

Ulster: purchase of land in 54–5

unemployment 76, 83

uniform 25, 110

United States of America 160, 166, 168

university scholarships 68, 160–1

V

Victoria, Queen 119; Golden and Diamond Jubilees 123

Virginia: emigration scheme 53–4

visits, annual: Godalming 57–8, 62, 65, 71, 96, 100, 131, 140, **171**, 173, 181; Rustington 181, 182; Twickenham 100, 143

voting *see* elections

W

Wace, Henry 129

wages: fall in after Great Fire 76; rates 13, 21, 24, 30; rise in due to population decrease after plague 28

Wales, Prince of *see* Charles, Prince; Edward VIII; George IV

Wardens 33; Account Book (1438) 146; cup **60**; and election day 13, 15, 16, 17–18; method of selection 147–8, 180: defeat of Court's nomination for Junior (1903) 151–2; difficulty over choice of during Second World War 152; and Ordinances 31, 32, 53; promotion to Master 148, 149; rankings 15; responsibility for almshouses 100; *see also* Appendix III

Warham, Thomas 147

wars *see* First World War; Second World War

Wars of the Roses 32

wealth: increase in 29, 52, 86–7, 99, 100, 123; *see also* income

Weavers' Company: formation 23; letting of Carpenters' Hall to 74

Wellington, Arthur Wellesley, 1st Duke of 107

Wharrie, Mary Woodgate **132**, 133

Wheatley, William **18**

Wheeler, Sir Charles 164, 165

Wheelwrights' Company 35

Whigs 76–7, 80, 93, 107

Wilkes, John 94

William III, King 80, 81, 83, 162

wills: Sir John Cass 87–8; John Read 68, 161; Thomas Smart 30; Richard Wyatt **54**, 56, 100, 172–3

Wilson, Harold 115–16

wine **174–5**, 176; expenditure on 64, **175**

winter (1683–4) 77

Wolsey, Cardinal 40, 41

women: admission 181, 182–3; admittance to Rustington Convalescent Home 171; Honorary Freedom conferred on **132**, 133, 162–3; Ladies dinners: *see* dinners; participation in social events 110, 181–2

Wood, Matthew 94

Woodmongers' Company 56

woodwork competitions 127

wool trade 28–9

Woolley, Robert 183

World War I *see* First World War

World War II *see* Second World War

Wren, Christopher 75, 76

Wyatt, Richard **54**, 54, 147; background 55–6; and Godalming almshouses **54**, **55**, 56–7, 100; tankards **63**; will 56, 88, 172–3

Y

Yallowley, Joseph 94–5, 96–7

York, Duke of *see* James II

York Minster 170